Homer and the Poetics of Gesture

Homer and the Poetics of Gesture

Alex C. Purves

OXFORD

UNIVERSITY PRESS

OXFORD
UNIVERSITY PRESS

Oxford University Press is a department of the University of Oxford. It furthers
the University's objective of excellence in research, scholarship, and education
by publishing worldwide. Oxford is a registered trade mark of Oxford University
Press in the UK and certain other countries.

Published in the United States of America by Oxford University Press
198 Madison Avenue, New York, NY 10016, United States of America.

© Oxford University Press 2019

First issued as an Oxford University Press paperback, 2022

Library of Congress Cataloging-in-Publication Data
Names: Purves, Alex C., 1972- author.
Title: Homer and the poetics of gesture / Alex C. Purves.
Description: Oxford : Oxford University Press, 2019. | Series: Oxford studies
in late antiquity | Includes bibliographical references and index.
Identifiers: LCCN 2018027945 (print) | LCCN 2018029132 (ebook) |
ISBN 9780190915483 (oso) | ISBN 9780190915469 (updf) | ISBN 9780190915476 (epub) |
ISBN 9780190857929 (hardcover : alk. paper) | ISBN 9780197651193 (paperback)
Subjects: LCSH: Homer—Criticism and interpretation. | Gesture in literature.
Classification: LCC PA4037 (ebook) | LCC PA4037 .P979 2019 (print) |
DDC 883/.01—dc23
LC record available at https://lccn.loc.gov/2018027945

1 3 5 7 9 8 6 4 2

Paperback printed by Marquis, Canada

For Lionel

Contents

List of Figures

Acknowledgments

It is a pleasure to acknowledge the many people who have helped and inspired me in writing this book. Several chapters have been significantly improved by the perceptive comments of readers, including but not limited to Karen Bassi, David Blank, Anne Duncan, Emily Gowers, Joshua Katz, Kathryn Morgan, Sheila Murnaghan, Kirk Ormand, Mark Payne, Verity Platt, Charles Stocking, Ralph Rosen, Mario Telò, Victoria Wohl, and Nancy Worman. I reserve special thanks for Jim Porter and Seth Schein, who both revealed themselves to me as readers for the press after the fact, and who have remained in close contact with me since, offering invaluable advice and ideas.

Sheila Murnaghan first gave me the confidence to move forward with this project when I tentatively suggested it to her at a meeting of the (then) APA and she has remained an important guiding force throughout. Kathryn Morgan helped me to piece together its earliest chapters, on falling and running, and thereby to see my way to the whole. Joshua Katz and Verity Platt each stepped in and gave me just the direction I needed during key moments of uncertainty. I wrote the last chapter as the visiting Spinoza fellow at Leiden University. I'll be forever grateful to Ineke Sluiter not only for her intellectual energy, but also for providing me with a space to work and think among such a warm community of students and colleagues.

Victoria Wohl has gone above and beyond as a reader and interlocutor for this book. I have been humbled by the critical insight she brought to this project, and by her generosity in helping me to make it better. Jim Porter's ability to step back and assess the whole through a series of thoughtful and penetrating questions has helped me to finesse my argument considerably, and he has been a frequent source of creative input over email. As for Seth Schein, I can't imagine having written this book without his intellectual guidance. Although all the errors that remain are my own, he has left a lasting impression on me about how to think and write about Homer, and his generosity as a scholar and a person is unmatched. After retiring at UC Davis, and just as I was beginning this book, he gave me a good part of his Homer library; it has been deeply inspiring to see his name on the inside cover of the books I have consulted for this project.

I also owe a great intellectual debt to my colleagues and students at UCLA. They have provided a community where ideas are celebrated and shared. In particular, David Blank, Francesca Martelli, Kathryn Morgan, Amy Richlin, and Mario Telò (now at UC Berkeley) have all left an impact on this book over the course of several memorable discussions. I have also benefited enormously from conversations in seminars with students, and especially from those who have written dissertations with me on Homer—Charles Stein, Craig Russell, Celsiana Warwick, and Ben Radcliffe—all of whom have changed my thinking and approach to the topic of this book in important and productive ways.

Stefan Vranka, my editor at OUP, has been wonderful to work with; I thank him for his patience, generosity and clear-sighted advice. At UCLA, Chrysanthe Pantages, Silvio Curtis, Zachary Borst, Ana Guay, and Ben Radcliffe provided invaluable research assistance at different points, funded by generous annual grants from the Council on Research at UCLA.

Finally, I am grateful to all of the members of my family. My parents have always encouraged me and have helped me in several ways, large and small, to finish this book. Orlando and Lionel, both much more expert readers of bodies than I am, have made the writing of this book a joyful experience for me, even if it wasn't always for them. I can't really thank Lionel adequately for all the time, encouragement, and ideas he has put into the book. It's an old joke (and true) that I stole the concept for it from him, and he has been the one who has inspired me and talked me through every one of its stages.

List of Abbreviations

DELG   P. Chantraine. 1968–1980. *Dictionnaire étymologique de la langue grecque: Histoire des mots*. Paris: Klincksieck. 2nd ed. with Supplement, 1999.

Denniston   J. D. Denniston. 1966. *The Greek Particles*. 2nd ed. Revised by K. J. Dover. Indianapolis, CA: Hackett.

Dindorf   W. Dindorf. (1855) 1962. *Scholia graeca in Homeri Odysseam*. 2 vols. Amsterdam: Hakkert.

Erbse   H. Erbse. 1969. *Scholia graeca in Homeri Iliadem*. 5 vols. Berlin: de Gruyter.

GH   P. Chantraine. 1958–1963. *Grammaire homérique*. 3rd ed. 2 vols. Paris: Klincksieck.

LfgrE   B. Snell et al., eds. 1955–2010. *Lexikon des frühgriechischen Epos*. Göttingen, Germany: Vandenhoeck & Ruprecht.

LIMC   *Lexicon Iconographicum Mythologiae Classicae* (1981–99). Zürich, München, and Düsseldorf: Artemis and Winkler Verlag.

LSJ   *Greek-English Lexicon*. 1925–1940. 9th ed. Compiled by H. G. Lidell and R. Scott, rev. H. S. Jones. Oxford: Clarendon. Rev. *Supplement* by P. G. W. Glare, 1996.

Introduction

I thought, as I wiped my eyes on the corner of my apron:
Penelope did this too.
                    —Edna St. Vincent Millay, "An Ancient Gesture"

In Edna St. Vincent Millay's "An Ancient Gesture" (1954), we are invited to contemplate how the gesture of wiping away tears with the corner of a piece of clothing is shared between the bodies of Penelope, Odysseus, and the poet. The poem's speaker is reminded of the *Odyssey* after performing a gesture she imagines for Penelope when she, exhausted from long nights unweaving her shroud, wept in longing for her husband. Although this exact gesture is more Millay's than Homer's, her poem registers a way of reading and remembering the epic through an association between her own body and Penelope's. Her protagonist's simple act, cast here as domestic and ordinary (perhaps it is performed in the kitchen by a woman cutting onions), acquires, through correlation to Homer, a certain resonance.[1] As she will go on to write, "This is an ancient gesture, authentic, antique, / In the very best tradition, classic, Greek." By overlaying her [own] gestures onto those of a fictional character, Millay also suggests some form of a shared experience; a common understanding or empathy that can momentarily occur through the reenactment of a bodily phrase.

But if gestures can be "authentic" they can also be copied and made false. For the poet proposes, in the second and final stanza, that Odysseus stole the eye-wiping motif from his wife and turned it into a rhetorical device. In Odysseus' hands, it is now performed "only as a gesture," in contrast to "Penelope, who really cried:"

And I thought, as I wiped my eyes on the corner of my apron:
This is an ancient gesture, authentic, antique,
In the very best tradition, classic, Greek;
Ulysses did this too.
But only as a gesture,—a gesture which implied
To the assembled throng that he was much too moved to speak.
He learned it from Penelope . . .
Penelope, who really cried.

---

1. On Millay's adoption of various markedly feminine personae in her poetry, including that of the wife, see Gilbert 1993; Cucinella 2010: 27–53.

All at once, therefore, the gesture—although it had seemed at first to retain its meaning as it traveled from person to person—is revealed to share only a formal resemblance between the three. It may involve the same mechanics in each case, but the context and emotional impact differ widely as it cycles through Homer's various characters and readers (even the connection between the poet and Penelope is frayed at the end, as we are left wondering what kind of tears Millay means her speaker-self to have wiped away). Finally, too, the gesture's initially intrinsic status, as something that was once original to the body of Penelope, is belied by the poem's marked use of repetition, not only in the formal structure of its rhyming and mirroring within and between the stanzas,[2] but also in its relaying of the gesture from subject to subject ("Penelope did this too;" "Ulysses did this too"). And since Penelope, as we are told, did it "more than once" it becomes clear that the gesture only really *becomes* a gesture through reperformance, whether by others or oneself.[3]

For Millay, then, the simple act of drawing a corner of material up to the face becomes a vehicle not only for engaging with Homeric epic in a personal way but also for thinking through the implications of a genre in which the same gesture can be both deeply meaningful in one case and learned or formulaic in another. The gesture is stored in the body as a kind of muscle memory, one that Millay herself can tap into as a resource for recalling Penelope, but that can also be re-enacted by other characters within the Homeric corpus, leading to an alignment between bodies that is at times unexpected.[4]

Although my reading of Homer is less personal than Millay's, in this book I too use specific bodily positions or actions as starting points for interpreting the *Iliad* and *Odyssey*. Each chapter begins from a movement phrase (falling, running, leaping, standing, or reaching) and then traces the iteration of that phrase through one or both of the poems. By reading a single or limited number of postures per chapter, I track the sequences and modulations into which a gesture can fall. At times, I follow a thread similar to the one from Millay I have just outlined, such as when I chart the emotional complexities of

---

2. In addition to the rhyming patterns within the poem (too/do/too; night/tight/light; years/tears; antique/Greek/speak; implied/cried), Millay frequently uses "and" at line-beginning to create a mirroring effect, especially with the opening line of each stanza (e.g., "I thought, as I wiped my eyes on the corner of my apron:" [1]; "And I thought, as I wiped my eyes on the corner of my apron:" [10]), although this symmetrical effect is on occasion deliberately broken (e.g., the second stanza has one fewer line than the first).

3. On the reperformance of gesture, especially gendered gesture, see Butler 1988 (and further in this Introduction).

4. Penelope's and Odysseus' contrasting use of gesture in Millay looks toward the long-standing debate over whether gesturing is a "natural" or "artificial" practice, as I discuss later in this Introduction.

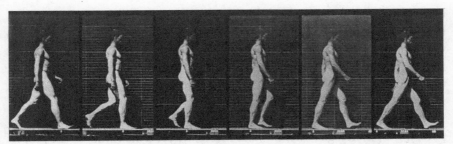

Figure 1.1. Eadweard Muybridge, *Animal Locomotion*. vol. 1, plate 2, *Walking* (excerpt), 1887. *Source:* Boston Public Library. Wikimedia Commons.

reaching one's arms out toward another person. But many of the gestures I consider also focus on the whole body, in sequences somewhat akin to Eadweard Muybridge's famous capturing of movement phrases in a series of stills, as in Figure 1.1.

Like Muybridge, I have been drawn to forms of pedestrian activity whose intricacies are only fully revealed when they are isolated or reframed.[5] Indeed, many of these types of activity occur so many times in Homer that they rarely stand out as marked sites for interpretation and analysis. We might instead describe them as providing a background rhythm to the poems, a kinetic structure that is intricately tied to Homer's engineering of temporality and plot while they in themselves pass largely unnoticed. Action of this kind often blends so imperceptibly with formulaic language ("he came up to him at a run"; "he jumped down with his armor from his chariot to the ground"; "she stood beside the pillar")[6] that their familiarity may condition us to paying barely any attention to them at all. My aim is to challenge that notion by isolating gestures and attempting to capture their kinaesthetic effects within the poems as a whole.

Gesture, though, is a difficult term and one that I want to be careful to categorize both broadly and flexibly. Following the work of scholars such as Vilém Flusser and Carrie Noland, I mean by it whole-body movement phrases rather

5. Many other examples that defamiliarize walking in particular could also be adduced. See, for example, the Judson Church dance collective's experiments with walking and other pedestrian movements (e.g., Trisha Brown's 1971 piece "Walking on the Wall") and my Chapter 5. Agamben's classic essay "Notes on Gesture" begins with Tourette's 19th-century medical research into the human walk (Agamben [1992] 2000, and further in this chapter).

6. ἀντίος ἦλθε θέων, three times, *Il.*; ἐξ ὀχέων σὺν τεύχεσιν ἄλτο χαμᾶζε, eight times, *Il.*; στῆ ῥα παρὰ σταθμόν, five times, *Od*. All translations are my own unless otherwise noted; all citations of Homer are taken from the Oxford Classical Text, vols. 1 and 2 (3rd ed., 1920) edited by David B. Munro and T. W. Allen, vols. 3 (2nd ed., 1917) and 4 (2nd ed., 1919) edited by T. W. Allen. On verb-subject formulas, see Parry [1928] 1971: 43; on minimal statements of the kind "strike with the spear" or "his limbs collapsed," which admit extensive variation, see Hainsworth 1993: 12–13.

than, specifically, facial or hand movements used in the service of communication.[7] In some contexts, a more suitable term would be *schēma*, which is used in Classical Greek to refer to the gestures or form of the human body, as well as—in rhetoric—to a figure of speech.[8] This meaning is complementary to my own use of "gesture" and helps to expand the term into a figurative and thematic, rather than purely literal, sense.

In Figure 1.2, a "chronophotograph" produced by Muybridge's contemporary, the physiologist Étienne-Jules Marey, we see a man who, in the process of walking, represents an abstract pattern of movement. The effect is produced by Marey's choice of where on his subject's body to place lighted strips, and by the systematic multiple exposure of the same figure on a single plate.[9] Whereas Muybridge's experiments create a freeze-frame effect, capturing a sequence of individual moments within separate grids of time and space, Marey's photographs result in a fluid running together of the various gradients of a gesture through time. It is worth noting, though, how both images bring to prominence certain parts of the body: the face and hands (our prime denominators of individuality) have disappeared, and instead the limbs alone reveal the contours of human movement.[10]

---

7. Flusser [1991] 2014: 1 ("gestures are to be considered movements of the body and, in a broader sense, movements of tools attached to the body"). See also Thomas 1991; Agamben [1992] 2000; Corbeill 2004; Noland 2008 and 2009: 1–17; Väliaho 2010; Olsen 2016 and forthcoming. For gesture limited to communication and thus akin to speech (nonverbal communication), see Kendon 1981 and 2004. Kendon's reading, which is concerned with semiotics, better relates to Lateiner's work on the Homeric body than mine. See Lateiner 1992 and 1995 and de Jong 2012 for analysis of gesture as a social and communicative practice in Greek epic. For gesture in other classical genres as well, see Boegehold 1999; the essays collected in Clark et al. 2015; O'Connell 2017: 53–79.

8. See further Schmitt 1990: 34–35 on *gestus, motus, kinēsis, habitus*, and *schema*. Greek σχῆμα and Latin *schema* are used by ancient critics to denote gesture in drama and rhetoric (see also n.28, this Introduction). Quintilian, *De oratore* 9.1.10–11, says the following of the term *figura* ("figure"): *Nam duobus modis dicitur: uno qualiscumque forma sententiae, sicut in corporibus, quibus, quoquo modo sunt composita, utique habitus et aliquis; altero, quo proprie schema dicitur, in sensu vel sermone aliqua a vulgari et simplici specie cum ratione mutatio* ("the word is used in two senses. In one, it means any shape in which a thought is expressed—just as our bodies, in whatever pose they are placed, are inevitably in *some* sort of attitude. In the second sense, which is the proper meaning of *schēma*, it means a purposeful deviation in sense or language from the ordinary simple form," trans. D. A. Russell).

9. On Marey's photographic method, see Braun 1992: 42–149. In cases such as Figure 1.2, the human figure is dressed all in black, so as to effectively disappear behind the illuminated strips on his limbs.

10. On the body "disappearing" in Marey's choronophotography, see Michaud 1998: 86, as discussed in Didi-Huberman 2002: 119–20. As the latter puts it, "[i]l faudra donc que les 'points caractéristiques'—par nature séparés, discrets, discontinus—parviennent à épouser le *continuum* temporel du mouvement" (emphasis original, 2002: 122), and discussed further in this Introduction.

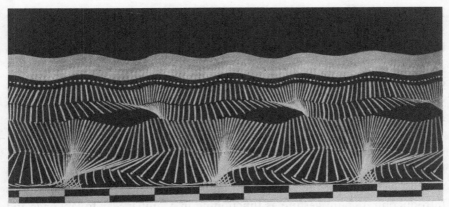

Figure 1.2. Étienne-Jules Marey, "Marche de l'Homme: Épure; Graphique obtenu au moyen de la chronophotographie géométrique partielle," 1882–1886. *Source:* Collège de France. Archives.

The sweep of the image produced by Marey's photographic experiments perhaps goes partway to explaining my own emphasis on gesture as "poetics," as I put it in this book's title, insofar as I want to suggest that bodies move in formal patterns in Homer and that those movements weave together complex patterns of meaning. The repeated actions and various nuances that make up these gestures have a way of gathering key elements of Homer's narrative logic into their own sweep or arc. I do not use gesture's various parts or units, therefore, as an attempt to think of the body as something that exists in pieces,[11] but rather as an attempt to explore movement's connection to the body (and the poem) as a whole. The *Oxford English Dictionary* defines gesture first as "a manner of carrying the body,"[12] and this meaning is important because it shows how deeply gesturing is tied to one's sense of self (as is also true when gesturing is shared between bodies, I go on to argue). The gesture of falling, for example, takes the whole body down with it, and in a certain way this action is what all gestures do: they remind us that we have a body, and that they are the devices, the vehicles, which "carry" or "bear" (*gerere*) it.[13]

---

11. On "the body in parts," see the collection by Hillman and Mazio (1997). Snell 1953 famously described the Homeric body as "a mere construct of independent parts variously put together" (6). I discuss the relevance of Snell's ideas of the Homeric body as an aggregate of parts (1953: 5–8) to my own arguments later in this Introduction.

12. Oxford English Dictionary, s.v. *noun,* 1a.

13. Agamben [1992] 2000: 57, quoting Varro *On the Latin Language* 6.8.77 and following the derivation of gesture from *gerere.* See also Agamben [1991] 1999b and [2005] 2007 and my Chapter 6.

In one case, therefore, gesture might emerge as an effortless, intrinsic expression of the body as a whole, but, in another it might be felt differently—as the burden of oneself, or as something the body has to carry around with it. When Poseidon in *Iliad* 13 tries to imitate mankind, for example, he cannot quite acquire the ease or "naturalness" of the human walk,[14] yet by the last book of the *Iliad,* gesture operates more as a weight or load to be borne by Achilles and Priam in their grief.[15]

One of my concerns in this book is to show how the poet structures his narrative in relation to the coordinates and positions of his characters' bodies. But since gesturing is everywhere in Homer, how and when does it matter and when does it count for the purposes of this book? As I explain further in this Introduction, I count gesture as functioning in a similar way to language and style in the epics, and I focus on those instances of misalignment among the three in which gesture's importance stands out. When there is a divergence between body and narrative form it can provide unexpected turns in the plot and reveal previously unrecognized temporal and spatial dynamics at work in the poem. For this reason, again, I attach myself to the notion of a "poetics of gesture"; I am each time following a gestural thread, not creating a taxonomy, and that thread takes each chapter in a different direction to make an independent argument. My choice of gesture chapter by chapter can be explained in that, in each case, I trace a movement through repetition that redirects or illuminates the meaning of the poem.

The second way in which the ubiquity of gesture matters to my project is specifically related to epic language and composition, since, as I go on to explain, I understand Homer's bodies to be formulaic in much the same way as scholars have long understood Homer's verses to be.[16] The ordinariness of actions like walking and standing accords with the ordinariness of formulas repeated numerous times in the poems. The connection between the language of gesture and the language of Homeric formula can thereby help us to think differently about the role of repetition within archaic Greek epic. Although gestures matter to the critical reading of any text,[17] it is my contention that they matter in a distinctive way to the *Iliad* and *Odyssey*, since they bear a special relationship with, and are indeed in many ways analogous to, the structure and sequence of formulaic speech.

---

14. *Il.* 13.70–72. As discussed in my Chapter 2 (51).
15. See my Chapter 6.
16. Since the discoveries of Milman Parry almost a century ago (further references follow).
17. See, e.g., Bolens [2008] 2012.

FORMULAIC BODIES

Many ritual and social acts in Homer can be analyzed through their adherence to a prescribed set of gestures (supplication, sacrifice, or hosting, for example), as can activities like fighting in battle.[18] In this section, I consider gestures as linking phrases that the body may remember and rehearse by a process of second nature, just as formulas are made from a series of words and metrical units that the poet recalls with little apparent effort through habituated training.[19] I have already suggested that epic's gestural units fit together into sequence and combine with other movements in a manner that is analogous to the process of formulaic expression. We can now go a step further and think of gestures *as* formulas, since the two have remarkably similar properties.[20] We are used to looking for phase patterns, formulas, and repeated sequences in Homeric composition, but I propose shifting some of these methodologies over from the formal structure of the poem (its language and meter) to the formal structures (particularly the formulaic gestures) of the bodies within it.

Gesture, then, can be understood to stage a process of articulation through limbs and joints just as epic verse does through verse and meter. Indeed, epic repetition not only comprises words, formulas, and type scenes, but also the oft-repeated postures, gestures, and stances of the epic figure. The Homeric body, like the Homeric line of verse, cannot help recalling and repeating earlier versions of itself, and, just like Homeric language, it has its own movement vocabulary and rhythm, its own way of fitting into the space of the line. Much like a poet who builds on an oral repertoire of stock themes and words, as, through habit, he is called upon to repeat them over and over again, the Homeric hero's physical repertoire is shored up by a process of somatic repetition, which he then carries with him in the form of habits, acquired gestures, and impulses over the course of the poem.[21]

How, then, does our understanding of Homeric repetition change when it is plotted not through language or theme but through the dynamics of a moving body? How can our reading of gestures repeated twice, ten, or a hundred times

18. See also Bell [1992] 2009, esp. 69–117, on ritual practice and the body.

19. On cognitive processing in oral composition, see Minchin 2001.

20. There is a danger of falling into a tautological trap here: in a formulaic poem—we could say—everything by its nature will be formulaic. Yet gesture and formula share striking parallels as modes of expression, and I argue that this association is particularly thought-provoking and unique.

21. That is not to say, of course, that there will not be things "only done once" (see Chapter 6) but for the most part, as Fenik 1968 long ago showed us, action in Homeric epic, especially on the battlefield, is deeply repetitive. What I am seeking to capture here, to quote Noland, is the "motivated connection between the kinesthetic experience of performing the gesture ... and the figurative meaning the gesture conveys" (2009: 60).

across the epics inform our understanding of Homer's poetic sensibility? How, finally, are the choices of the poet or of characters within the narrative informed by the pull of repetition, its urge to direct the body along particular channels toward the exercising of familiar and well-practiced positions?

Donald Lateiner's exploration of Homeric gesture as a form of nonverbal communication has shown that epic body language can be read as a text of its own, cueing us to elements of the poem that might otherwise be missed.[22] While his research has focused on the social signs that the Homeric body conveys, I am interested in identifying how Homeric movement figures into and complicates the way that the story is told, particularly insofar as it orients itself toward and away from other modes of narrativization at work in the poem. At the same time, in trying to uncover the gestural system at the core of epic language, this book also acknowledges our own physical sensibilities as readers (or listeners) and the sensorimotor modes by which we experience movement. This experience applies to our own kinetic system—the embodied sense of *what it feels like* to gesture[23]—but also to our perception of the movement of others, which recent studies suggest we similarly "feel" through kinaesthetic empathy and the processing of so-called mirror neurons in the brain.[24]

The gestures that a Homeric character—let's say a warrior on the Iliadic battlefield—performs are thereby dependent on two formulaic systems: both the practice of oral composition in performance and the habits and training of his own (fictional) body as it reacts to the circumstances in which the narrative places him. At the very beginning of *Typical Battle Scenes in the Iliad*, Bernard Fenik explains that "verse building and action narrative ... represent two aspects of basically the same compositional technique,"[25] and this analogy between verse and action applies, both externally and internally, to the poet's choice of words and to the character's choice of movement.[26] One could argue

22. Lateiner 1992, 1995. See also Boegehold 1999, on the importance of gesture to the ancient Greeks particularly insofar as it supplements (and explains gaps in) speech, as well as Bremmer 1991; De Jong 2012; Clark et al. 2015.

23. Noland 2009.

24. See Craighero 2004; Foster 2008, 2011; Bolens [2008] 2012; Rizzolatti and Sinigaglia 2008; Noland 2009: 14; Shapiro 2011: 109–11; Craighero 2014; Olsen 2017a. Mirror neurons have been shown to fire in imitation when we perceive, read, or hear about an action. On bodily action stimulating the reader's imagination (enactivism), see Grethlein and Huitink 2017, and the essays, especially the introduction, in Kukkonen and Caracciolo 2014. It would be possible to write this whole book from the perspective of embodied cognition (cf. Clark 2013 on "action-oriented predictive processing," and Kukkonen 2014) but I am more interested in formal problems concerning the relationship between gesture, style, and narrative.

25. Fenik 1968 ("Summary of Contents").

26. See Martin 1989: 10 on the overlap between external (poet) and internal (character) speech and his observation that heroes are poetic performers in their own right. I develop this point further in Chapter 4.

that both are essentially the same or that we could not have one without the other, but the doubling effect—that it is not just Homeric language that tends to repeat, but also the Homeric body—is important. The highly stylized nature of epic verse brings to the surface the repetitive underlayer of all gestural practices, what Marcel Mauss refers to as "techniques du corps."[27] Formula and gesture thus stand in tandem, as parallel and mutually reinforcing forms of expression.[28] As has long been argued, and as I discuss further here, our gestures represent habits that emerge from social conditioning and repeated practice.[29] But if all bodies are formulaic, the Homeric body is especially formulaic, for, like the poet, it knows and recalls its own sequences, its own movement vocabulary and phraseology. And like the Homeric poet, the body "remembers" (what is often referred to as muscle or motor memory) through a process of learned or habitual repetition.

The formula, therefore, once famously defined by Milman Parry as "a group of words which is expressed under the same metrical conditions to express a given essential idea,"[30] provides us with a framework through which to consider gesture in Homeric epic as, instead, "a group of [movements] expressed under the same [physical] conditions to express a given essential [event]."[31] Indeed, the kinship between formula and gesture as they are discussed in their respective fields is surprisingly strong. They both emerge through a kind of habitual training and both are troubled by claims that they are overly mechanical and too dictated by forces beyond one's personal control.[32] The bard, who relies on a process of training acquired over many years, can be seen to draw on a repertoire of words, phrases, and scenes much as the Homeric character draws on a repertoire of actions or gestures. In both cases, it is acknowledged, there is room for variation and flexibility, but there is also a prevailing sense that the

---

27. Mauss [1935] 1992, who categorized these techniques much as I (and others) classify gesture.

28. They resemble the later use of the term *schēma* in oratorical practice as discussed earlier, which refers to both the form or posture of an athlete as well as a figure of speech (Isoc., *Ant.* 182–83; Hawhee 2004: 35; O'Connell 2017: 53–79). On style and bodily deportment in general, see Worman 2015.

29. On ancient athletic bodily practice and training (ἄσκησις) see Hawhee 2004; Stocking 2016.

30. Parry [1930] 1971: 272.

31. I thank Charles Stocking for helpful discussion on the problem of the term "idea" in Parry's definition (also explicated in Bakker 2013: 159–60).

32. That these gestures and phrases repeat has traditionally devalued them (for a movement like walking because we execute thousands of steps a day, and for Homeric formulas because of what tends to be seen as their metrically determined or "automatic" placement within the dactylic hexameter). This take on the formula has been well articulated, and challenged, by Bakker. See, e.g. (2013: 10): "The acknowledgment that Homeric language is formulaic, however, does not mean that the utterances of a formula is always done without the memory of other occurrences. Language (whether or not formulaic) is not autonomous, and utterances are never made in isolation, independently of a given context" (see also 157–69).

choices that the Homeric bard or the Homeric figure makes are not really his or her own.

Not only does Albert Lord use the term "habit" frequently in his discussion of oral-formulaic training and technique,[33] but he also explains the process of oral composition as a reliance on the "trained reflexes" of the poet.[34] Similarly, on the Homeric battlefield—where we see these kinds of reflexes realized in the body of the warrior—action sequences are determined by the physical situation in which a fighter might find himself and there are only a set number of gestures he will perform each time he is confronted with the same situation.[35] Both warrior and bard have a repertoire that has become natural over time, but only through a careful process of training and repetition.[36] The analogy between the habitual summoning of language and the habitual summoning of gesture is particularly appropriate to the battle narrative of the *Iliad,* moreover, since this kind of stylized use of the body—whether we want to call it "technique," "dressage," or "habitus"—is especially reinforced by military training.[37]

This is not to suggest, as Michel Foucault did for the eighteenth-century soldier, that Homeric warriors were no more than docile machines, or "automatisms of habit."[38] To do so would bring us back to earlier unproductive arguments defining Homeric characters as puppets without agency and the oral poet as entirely lacking in creativity or spontaneity.[39] Yet it is worth bearing in mind that charges of mechanical repetition are brought equally against both gesture and traditional oral style.[40] In their reading of gesture, some theorists

---

33. Lord [1960] 2000: 34, 36, 37, 53, 57, 58, 60, 63, 65, and passim. See also Parry [1928] 1971: 14, 22, 69.

34. Lord [1960] 2000: 58. Despite Lord's overall push toward a largely mechanical understanding of formula, I have no problem allowing for improvisation and originality within the notion of training, repetition, or reflex. On the resistance to the mechanics of oral-formulaic theory as originally conceived, see Bassett 1938; Kakridis 1949; Nagler 1974; Griffin 1986; Slatkin 1991; Minchin 2001: 33; Elmer 2015. On Homeric repetition and analogy, see Anderson 1957; Lohmann 1970; Austin 1975: 115–29; Edwards 1991: 11–23; Lowenstam 1993: 1–30. For a good discussion of the formula, see Hainsworth 1993: 1–31; Russo 1997. Important work in the history of its analysis, following Parry [1928] 1971 and Lord [1960] 2000, include Hoekstra 1965; Hainsworth 1968; Nagler 1974; Kahane 1994: 5–16; Watkins 1995: 471–504; Stocking 2010; Elmer 2010 and 2015, all with further references.

35. Fenik 1968.

36. See also Ingold 2011: 51–62; Noland 2009.

37. "Technique": Mauss [1935] 1992; "dressage": Lefebvre [1992] 2004: 38–45; "habitus": Mauss [1935] 1992: 458; Bourdieu [1972] 1977: 72–95, [1980] 1990a: 52–79; Crossley 2013; cf. Brecht on social *gestus* ([1930] 1992: 104).

38. Foucault [1975] 1995: 135 and 135–69. On the Foucauldian body in relation to the ancient and modern subject, see Porter 2005.

39. The scholarship on both topics is extensive. For recent assessments, with bibliographies, see Haubold 2007 on the poet, Purves 2015 on "Homeric man," and Holmes 2010: 1–83 on the Homeric body.

40. Gestures, like epithets, have been called "iterable and easily detached from the specific contexts of their performance" (Noland 2008: xi–xii).

propose that the body entirely conforms to social regulation and conditioning and that *all* gesture is therefore unnatural and stylized. Pierre Bourdieu is well known for his argument that physical deportment in general (*hexis, habitus*) can be understood as a result of the invisible enforcement over time of dominant ideologies,[41] while Judith Butler has persuasively maintained that gestures are performed and consolidated according to the cumulative re-enactment of a gendered script.[42] Gesturing may be unconscious, but it is still a social act. As Henri Lefebvre has put it ([1992] 2004: 39),

> [t]o enter into a society, group or nationality is to accept values (that are taught), to accept a trade by following the right channels, but also to bend oneself (to be bent) to its ways. Which means to say: dressage [*breaking-in*]. ... One breaks-in another human living being by making them repeat a certain act, a certain gesture or movement.

If we follow these arguments to their extremes, human gesture becomes aligned with the repetitive work of puppets or machines and the notion of an active, creative subject starts to fade away.[43] Such arguments are familiar to scholars of Homeric poetry, who have wrestled with precisely the problem of the individual's agency, both in narrative terms and along the lines of more formal properties such as theme, type, and language.[44] The challenge then becomes finding a way to read the Homeric body for both its repetitive *and* autonomous natures, both its "traditional referentiality" *and* its originality.[45]

A similar problem persists in reconciling the deeply repetitive and sometimes "automatic" nature of Homeric style (one third of both epics is made up of repeated phrases) with literary interpretation. Arguments as to how ornamental or unthinkingly reflexive an epithet is, or how problematic or accidental wholesale repetitions of scenes are, especially when they seem to take the plot off track, have led to suggestions that the poet is unsophisticated in the art of literary composition, rapidly plugging in bits and pieces of various scripts without making

41. The idea goes back to Aristotle, where it is cast in a positive light, as the practice of *euexia* (good bodily disposition). See further Hawhee 2004: 4; Sloterdijk 2009 (2013).

42. See, for various different approaches to and extremes of this position: Bourdieu [1972] 1977, [1980] 1990a; Foucault [1975] 1995: 135–69; Young [1980] 2005; Butler 1988 ("[gender is] an identity instituted through a *stylized repetition of acts*," 519, emphasis original), 1997; Agamben [1992] 2000; Lefebvre [1992] 2004: 38–45. See Corbeill 2004 on Bourdieu's habitus in relation to Roman gesture.

43. Noland 2009.

44. Purves 2015: 76–78, with references. On the question of the hero's agency beneath the controlling hands of the gods, see esp. Snell 1953; Lesky 1961; Williams [1993] 2008.

45. The phrase "traditional referentiality" is applied by J. M. Foley to Homeric poetics in an effort to privilege the immanent inherent meaning of repeated words and to de-emphasize any situation-specific meaning (1991, 1999). See further Danek 1998: 1–22, 2002; Kelly 2007a.

intelligent choices or providing a considered sense of the poem working as its own autonomous whole.[46] Parry claimed that, before his own work, repetition in Homer was considered no more than imitation and judged wholly negatively, yet he also argued forcefully for the absence of Homeric originality.[47] Since then there have been several studies of traditional repetition's value,[48] many of them offering considerable insight into its formal properties and laying out the issue in terms similar to those articulated by Walter Arend (who argued that there is always "play between fixed form and varying embellishment, ... between necessity and chance, between the typical and the individual, between repetition and variation").[49] But questions as to its use remain. For example, when is Homeric repetition significant and when not?[50] Should we distinguish between the type of repetition that occurs within formulas and the type that occurs within specific scenes? Is it possible to argue for intertextuality (and intratextuality) within a genre that is composed largely through a system of repetition?[51]

My approach to these questions is on the one hand indebted to the work of Pietro Pucci, who has demonstrated that a sophisticated intertextual relationship exists between the *Iliad* and *Odyssey*.[52] But when it comes to the kind of habituated and embodied repetition I am considering in this book, it is also helpful to think about intertextuality according to Egbert Bakker's "scale of interformularity," which looks specifically at the significance of repeating

46. On the ornamental epithet, "which has no relation to the ideas expressed by the words of either the sentence or the whole passage in which it occurs," see first Parry [1928] 1971: 21. Lord's adherence to Parry's views meant that he claimed that literary interpretation of formulas was an instance of pathetic fallacy (Lord [1960] 2000: 66), a position with which most scholars now disagree. For a good introduction and modification of Parry's and Lord's views on Homer's lack of individuality as a poet, see Lowenstam 1981: 1–30 (esp. 10–12 on ornamental epithets); Vivante 1982; Clark 1997: 214–15; Elmer 2010, 2015.

47. Parry [1928] 1971: 8. The scholia often marked repeated lines as spurious. The practice of determining which of two passages was "original" and which repeated (e.g., *Il.* 6.506–11 and 22.263–68; see further Calhoun 1933: 2–4) has now largely been abandoned.

48. Calhoun 1933; Kahane 1994; Watkins 1995: 28–49, 97–108. Bowra 1930: 87–113 argues that repetition is vital for improvisation (87); Nagler 1974 similarly draws literary value from repetition. See further Lowenstam 1981; Kelly 2007b.

49. Arend [1933] 1975: 27 (my translation). The full quotation in the original is "So entsteht das Eigenartige und Einzigartige der homerischen Kunst, der Wechsel von fester Form und verschiedener Ausschmückung (εἶδος und ποικιλία in der Sprache der alten Erklärer), von Notwendigem und Zufälligem, von Typischem und Individuellem, von Wiederholung und Variation."

50. Clark 1997: 213–37.

51. Nagy 1979; Pucci 1987; Danek 1988, 2002; Schein [1999] 2016: 81–91; Graziosi and Haubold 2005: 48–56; Tsagalis 2008; Burgess 2009: 56–71, 2011; Ormand 2014b: 12–14; Currie 2016. See also Elmer 2015 on the marked misplacement of formulas in the *Iliad,* which he identifies as a case of deviant focalization. On mythological allusion, see Slatkin 1991; Danek 1998 and 2002; Clay 2002b.

52. Pucci 1987; See also Tsagalis 2008.

formulas.[53] Some of the gestures I consider in this book fall at the high or meaningful end of Bakker's scale, such as leaping in the verse "he leapt having crouched like a high-flying eagle," which occurs only once in the *Iliad* and once in the *Odyssey,* and in the *Iliad* at an especially memorable moment in the poem (the death of Hector). But others, such as "he fell with a thud," are variable in their terminology and densely repetitive in their occurrences. In this case, repetition is not allied with quotation or allusion, but can be better described as arising from the repetitive structure (what we might call the nervous system) of the poem itself. Falling, like running, marks an important tempo for the *Iliad*; its frequency provides a groundwork for the epic.

In the case of other formulaic gestures, I sometimes argue for a practice of "rebellious repetition," that is, a repetition whose incongruous placement disrupts the trajectory of the narrative.[54] Alternatively, I consider instances in which a repeated gesture, such as standing, can lead to stasis and the threat of repetition without variation. Finally, against the background of Homeric repetition, scholars have long identified *hapax legomena,* or things said only once. In this book, I identify marked instances of what I term *hapax poioumena,* gestures performed only once.[55]

HABIT, GESTURE, AND FREEDOM

> It is time to acknowledge humans as the beings who result from repetition.
> —Peter Sloterdijk, *You Must Change Your Life*

The human capacity to gesture can be seen as contributing a crucial dimension to one's sense of self. For some it is the sign of one's unique idiosyncrasies, intentions, and alertness to the present moment, but for others, as I have previously noted, the body is conditioned in its gestures by habit and *habitus* as much as by its own original sense of "kinetic spontaneity."[56] Indeed, the notion that the nervous system is conditioned by force of habit dovetails with nineteenth-century explorations into the body's seriality that we touched on previously

---

53. Bakker 2013: 157–69. As he writes (168), "'intertextuality'. . . runs the risk of underemphasizing the fact that the intertextual allusion takes place entirely within the system of epic formulaic diction."

54. See Chapter 4. See Graziosi and Haubold 2005: 48–56 on the incongruous repetition of epithets for poetic purposes.

55. See Chapter 6.

56. See further Noland 2008: xi, with references, and Väliaho 2010: 25, quoting Sheets-Johnstone 1999 on "kinetic spontaneity." In Book 3 of Plato's *Republic*, Socrates argues that imitation through speech or gesture (κατὰ φωνὴν ἢ κατὰ σχῆμα μιμεῖσθαι, 393c5–6) is inadvisable, insofar as "imitations practiced from youth become part of nature and settle into habits of gesture, voice, and thought" (αἱ μιμήσεις, ἐὰν ἐκ νέων πόρρω διατελέσωσιν, εἰς ἔθη τε καὶ φύσιν καθίστανται καὶ κατὰ σῶμα καὶ φωνὰς καὶ κατὰ τὴν διάνοιαν, 395d1–2, trans. Grube and Reeve in Cooper 1997). See further O'Connell 2017: 62.

in the work of Muybridge and Marey (Figures 1.1 and 1.2). As Marey states in *Animal Mechanism* ([1873] 1893: 29),

> Many physiologists think, and we are of the same opinion, that there exist in the brain, and in the spinal marrow, centres of nervous action which acquire certain powers by force of habit. They attain to the command and co-ordination of certain groups of movements without the complete participation of that portion of the brain which presides over reasoning and the consciousness of our actions.

This argument is contemporary with that of the psychologist William James, who in his essay "On Habit" ([1890] 1950: 127) calls mankind "mere walking bundles of habits." Classifying habit as "the enormous fly-wheel of society, its most precious conservative agent," James argues for the plasticity of our organic matter and its susceptibility to influence over time (121). Habit, he argues in an example that works especially well for the *Odyssey*, is a kind of scar: a site of return in the nervous system that tracks the body's gestural practices back into previously inscribed pathways or grooves.[57]

Like clothing that seems to remember its wearer (another of James's evocative images),[58] habit—especially gestural habit—relates directly to *habitus*, the term popularized by Bourdieu to describe everyday practices and movements that appear natural but that are, rather, durably installed within bodies by history as an invisible and immanent law (*lex insita*) that directs the individual toward conformity.[59] Habitus, in Bourdieu's formulation, is wide ranging in its scope, but, like Marey's and James's habit, it also applies to bodily deportment and the exercise of gestural routines. First explicated by Mauss in *Techniques du corps* (the essay, as I have previously discussed, that identified gesture as the key factor in the cultural construction of the body), the habitus is constituted through a principle of "regulated improvisation."[60] For Mauss, habitus is best

---

57. Each of these grooves leaves a little scar or path, paving the way for its next iteration (106). This notion can be found in many subsequent writers, too (e.g., Bergson 1988: 83 talks of action recollection "as of an impress graven deeper by repetition").

58. James [1890] 1950: 105, quoting Léon Dumont: "Every one knows how a garment, after having been worn a certain time, clings to the shape of the body better than when it was new; there has been a change in the tissue, and this change is a new habit of cohesion." On habit and neuroplasticity (that "habit takes a physical form [and] needs constant reinforcement to be structurally maintained,") see Sparrow and Hutchinson 2013: 14.

59. It is difficult to sum up Bourdieu's theory of the habitus, which evolved over time and was complex in its parts, in a single paragraph. At one point, he describes it as "embodied history, internalized as second nature, and so forgotten as history" [1980] 1990: 56. See especially Bourdieu [1972] 1977: 72–95, [1980] 1990a: 52–79 and passim, [1987] 1990b: 157–67.

60. Bourdieu [1980] 1990a: 57; Mauss [1935] 1992: 458: "Hence I have had this notion of the social nature of the habitus for many years. Please note that I use the Latin word—it should be understood in

identified in the movements of the whole body, such as swimming, marching, or simply walking; movements that count as techniques because, as he was one of the first to argue, each is inherently unnatural (or nonbiological) and definitively culturally inscribed.[61]

These and other scholars have proposed—to differing degrees—that gestures are born from and through social conditioning and repeated practice. In each case we see gesture emerging as a process of acquired or imprinted movements over time. Without this habitual process of sedimentation, though, the body would also be at a loss. This leads Maurice Merleau-Ponty to suggest that habituated gesture, rather than disciplining or depriving the body, offers it a set of possibilities for addressing the present moment. For him, habit is a form of bodily knowledge that enables the self to face whatever task is at hand, by drawing on a deeply rooted and private "kinaesthetic background."[62] This background (*fond*) is rich with possibilities for both the future and the past. Edward Casey explains it this way (2013: 218):

[Habit] establish[es] the special ways the lived body comes to inhabit the world in a regular and repeatable (rather than purely spontaneous) fashion. Put differently: it gives the special depth of virtuality to a body that, lacking it, would be bound forever to the merely episodic and unrepeated.

Similarly, in her extensive work on gesture Carrie Noland writes (2009: 80, italics mine),

Merleau-Ponty, Bergson and the neuroscientists who follow in their path understand *movement, like thought, to be shot through with retentive patterning*, the sedimentation of previously executed gestural routines, *and at the same time future-oriented*, groping through the space of the present in

France—'*habitus.*' The word translates infinitely better than '*habitude*' (habit or custom), the '*exis*' [*sic*] the 'acquired ability,' and 'faculty' of Aristotle (who was a psychologist) ... These 'habits' do not just vary with individuals and their limitations, they vary especially between societies, educations, proprieties and fashions, types of prestige. In them we should see the techniques and work of collective and individual practical reason rather than, in the ordinary way, merely the soul and its repetitive faculties."

61. Mauss [1935] 1992: 459: "there is perhaps no 'natural way' [of walking] for the adult." Mauss claimed that of all gestures, only the squat might be truly natural (463).

62. Merleau-Ponty [1945] 1962: 166, 202–32. Cf. Ravaisson [1838] 2008: 55–56: "Ultimately it is more and more outside the sphere of personality, beyond the influence of the central organ of the will—that is to say, within the immediate organs of movement—that the inclinations constituting the habit are formed, and the ideas are realized. Such ideas become more and more the form, the way of being, even the very being of these organs."

search of the movements that will best address the demands of the next lived moment.

Indeed, as Henri Bergson puts it in *Matter and Memory*, the forward movement of the body's gestural memory "bears [the subject] on to action and to life."[63] The structure of habit is useful, indeed crucial, therefore, insofar as it allows us to re-embody the past, to draw the past back into our bodies and thereby engage in action. But it is also important to note that this is a nonspecific and a temporal form of "remembering," and one that is markedly different from the remembering of specific events.[64] In this sense habit and intertextuality (where the latter alludes to a specific moment in time) engage in a complicated relationship.

The form of embodied repetition recalled by habit affects not only the actor but also the reader or listener of the poem. As Gillian Beer has said of rhyme in English verse, and as we can also say of gesture and formula in Homer, it "makes memory within the poem" by aiding recollection and bringing things back for the listener as well as the poet.[65] Habitual acts thereby ground ("sediment") the Homeric body within a series of temporal layers, but they also provide for the future, modulating between the twin poles of—as Noland puts it—"kinaesthetic memory and kinetic potential."[66] For epic, this means that the formulaic behavior of its bodies binds the poem and forces it to cohere. Homer's use of repetition, both on the lexical and gestural level, works as stitches or folds in the poem that gather it together.

We can say, then, that the patterns and tendencies of past experiences orient the body in certain directions, guiding it through a principle of somatic memory toward certain choices and behaviors. But the pattern is not fixed, and there is always the potential for risk and deviation within repetition, just as there is always the capacity for resistance within gesture.[67] To translate this idea to epic poetry, we might say that its formulaic style underwrites a certain pattern of

63. Bergson [1896] 1988: 83. See also 84: "It is true that the example of a lesson learned by heart is to some extent artificial. Yet our whole life is passed among a limited number of objects, which pass more or less often before our eyes: each of them, as it is perceived, provokes on our part movements, at least nascent, whereby we adapt ourselves to it. These movements as they recur contrive a mechanism for themselves, grow into a habit, and determine in us attitudes which automatically follow our perception of things. This, as we have said, is the main office of our nervous system." Cf. Bourdieu on the habitus, which "at every moment structures new experiences in accordance with the structures produced by past experiences." [1980] 1990a: 60.

64. For Bergson, the one *acts* our past, the other *represents* it (1988: 82).

65. Beer 2007, as discussed in Flint 2014.

66. "Sedimentation" is a favorite term of both Merleau-Ponty and Butler, used to describe the accrual of certain patterns within the body over time. On "kinaesthetic memory and kinetic potential," see Noland 2009: 66.

67. See Butler 1997: 30: "'becoming' is no simple or continuous affair, but an uneasy practice of repetition and its risks ..." and 1988: 520 on the possibility of a different sort of repeating. Noland 2009: 8 "Individual bodies develop 'tactics' that successfully belie the 'durable' body *hexis* to which

gestures and behaviors that the Homeric body is to an extent expected, or even programmed, to follow. Yet what we have here is not, as Bourdieu said of the habitus, "a near-circular relationship of near-perfect reproduction" ([1980] 1990: 63). Formula and gesture can always become unfixed and, with every iteration of the body, movement has the capacity to speak in a slightly different way. As a form of expression, a gesture—no matter how formulaic—cannot help changing its meaning each time it is transferred between bodies and places. Each individual body and each different circumstance will bring its own measure of vitality, creativity, and affect to a gesture's performance.

BODIES IN MOTION

As a means of illustrating some of the questions I am trying to answer in this book, I turn now to consider more thoroughly how attempts by scientists, physiologists, and inventors to capture the successive phases (and intermittent gaps) of the human figure in motion in the late nineteenth century have opened up various avenues of inquiry for this project. Scholars such as Giorgio Agamben and Friedrich Kittler have shown how the research of physicians of that period into anatomical locomotion brought to light something extraordinarily distinctive about gesture. These discoveries, such as the Weber brothers' early analysis of walking by scientifically analyzing the joints and musculature of cadavers (Figure 1.3), or de la Tourette's 1886 experiments tracking the path of human footprints left by charcoaled soles on white paper, were instrumental in revealing previously invisible aspects of the gesturing body.[68]

This work, along with a renewed interest in Marey and Muybridge, has proven particularly important to the study of gesture since the late twentieth century.[69] Indeed, some of the most interesting writing on gesture has taken

they have been subjected" and 2008: x: "gesturing may very well remain a resource for resistance to homogenization."

68. The physiologists Wilhelm and Eduard Weber published *Mechanics of the Human Walking Apparatus* in 1836 (on which see Väliaho 2010: 48; Kittler 2003). Later, Braune and Fischer in *The Human Gait* [1895–1904] 1987 continued Weber and Weber's investigations into walking by the use of experiments with both cadavers and photography. Muybridge's eleven-volume *Animal Locomotion* was first published in 1887, while Marey published *Animal Mechanism: A Treatise on Terrestrial and Aerial Locomotion* in 1878 and *Movement* in 1895. In the same period, Gilles de la Tourette published *Études cliniques et physiologiques sur la marche*" (1886), on which see Agamben [1992] 2000: 49–53. On overlaps between Muybridge and Marey, who worked in different countries but knew and influenced each other, see Braun 1992: 228–62.

69. See, particularly in relation to gesture and the nineteenth century, Agamben [1992] 2000 (on Tourette), Väliaho 2010; Doane 2002: 46–68 (on Muybridge, Marey, and early film); Kittler 2003 (on the Weber brothers), and further references to follow.

PLATE XVI

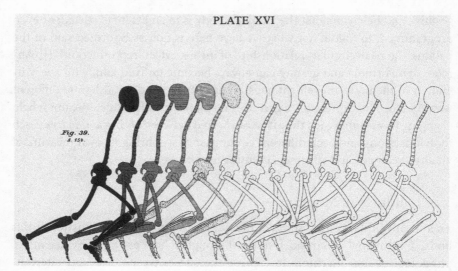

Figure 1.3. Table XVI from Wilhelm and Eduard Weber, *Mechanics of the Human Walking Apparatus*. Berlin and New York: Springer-Verlag, 1992. First published in 1836.

shape around the invention of the moving picture at the turn of the twentieth century, for which these practitioners and physiologists serve as important precursors. Early film, as scholars such as Väliaho and Doane have shown, radically altered our understanding of the relationship between action and form, partly because the silent medium exaggerated it from the start and partly because the camera's ability to displace, multiply, and otherwise play tricks with the body turned gesture into a strange and curious mode of expression.[70]

Muybridge's experiments with stop-action photography in Philadelphia and Marey's zootropic research into physiology in Paris crystallized around the recording of movements such as walking and running that are the most ordinary in daily life. In cataloguing these formulaic sequences as a series of intermittent phases and tracking them through time, both revealed novel aspects of the relationship between body and form. Marey's original desire was to record the flight of birds ("to seize the bird in a pose, or even better, in a series of poses, marking the successive phases of the movement of its wings"),[71] and in the process of

70. Burch 1990: 162–85; Doane 2002; Gunning 2003a: 48–49; Väliaho 2010. According to Agamben ([1992] 2000), cinema records the "loss of gesture" that began in the nineteenth century.

71. Braun 1992: 47, quoting Marey's letter to *La nature* in 1878. Cf. Muybridge's early experiments with horses, which prompted Marey to move from the "graphic" to "chronographic" method (Gunning 2008: 30–31). Although I am focusing on gesture here as a human expression, both Marey and Muybridge conducted much of their research on animal as well as human locomotion. On Marey's near-exclusion of the female body from his work, see Gunning 2003b, with further references.

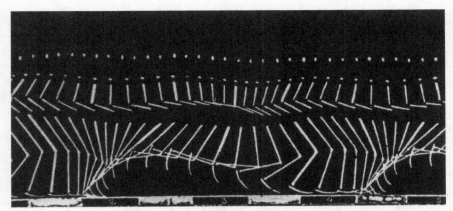

Figure 1.4. "Man Running," c. 1880, a chronophotograph by Etienne-Jules Marey. Marey (1830–1904) was a French scientist, physiologist, and pioneer of early photography. In this early experiment, a man wearing a black suit with a white stripe painted on it was recorded. *Source:* Science History Images/Alamy Stock Photo.

attempting to do so he invented a technology capable of capturing on a single plate the kinetic structure of human movement.[72]

The numbered markers at the bottom of the photographic strip at Figure 1.4, for example, allow us to study in isolation a number of gestural "steps" or "units," as they also capture distinctly the repeated, iterative nature of the movement itself. As can be seen both here and in Figure 1.2, Marey's use of lighted strips against a dark background abstracts the moving body into an almost two-dimensional skeletal form, that traces a sweeping, mesmerizing pattern of extraordinary subtlety and precision. The patterns that emerge from Marey's experiments are particularly important to my project, for they reveal a kind of poetic or narrative arc embedded in all movement, especially insofar as it emerges from the inherently repetitive nature of kinaesthetic experience.

By overlaying several frames of the same human figure onto a single plate, Marey brings to light a kinetic liveliness that contrasts with Muybridge's practice of splitting movement into stills separated by vertical lines (Figures 1.1 and 1.5).[73]

72. See further Didi-Huberman 2002: 117–23. As he puts it (122–23), "tous ces appareils, décrits par Marey, avaient pour fonction de restituer le *trait de temporalité* des phénomènes les moins faciles à observer …" ("all these devices, described by Marey, had the function of restoring the *trait of temporality* of phenomena that are the least easy to observe … ," translation mine, emphasis original).

73. See further Doane 2002: 209 on photography, "'capturing' a moment that does not really exist. It immobilizes the runner forever in the midst of a stride, the jumper in midair, the discus thrower at a moment in the process of winding up." Earlier anatomical explorations by the Weber brothers (see n.68, this Introduction) had led to similar effects, such that one of their drawings that captured the human figure in mid-step was said to make him appear to lurch awkwardly "as if a drunken town-musician" (Kittler 2003).

Figure 1.5. Eadweard Muybridge, *Animal Locomotion,* vol. 1, plate 62, *Running at full speed* (excerpt), 1887. *Source:* Boston Public Library. Wikimedia Commons.

We can find in the contrast between the two effects two complementary ways of understanding gesture. In Figure 1.4, we see gesture as a movement phrase or "wave": a form of energy that travels down the line. In Figure 1.5, the effect of isolating gesture into a series of freeze-frames draws attention to those aspects of movement that are ordinarily impossible to see. Muybridge's "cuts," moreover, make his figures detachable from the whole, giving the viewer time to consider them in detail.

We might note here the resemblance between the images of running at full speed depicted on sixth-century Panathenaic prize amphorae (Figure 1.6) and both Muybridge's serialization of slices of time and Marey's experiments with chronophotography plotted on a single plane.[74] Marey and Muybridge use the repetition of a single figure through space to create a synchronic impression of serialization, where the articulations of a gesture "travel" through the sequence of the plate, from left to right, enabling us to "see movement" through a sequence of stills. In this sense, their mechanics operate in an almost exactly inverse way to the Greek vase painters, who capture *several* figures running through time at one precise or "pregnant" moment in the race (note that each runner's feet are approximately the same distance from the ground), but who in doing so nevertheless create an impression of movement across the vase.

Although the athletes on the Panathenaic amphorae are in competition with one another, the manner in which they are represented also creates the effect of the repetition through time of a single figure. I find this formulation particularly helpful when considering Homeric characters because epic bodies are similarly both separate and the same, insofar as they share the same gestures and movement patterns. Such a sharing of near-identical poses and gestures is well known from geometric vase painting, as in Figure 1.7, in which a row of mourners on the Dipylon amphora (c. 750 BCE) hold their hands to the tops of their heads

74. On the Panatheanaic prize amphorae, see further Kyle 1993: 33–35. I am grateful to Charles Stocking for suggesting to me the Panathenaic amphorae as a parallel to Muybridge and Marey.

Figure 1.6. Terracotta Panathenaic prize amphora, attributed to the Euphiletos Painter. Attica, c. 530 BCE. *Source:* Metropolitan Museum of Art. Wikimedia Commons.

Figure 1.7. Dipylon Master (fl. 760–c. 735 BCE). Geometric-style amphora, 750 BCE. Greek. From the necropolis of Dipylon at Athens. Detail: prothesis scene (exposure and lamentation of the dead). *Source:* National Archaeological Museum, Athens, Greece. ART531993 (© DeA Picture Library/Art Resource, NY).

Figure 1.8. Étienne-Jules Marey, *Demeny Walking*, 1883. *Source:* Collège de France. Archives.

with elbows bent. As other have shown, there is a reciprocity between the repetition of figures on geometric vases and the repetition of formulas in early Greek epic; in both media we see repetition tracked through the angles and coordinates of the human body.[75]

The attempts of Marey and Muybridge to capture and record gesture's phases led to two important insights about the body, both of which apply to my project in this book. The first is its relationship to time.[76] Not only did the ability to analyze movement in increasingly smaller units allow for a process of deceleration and dissection, but it also presented two contrasting modes of viewing human action: stillness, on the one hand, and seriality, on the other.[77] In terms of seriality in particular, both photographers made visible the process of repetition at work in ordinary movement. The iterative cycle is especially well illustrated by the patterned modulation of arms and legs in Figures 1.2 and 1.4, but it is also dramatized by the viewer's initial confusion in Figure 1.8 as to whether she is looking at several *different* figures moving simultaneously in space (as in Figures 1.6 or 1.7), or one body moving repetitively and sequentially across a series of frames.[78] At the same time, the more repetitive Marey's mapping of movement becomes, the more mechanical it appears, undoing the sense of autonomy and spontaneity that one normally associates with individual motion.

The second way in which these images helped in the understanding of human movement and form was that they directed attention specifically to gesture as a category and provided an opportunity for it to be studied in isolation. By means of the alienating effect of scientific and technological experiments, limbs could now become, as Kittler has put it, "abstract" and "lonely"; held apart and incomplete in time or separated from their bodies

75. Schein 1984: 33, with further references.
76. See further Didi-Huberman 2002: 117–23; Doane 2002; Väliaho 2010: 40–51.
77. Doane 2002: 35 on the opposition between continuity and discontinuity.
78. Doane 2002: 49. Cf. Dagognet [1987] 1992: 173.

in space.[79] Or, as with Marey, they may lose their thickness and contours, being reduced to the bare bones of the graph system into which they are abstracted.[80] The gestures separated in this way function as indices for movement, helping us to track its variables and possibilities through a kind of cataloguing of gesture's formal properties.

Finally, in contrast to the abstract and mechanical presentation of gesture in Marey and Muybridge, we might consider Aby Warburg's unfinished *Mnemosyne Atlas* (1924–1929), whose aim was to capture gesture's emotive trace, its memory "engram," across widely disparate bodies and times (Figure 1.9).[81]

The black canvas boards upon which he placed a selection of images and texts explicitly eschew notions of seriality and sequence; instead Warburg strives to isolate the energy or intensity of a gesture by presenting it at moments of extreme emotion as depicted in, for example, Renaissance art, classical antiquity, or modern photography. Warburg's goal was to express the "representation of life in motion" (*Darstellung bewegten Lebens*)[82] by focusing on those "stages that lie in between [the] extremes of orgiastic seizure—states such as fighting, walking, running, dancing, grasping."[83] He coined the term *Pathosformel* ("pathos formula") to describe this preservation of affect and experience in gesture, and his attempt to capture the emotional (*Pathos*) within the formal and abstract (*Formel*) is crucial to our understanding of the gap between impulse and rational action that each of his panels stages.[84]

The images that Warburg included on the screens, such as various representations of the body striding in motion (Figure 1.10), or a photograph of a woman golfer with club raised alongside an image of Judith holding the head

---

79. Kittler 2003: 646; See also Gunning 2003b on the first objections to Muybridge's horses in motion because of their ungainliness as captured by his photographs, contrasting with the symmetrical images of galloping horses in equestrian paintings of the era.

80. On Marey's photography stripping away the "thickness" and "contours" of human form, see Väliaho 2010: 47–50, with further references; Michaud [1998] 2004: 86–91; Didi-Huberman 2002: 120–21.

81. Special thanks to Leopoldo Ibarrin for alerting me to Warburg's treatment of gesture.

82. Johnson 2012: 21.

83. Warburg "Einleitung" (1926–29), emphasis mine, as translated in Warburg and Rampley 2009: 277.

84. Warburg and Rampley 2009: 280; Johnson 2012: 63. This concept has been described by Rampley (Warburg and Rampley 2009: 274) as part of the Apollo-Dionysus opposition that informs Warburg's project, which emerges in "the contrast between the maintenance of rationalizing distance and empathetic absorption in the objects of perception." Cf. Agamben [1975] 1999a. Gombrich argues that Warburg's engram conserved "potential energy" that "may, under suitable conditions, be reactivated and discharged—we then say the organism acts in a specific way because it *remembers* the previous event" (italics original), Gombrich 1986: 242, quoted in Agamben [1975] 1999a: 93–94; cf. Barasch 1991: 126 on a gesture's "energetic inversion" across two different depictions. See further Didi-Huberman 2002 and my Chapter 6.

Figure 1.9. Aby Warburg, *Mnemosyne Atlas*, plate 39. *Source:* Copyright: The Warburg Institute.

Figure 1.10. Aby Warburg, *Mnemosyne Atlas*, plate 76 (excerpt). *Source:* Copyright: The Warburg Institute.

Figure 1.11. Aby Warburg, *Mnemosyne Atlas*, plate 77. *Source:* Copyright: The Warburg Institute.

of Holofernes (Figure 1.11),[85] provide, as Philippe-Alain Michaud has suggested, Kabuki-like "cuts"—mid-frame, mid-stride, or mid-swing—of action "immobilized at the height of gestural intensity" ([1993] 2004: 272).

But the logic of Warburg's *Mnemosyne Atlas* is also difficult to decipher in a way that the plotting and freeze-framing of movement in the Muybridge and Marey photography are not. For Warburg arranges his images and text on the canvas with no concern for diachronic sequence. Instead we are left to contemplate the blank spaces between the images and to use his "iconology of the intervals" to work out the meaning that binds this arrangement of gesture's inherent force (engram) into a disassembled encyclopedic form.[86] The juxtaposition of images across time and movement based on a quality that they together share (and whose meaning is revealed only in their juxtaposition) relates to my

85. On the motif of "nymph as head-hunter" and a depiction of the Jewish woman Judith raising her sword and holding the enemy general Holofernes by the hair, see Panel 47.

86. Warburg wrote in his journal of 1929 of his interest in the "iconology of the intervals," as quoted in Gombrich 1986: 253. See also Michaud [1993] 2004: 251–76. On points of contact between Marey and Warburg, see Michaud [1998] 2004: 88; Didi-Huberman 2002: 119–20.

stacking of certain gestures in the Homeric poems one upon the other, so that further patterns of meaning can emerge.

CHAPTER OUTLINE

The book arranges a select number of gestures into separate constellations, and attempts from that starting point to offer a new argument about Homeric epic in each of the chapters. The chapters are arranged here in the sequence in which they were written.[87] As a result, they become more and more explicit as they move along as to gesture's theoretical significance to the project as a whole, ending with a chapter that tries to tackle the larger problem of what it means to inhabit a body that gestures. Two of the chapters (the first and last) deal solely with the *Iliad*, while the three in the middle juxtapose forms of gesturing that occur in different but related ways in both of the epics. In the last three chapters, I pay attention to the precise moments at which the epics begin and end, while the first two chapters are more concerned with how particular gestures or actions propel the narrative through the middle parts of the poems. In all of these cases, although I look at clearly defined occurrences of gesture as I move through each chapter, I also take my interpretations beyond the body, aiming to show that the positions and stances I identify are—like "figures" or *schēmata*—often suggestive of an underlying thematic or narrative logic at work in the epics.

Chapter 2, "Falling," considers a gesture that is not only highly repetitive in the *Iliad* but also marks the kinetic drive of the battle scenes, in which falling to one's death is a dominant motif. I begin by arguing that falling serves as a point of reference throughout the poem for a concept of time that is specifically human. It is well known that mortals fall at the moment of death in the poem, but it has not been recognized that the movement of the fall is also connected with the time of birth, aging, and generation. In light of the significance of falling for mortals, I then go on to examine the problematic case of two particular gods who fall in the *Iliad*. When Hephaestus tumbles to earth from Olympus, and when Ares is knocked flat on the battlefield, both gods, I argue, also "fall into" human time. This action complicates their status as ageless and eternal beings and draws into question the different temporal registers at work in the narrative, such as repetition, "long time," and time that is steady or continuous. The single gesture of falling brings together several key concepts in

87. Earlier versions of Chapters 2 and 3 have been previously published as articles (Purves 2006 and 2011).

the poem that hinge on the issue of the separation between the mortal and immortal spheres in the *Iliad*.

Chapter 3, "Running," examines speed and the difference between catching up and overtaking as it occurs in the *Iliad* and *Odyssey*. I begin by exploring how the *Iliad* foregrounds the problems and strategies involved with catching up with one's opponent and getting ahead. I then go on to show, by contrast, how the *Odyssey* presents a world where the act of overtaking and the alternation between the categories of first and last are of central concern to Odysseus on his way home in Books 8 and 9. This focus on the thematics of running reveals not only something about the kinetic sensibility of both poems, but also about the difference between time as it is experienced through the body and time as it unfolds in the plot. As I argue, the different running styles of the protagonists of the *Iliad* and the *Odyssey* speak also to important conceptual differences between the two poems.

My fourth chapter, "Leaping," considers the last gesture that Odysseus performs in the *Odyssey*: a single leap just ten lines before the poem's end. It understands that leap within the context of the relationship between gesture and repetition in Homeric epic by paying particular attention to the ways in which gestures work as a series of habituated impulses that almost automatically drive their characters forward. In the case of Odysseus, I argue that his final leap expresses an instance of rebellious repetition, whereby the kinaesthetic impulses of the warrior's body run counter to the demands of the narrative (in simple terms: he wants to keep going while the poem wants to end). There is a kind of muscle memory at work in Odysseus' body that unexpectedly emerges as an expression of autonomy when he disobeys Athena's command and keeps on fighting, even as his story draws to a close. In this chapter, I follow the trajectory that Odysseus launches with his leap, by reaching forward through this verse to the notion of alternate plot lines and competing authorial impulses. As such, I trace Odysseus' leap through two passages in the *Iliad* (Achilles' partial drawing of his sword in Book 1 and Hector's last leap in Book 22) and, briefly, one in the *Aeneid* (the death of Turnus), in order to show how this final leap falls into a small category of gestures or actions that reveal a moment of divergence between body and narrative form.

Chapter 5, "Standing," looks at two separate and enduring acts of standing in the *Iliad* and the *Odyssey*. The first is the standing apart (διαστήτην) of Achilles and Agamemnon in the seventh line of the *Iliad*, a gesture that sets in motion a subsequent series of "standing aparts" between Achilles and the Achaeans. The gap that this opening *dia-* forges in the poem allows us to understand more clearly the role played by standing's other prefixes (notably *para, amphi, anti,* and *ana*), which so often set one figure in a relational aspect with another. Throughout this first part of the chapter, we see how various manifestations of standing on or near the battlefield reveal the loneliness of the warrior after the structure of "standing beside" has been broken.

That Achilles expresses defiance through an opening stance that shuns physical movement through space leads to certain problems to do with narrative progression in the *Iliad,* but that issue is only compounded by Penelope's signature pose of "standing by the stathmos," repeated four times in the *Odyssey* and symbolizing her reluctance to move forward through time. I explore how this fourfold repetition of a static scene maps out a notably restricted route and set of expressions for her body, as I also identify a particular agency that comes with her own unusual style of epic gesturing. Penelope is an interesting challenge for this book, because unlike the other characters, she repeats without variation. Her repetitive kinetics are thus an articulation of standing-as-stopping, an interruptive force that focuses the poem and articulates her resistance to the ongoing events in Ithaca.[88]

My final chapter, Chapter 6, takes as its central scene Priam's gesture of reaching Achilles' hands to his own mouth when he comes to ransom the body of his son. The gesture has mostly been noted for its emotional effect on the poem's audience, but I try to frame it within the context of other gestures at work in the *Iliad*'s final book. In particular, I consider the difficult notion of bearing one's own body (as in the *OED*'s definition of gesture previously discussed) as well as the body of others. This notion can be seen both in Priam's desire to lift the body of his son in his arms and in Achilles' dragging of the corpse at the beginning of the book, in a scene that transfers the heavy gestural "drag" of grief onto the body of Hector. The scene shared between Priam and Achilles emerges in my telling as an attempt to bear their own bodies—to hold up under the pressure of grief—and this attempt is modulated by the inherent ambiguity of the word for reach (ὀρέγεσθαι) in the famous phrase spoken by Priam, "[I have endured] to reach to my mouth the hands of a son-killing man," (ἀνδρὸς παιδοφόνοιο ποτὶ στόμα χεῖρ' ὀρέγεσθαι, 24.506). It is essentially unclear which direction ὀρέγεσθαι is moving in this scene, for in addition to meaning "reach *your* hands to *my* mouth," it could also mean "reach with *my* hand to *your* mouth." An ambiguity is therefore revealed by the pose that Priam and Achilles share, an ambiguity that, I argue, creates an opening for reconciliation through the joint practice of holding (on) and letting go. The physical forms of expression shared between the two

---

88. Foley 1978 argues that the people and events on Ithaca are frozen in time while Odysseus is away.

eventually show how the experience of grieving is affectively translated from the dragging of Hector's corpse to its lifting, ritual cleansing and anointing, and final carrying home.

HOMERIC BODIES

In the last part of this Introduction, I briefly indicate how my work intersects with two related areas in studies of Homer and the body. The first is the performative gestures of the Homeric rhapsode, and the second addresses the question, raised most notably by Bruno Snell, of how we can conceptualize the Homeric body as a fully realizable and visible "whole."

Rhapsodes and the Body in Performance

If the relationship between Homeric composition and Homeric movement is as intricately connected as I have suggested, what then of the body of the singer or rhapsode who performs these poems? Homer was said by Aristotle to have "composed dramatic imitations" (μιμήσεις δραματικὰς ἐποίησεν, *Poetics* 1448b37) and by Plato to have "made his narration through mimesis (διὰ μιμήσεως)" and "likened himself, whether in voice or in gesture (ἢ κατὰ φωνὴν ἢ κατὰ σχῆμα)" to his characters (*Republic* 393c5–6).[89] Since Socrates elsewhere puts rhapsodes and actors into the same category,[90] how should we interpret the physicality of the rhapsode as he recites Homeric epic? Since the evidence on Homeric performance is meager,[91] I will focus on what can best be gleaned from late-fifth- and early-fourth-century sources. Even though these performers were not the same as the singers (*aoidoi*) described in the epics, who would have had their hands full with lyre and plectrum (and even though Plato's *Ion*, our primary source text, reaches toward parody), they still give us some information on how the poems were performed.[92]

89. Herington 1985: 10–15; O'Connell 2017: 62; Kretler forthcoming 2019; Thanks to Daniel McLean for helpful discussion on this question, and to Marcus Folch for first asking me to consider them.

90. Plato, *Ion* 532d6–7; 535e9–536a1; Herington 1985: 11–12 (and see n.98 in this Introduction); Murray 1996: 110; Nagy 1996a: 161.

91. Boegehold has made the case for rhapsodic gesture occurring at those moments in Homer in which the sense needs to be completed (1999: 36–47), but cf. De Jong 2012. Note also that Odysseus at *Il.* 3.218–19 is said to have stood so still, without moving his staff backward or forward, that the Trojans considered he must be a weak or inexperienced speaker.

92. De Jong 2012; see also Nagy 1990b: 19–28; and on evidence from vase painting, Shapiro 1993; Herington 1985: 14–15; Bundrick 2015; Kretler (forthcoming 2019: App. A). On Plato's negative approach to poetry, see Murray 1996: Rijksbaron 2007: 9–14.

In the *Ion*, we find evidence for the rhapsode's clothing and platform,[93] but—although reference is made to the emotions aroused in both Ion and his audience and to their bodily effects—nowhere does Socrates refer to any kind of gestural movement on the part of the rhapsode.[94] Instead, there is an emphasis on gesture *within* the epics (*Ion* 535b2–6):[95]

ὅταν εὖ εἴπῃς ἔπη καὶ ἐκπλήξῃς μάλιστα τοὺς θεωμένους, ἢ τὸν Ὀδυσσέα ὅταν ἐπὶ τὸν οὐδὸν ἐφαλλόμενον ᾄδῃς, ἐκφανῆ γιγνόμενον τοῖς μνηστῆρσι καὶ ἐκχέοντα τοὺς ὀϊστοὺς πρὸ τῶν ποδῶν, ἢ Ἀχιλλέα ἐπὶ τὸν Ἕκτορα ὁρμῶντα, ...

When you recite epic verse and you greatly astound your spectators, either when you sing of Odysseus leaping onto the threshold, being revealed to the suitors and shedding arrows at his feet, or Achilles charging at Hector ...

and these forms of poetic gesture lead not to imitation but rather to internal physiological effects for both the audience (who are described as "crying and looking terrified, and overcome with amazement at the things being said," κλάοντάς τε καὶ δεινὸν ἐμβλέποντας καὶ συνθαμβοῦντας τοῖς λεγομένοις, 535e2–3) and the speaker. For as Ion says (535c5–8),

ἐγὼ γὰρ ὅταν ἐλεινόν τι λέγω, δακρύων ἐμπίμπλανταί μου οἱ ὀφθαλμοί· ὅταν τε φοβερὸν ἢ δεινόν, ὀρθαὶ αἱ τρίχες ἵστανται ὑπὸ φόβου καὶ ἡ καρδία πηδᾷ.

For when I recite something pitiable, my eyes fill with tears, and whenever I recite something fearful or terrible, my hair stands on end from fear and my heart jumps.

---

93. Socrates frequently remarks on Ion's costume in the first pages of the dialogue (*Ion* 530–35) and at 535e1–2 the rhapsode recounts "look[ing] down on the audience from up on the rostrum" (καθορῶ γὰρ ... αὐτοὺς ἄνωθεν ἀπὸ τοῦ βήματος, 535e1–2).

94. *Ion* 535b2–e3 lists *ekplēxis*, weeping, hair standing on end, heart pounding, terror, and amazement. In chapter 26 of the *Poetics*, Aristotle says that the more cultivated audience of epic (as opposed to tragedy) "does not need gesture" (οὐδὲν δέονται τῶν σχημάτων, 1462a3). Although certain rhapsodes may be faulted for "overdoing the gesturing" (περιεργάζεσθαι τοῖς σημείοις, 6), Aristotle makes clear in this passage that epic best produces its effect "without movement" (ἄνευ κινήσεως, 11–12). See further Herington 1985: 12–13. De Jong 2012 argues that deictic pronouns in Homer do not call for gestures on the part of the narrator.

95. As Murray notes (1996: ad loc.), these actions refer to the climactic moments of both poems (Odysseus about to kill the suitors in *Odyssey* 22; Achilles killing Hector in *Iliad* 22).

This passage suggests that the kind of gestures I consider in this book do have a bodily effect on the rhapsode, but probably not a mimetic one. In fact, Socrates comments on the incongruity of Ion feeling afraid as he recounts these passages, even though he is "standing (ἑστήκως) among countless friendly people ... [and] no one is trying to strip him or do him harm" (535d4–5). Is the word "standing" meant to make us think of a correspondence between the body of the rhapsode and a figure like Odysseus who pauses on the threshold, or—perhaps more likely— of Ion's *inactive* pose in contrast to heroes who leap (ἐφάλλομαι) and charge (ὁρμάω)?[96] The emphasis on heroic rather than rhapsodic action is underscored a little later in the dialogue when Socrates asks Ion to recount Nestor's speech to Antilochus at the turning post (*Iliad* 23.335–40), and Ion replies by moving the verb "lean" to the prominent, initial position in the line: "Κλινθῆναι δέ," φησί, "καὶ αὐτὸς ἐϋξέστῳ ἐνὶ δίφρῳ ..." (" 'Lean,' [Nestor] says, 'Lean yourself over on the smooth-planed chariot ...'" 537b).[97] Here, as before, there is a suggestion that the gestures performed by Homer's characters provide the impetus for the rhapsode's ownership or embodiment of the poem. Indeed, as Katherine Kretler suggests, by focusing on embodiment in performance rather than on re-enactment we may gain a more productive sense of the rhapsode's relationship to Homeric gesture.[98]

Given the limited nature of the evidence and my own points of interest, I have therefore largely avoided the practice of reading Homeric actions onto the body of the performer, as I have also avoided attempting a reconstruction of the rhapsode's gestures as he recites.[99] We know that there was a time when Homeric epic was acted out as show pieces by the *Homeristae*, who dressed up in armor and fought as they recited sections of battle narrative in

96. See Chapter 4 for my discussion of leaping (and Chapter 5, for standing). That it is Ion's hair and heart that move and jump (πηδάω), rather than his body, is perhaps also a tongue-in-cheek commentary on his immobile stature. For hair standing on end and hearts beating in fear in Homer, see *Il.* 24.359, 22.461 (Murray 1996: ad 535c5–8).

97. Compare *Il.* 23.335: αὐτὸς δὲ κλινθῆναι ἐϋπλέκτῳ ἐνὶ δίφρῳ, where the word order is slightly different: "You yourself lean over in the well-made chariot."

98. Kretler forthcoming 2019, particularly her reading of curse gestures in *Iliad* 9. See also Herington 1985: 13: "Homeric poetry. . . seems to have been designed from the first to be *acted*. It demands impersonation; it demands skillful variations in tone, tempo, and dynamic; and there are some points, also, where it seems imperiously to exact from the speaker some form of physical gesture ... One is not prepared to believe that [the rhapsode] stood there like a tree-trunk and recited ... " (emphasis original). As Ralph Rosen points out to me, there is also an interesting point of contact between Plato's disingenuous Ion and Millay's Odysseus, both of whom use gesture in an artificial and imitative way.

99. For discussion on rhapsodic delivery and on the rhapsode as ὑποκριτής or performer, see González 2013. As he observes, our ancient sources overwhelmingly pay attention to the voice in delivery (533–43; Arist., *Rh.* 1403b20–25), although Aristoxenus notes that "there are three things that can be made rhythmic: utterance, melody, and bodily motion (κίνησις σωματική)," (2013: 541–42, n.78; Aristoxenus, *Elements of Rhythm.* 19.15). On all aspects of rhapsodic performance see now the essays collected in Ready and Tsagalis 2018, which regrettably appeared too late for me to consult for this chapter.

the theater.[100] But leaving such diversions aside, the question remains open as to whether we can relate such ordinary gestures as standing, walking, or reaching to actions that the bard or rhapsode might have adopted. One possibility, as I have touched on in my reading of the *Ion*, is to think in terms of cognitive and mnemonic sequences, whereby performers cognitively "store" different aspects of storytelling within different regions of the body or senses. Gestures could in this way be a useful aid for organizing or remembering a narrative.[101] Although the early use of a staff (*rhabdos*) by rhapsodes is contested, Kretler argues that its presence in the hand of a performer would have encouraged certain gestures as it also deflected others. In general, though, when it comes to attempting to visualize the rhapsode, there is no need to imagine the singer reaching or crouching when he narrates these gestures in order for the arguments to achieve their full impact. Indeed, in some senses, as I discuss in the final part of my Introduction, the inability to visualize the body in every instance may be productive, just as it may not always be helpful to take every instance of a gesture as something that can be conceived of only literally.

Snell and the Homeric Body

Earlier in the Introduction, I discussed the notion of gestural freedom as it has been debated by scholars such as Bourdieu, Foucault, Merleau-Ponty, and Noland. But the issue is also a particularly apt one for the Homeric body, a figure that has long been plagued by arguments concerning its supposed lack of agency and autonomy. Homeric man was best understood, according to Bruno Snell in the first chapter of *The Discovery of the Mind* (1953), as an assemblage of parts rather than as a single, independently operating and autonomous self. His argument, based on the lack of a single word for a "living body" in Homer, is well known and need not be rehearsed in full here.[102] As I have discussed elsewhere, however, his central claim that "the early Greeks did not ... grasp the body as a unit" (7)—although misleading in its simplicity and overly reliant on a soul-dependent theory of action—is also constructive for the way it directs our attention towards the idea of gesture as a category.[103]

---

100. See Nagy 1996a: 157–68 on the *Homeristae* and the performance of Homer becoming increasingly mimetic over time; González 2013: 447–65, esp. 451 and n.62; Ready and Tsagalis 2018.

101. Alice Oswald, who recites *Memorial* (a rendition of the *Iliad*) from memory, tells me that she does so by working through a kind of internal cognitive dance, with different parts of her body serving as different *loci* in the poem.

102. Snell 1953: 1–22; See also Fränkel [1962] 1975: 75–85; Holmes 2010: 5–9, 29–37, 41–83, with further references.

103. Purves 2015, esp. 76–78, 93.

Figure 1.12. Bruno Snell, "Fig. 2" (reproduction of the Greek concept of the human shape as found on Geometric vases). *Source*: In *The Discovery of the Mind: The Greek Origins of European Thought*, 1953. Cambridge, MA: Harvard University Press, p. 7.

The body, according to Snell, does not really exist in Homer. As his illustration of Homeric man, based on early Greek vase painting (Figure 1.12), attempts to illustrate, these "geometric figures lack [the] central part; they are nothing but μέλεα καὶ γυῖα, i.e. limbs with strong muscles, separated from each other by means of exaggerated joints" (6). But in contrast to the sequencing of movement we earlier considered on the Dipylon amphora, here Snell sketches a single, lonely figure in isolation from its pictorial context.

The illustration, which stands alone and at rest, traps the Homeric body within a static pose. To think of the epic or archaic body in these terms is—as I hope this Introduction has shown—antithetical to how Homer or the Dipylon Master themselves understood it. For both the poet and the vase painter, the body is multiple; it does not make sense to consider it as an individual unit in isolation from the other bodies that surround it and whose gestures it shares. Indeed, it would be better to envision the Homeric body as an entity not formed from "centers" or "parts" but *through movement*, as Snell goes on to state on the following page (8):

> Again and again, Homer speaks of fleet legs, of knees in speedy motion, of sinewy arms; it is in these limbs, immediately evident as they are to the eyes, that he locates the secret of life.

Whether or not the limbs of the Homeric figure do indeed hold "the secret of life," Snell pinpoints the manner in which the epic body as a whole comes into focus through the tracking of movement and gesture. His reading is valuable for its ability to recognize in Homeric characters a dynamic articulation of limbs, tendons, and muscles, whose various patterns trace the body's on-going processes of decision-making as well as, more generally, an articulation of self.[104]

In this book, I too conceive of the Homeric body as something that acquires a special kind of visibility through the choices it makes in movement.[105] I do not, therefore, consider the Homeric body for the intricacies of its parts (*thumos*, limbs, midriff),[106] but rather for the intricacies of its *actions* (standing close or far apart, running quickly or slowly, or leaping in to fight).

The final point to consider about Snell's reading, as Bernard Williams has shown, is that it is somewhat absurd to argue that there is no concept of a living "whole body" in Homer. When Priam sets out to recover Hector's body in *Iliad* 24, one of his central concerns is to know whether his son's corpse is still complete or has been torn limb from limb (24.408–9).[107] Williams writes of the scene that ([1993] 2008: 24),

> In wanting Hector's body to be whole, Priam wanted Hector to be as he was when he was alive. The wholeness of the corpse, the wholeness that Priam wanted, was not something acquired only in death: it was the wholeness of Hector.

His words reveal that it is not only Priam's concern for Hector's corpse, but also many of the gestural practices surrounding its care and destruction, that shed light on the question of how the body is moved and how—through that movement—it also moves us. Yet Priam's yearning to take hold of the "whole Hector" (as I discuss in my final chapter) speaks more broadly to an inability to *ever* grasp the body as a whole within Homeric epic, and this lack is perhaps part of a phenomenon that Snell correctly identified but also interpreted too literally. For it does not mean that Homer "could not" conceive of the self or the subject; it is rather that, taken together, gesture and formulaic action inevitably blur any attempt to focus on a single Homeric figure moving organically and autonomously through time.

Indeed, if we consider Snell's still geometric man (Figure 1.12) alongside the photograph of Marey's assistant, Georges Demenÿ, whom we saw in

104. Osborne 2011.

105. Cf. Austin 1975: 114.

106. On which see the valuable studies of Pelliccia (1995) and Clarke (1999). On the question of the Homeric body's relation to self, and whether we conceive of epic bodies as having "interiority," see Williams [1993] 2008: 21–49; Porter and Buchan 2004; Holmes 2010: 41–83; Purves 2015.

107. See Holmes 2010: 33 on how the idea of being "uncared for" is "more than incidentally important to the meaning of *sōma* in the Homeric poems." More regularly the human corpse is referred to as *nekus* or *nekros*.

Figure 1.13. Étienne-Jules Marey, "Demeny portent le costume noir à lignes et points blancs," 1883. *Source:* Cinémathèque Française.

Figures 1.2 and 1.4 in motion but see now, clad in the same black outfit, at rest (Figure 1.13), a similarity arises that may prove instructive. In his discussion of Marey, Philippe-Alain Michaud claims that paying close attention to gesture can lead, paradoxically, to an eclipse of the body *as a whole* ([1988] 2004: 88):

> When at rest, the figure appears, in his disappearing outfit, to be endowed with a paradoxical presence that allows only what annuls him to be seen. As he begins to run, a mutation affects his body, and in its place its spectral form appears on the plate—not its structure, but its passage, its vanishing, whose anti-figurative aspects Marey further heightened by tracing proofs made by photographic impression onto his images … Instead of representing the body devoid of movement, he represented movement through an eclipse of the body.

Marey's invisible body, like the disappearing waist in Snell's diagram at Figure 1.12, perhaps helps to reveal what is so enigmatic about the liveliness of gesture, whether we mean gesture within a single body, within a single moment in time, or gesture shared between bodies. Or, to take the kinetic dimension one step further, we might understand gesture's liveliness not only in terms of what it means for a Homeric character to move through the ordinary and urgent sequences of being alive, but also in terms of gesture's potential to bring to life its own forms of epic reading and expression.

2

Falling

Our human vision depends on gravity,
That is, on the fact that one does or does not fall.
—Paul Virilio, "Gravitational Space"

THE GESTURE OF FALLING—OF FEELING ONE'S CENTER OF BALANCE slip, one's limbs give way, and, eventually, of colliding with the ground—is central to the experience of mortality in the *Iliad*.[1] Although most characters experience falling only once over the course of the poem, phrases such as δούπησεν δὲ πεσών ("he fell with a thud") or λῦσε δὲ γυῖα ("he unstrung his limbs") occur regularly within the battle books.[2] In each of these cases, as something that happens *to* you, falling is a gesture without agency—a rapid and irreversible sweep toward death, as well as a forced submission to the rules of the epic: you will die, as all the others die, by descending to the ground.

For this reason, among others, we do not expect the Olympian gods to have the kinds of bodies that fall. Yet in the *Iliad* they do. At specific points within the poem, Hephaestus, Ares, and Aphrodite each join with humans in the act of having fallen. By imitating what is elsewhere in the poem a uniquely human gesture, these Olympian falls not only open up a new avenue through which to explore the much-discussed topic of "immortal death" in Homer,[3] but they also cast new light on the question of how differently gods and humans in the *Iliad* experience space and time through their bodies. For, as I go on to show, the significance of falling in the *Iliad* encompasses a complex interplay between different temporal registers at work in the poem.

Since the theme of falling on the battlefield of the *Iliad* is so rich and repetitive, in this chapter I limit myself to an examination of bodies falling in that

---

1. In Greek: δούπησεν δὲ πεσών or λέλυντο δὲ γυῖα. In the vast majority of cases in the *Iliad*, the time of one's death is fixed by the moment of one's fall. As Lowenstam (1981: 85, n.29) observes, λῦσε δὲ γυῖα ("he loosened his limbs") always signals death in the *Iliad*, as do λέλυντο δὲ γυῖα and ὑπέλυσε δὲ γυῖα, with the exception of 23.726. See further n.11 in this chapter and *LfrgE* s.v. λύω on the verb's considerable semantic range (see 3a on falling to the ground in death). On Iliadic death in general, see, e.g., Fenik 1968; Griffin 1980; Garland 1981: 43–60; Schein 1984: 67–88; Morrison 1999: 129–44.

2. λῦσε δὲ γυῖα (eight times, *Il.*), λέλυτο δὲ γυῖα (once, *Od.*), λύντο δὲ γυῖα (twice, *Il.*), δούπησεν δὲ πεσών, ἀράβησε δὲ τεύχε' ἐπ' αὐτῷ (six times, *Il.*; once, *Od.*), δούπησεν δὲ πεσών (nineteen times, *Il.*, twice, *Od.*), ἀράβησε δὲ τεύχε' ἐπ' αὐτῷ (nine times, *Il.*; once *Od.*).

3. On which see Braswell 1971: 16–26; Willcock 1977: 41–53; Levy 1979: 215–18; Vermeule 1979: 118–44; Loraux 1986: 335–54.

poem only. To veer into the *Odyssey*, although tempting (Elpenor falls from the roof; Eurycleia lets Odysseus' foot fall into the pail with a crash), would be to make a different argument from the one presented here. My reading in this chapter, therefore, follows a relatively fixed pattern of movements through which humans and gods together gesture toward death.

This chapter, like the one on running that follows it, takes as its primary focus the movement of the body through time.[4] On a purely physical level, falling sweeps the body up into its own sense of time, its own "free fall," beginning with the moment that it loses its secure, vertical standing on the earth and ending at the point when it hits the ground. To set our reading of the fall within the context of the *Iliad*, we can say that the experience of falling onto the Trojan plain subjects the body to two kinds of time at once. The first is the speed at which one falls, which is determined by the weight of one's body as it moves through space. The second, and the one that is most readily apparent, given the subject of the poem, is the time of death. In tracing a path from vertical to horizontal, falling takes the body from a firm, rooted position on the earth to one where it mixes in with the ground's physical matter, as the dust soaks up the blood of a fallen warrior or as his teeth bite into the earth at the moment of death. The physics of the Homeric fall can be explained by the principle that heavy objects must, eventually, drop downward toward the earth.[5] But if we go so far as to posit this as a "law" of the Homeric natural world, we are left with the problem of explaining how gods, who also have bodies and who also move downward through space, do or do not partake in the activity of falling.

Part of the difficulty here lies in seeking to identify what kind of bodies the gods inhabit. As divinities, they are immune from the usual vicissitudes and

---

4. For other approaches to time (not having to do with falling) in the *Iliad*, see, e.g., Fränkel [1931] 1955: 1–22; Bassett 1938: 26–46; Bergren 1980: 19–34; Bakker 1999: 50–65; Pucci 2000: 33–48; Kullman 2001: 385–408; Garcia 2007; Beck 2017. For approaches to falling and time from a modern perspective, see Virilio 1994: 35–60; Gilpin 1994: 50–55 (my thanks to Ann Bergren for alerting me to this work); Pagès 2012: 39–51. For a comparative study of falling in epic, see Greene 1963. Unsurprisingly, one area of literary studies that has paid a fair amount of attention to falling is work on Milton's *Paradise Lost* (Jones 1975: 221–46; Quint 2004: 847–81), but see also Nightingale 2011: "In Augustine's view, when Adam and Eve 'fell' into earthly bodies, they also 'fell' into time" (7).

5. This principle can be deduced from the way that objects fall to earth in Homer and Greek thought overall. See Aristotle, *Phys.* 216a13; Hes., *Th.* 722–23; West 1966: ad loc., and my n.56, this chapter. In the *Odyssey*, the description of Sisyphus' stone, which a "mighty force" compels to roll back down the hill, speaks to an ancient principle of the downward movement of weighted objects, translated by Lattimore as "the force of gravity" (τότ' ἀποστρέψασκε κραταιΐς, *Od.* 11.597). Only in Hesiod's χάσμα μέγα, located beyond the gates of Tartarus, does epic entertain the idea of a region, "terrible to gods and men," where objects that fall do not reach the ground, even after the passing of a year (*Th.* 740–44).

inconveniences of time and space, yet as anthropomorphic beings, they sometimes find their immortal status challenged by their corporeality. Falling is one movement that exposes the gods' somatic side—their "physics of presence," as Andrea Nightingale has put it in a different context[6]—and that prompts us to ask new questions about the way that divinities experience their bodies. For example, how do the effects of vertigo or velocity factor into Hephaestus' fall from Olympus? Is it possible for a god to lose control of her body and to fall victim to the effects of her own weight? Do gods' bodies change in some way when they come into contact with the earth?

The three Olympians who fall in the *Iliad* also do so in ways that are problematic for the cohesive structure of the poem. Their falls allow us to see a small but telling stumbling block in the passage between immortal and mortal time and space, which the gods otherwise appear to navigate seamlessly in their travels between Olympus and earth. I argue here that it is the physical engagement of two of these gods (Hephaestus and Ares) with the human sphere, and—specifically—with the human gesture of falling, that causes them accidentally to "fall into time."[7] By this I mean that, on certain rare but telling occasions in the poem, gods come close to experiencing, through the downward pitch of their bodies to the ground, what it is for time to have length and what it means to suffer through the mortal cycle of events that are connected with the earth.

In the first part of this chapter I examine the movement of the fall in the mortal sphere, showing how it serves as a temporal marker within the human time frame of the poem. I argue that falling is connected not only with the mortal time of death, but also with the time of birth, aging, and generation, and that, in turn, the falling of bodies in the poem drives the plot forward from one death to the next. In this section I also argue that the Olympians typically remain aloof from the mortal experience of time, inhabiting their own temporal zone that is set far apart from that of the mortals on the ground. In the second half of the chapter, I examine what happens to the gods' conception of time on the rare occasions when they are caught up in the human activity of falling. By comparing human and divine falls side by side we will be able to plot an outline for the ways in which the divine body, through the act of falling, destabilizes the idea of a clearly demarcated separation between the mortal and immortal realms.

---

6. Nightingale 2011: 16.

7. Cf. Schein 2016: 70–71 on Aphrodite engaging in a related "fall" into human time in the *Homeric Hymn to Aphrodite*.

MORTAL FALLS

The verb πίπτω, in all its forms, and the verb ἐρείπω in its aorist form (ἤριπε) occur over 150 times in the poem in connection with the falling and death of the warrior on the battlefield. As every reader of the *Iliad* knows, Homer tends to dwell on the actual moment of the fall, adding details that make it both graphic and familiar—such as the armor ringing out, hair being strewn in the dust, hands clutching the earth, bodies face up or face down, and blood soaking into the ground.[8] To lose one's footing in the *Iliad* is, in the vast majority of cases, to lose one's life. To fall is to be pulled into mortality—to be pulled appropriately downward toward death.

Elsewhere in archaic literature, particularly in Hesiod's *Theogony*, the source of that downward pull is often located beneath the earth, in the underworld.[9] In the *Iliad* it is located on the very surface of the earth. The plain at Troy can be thought of as a magnetic field that draws the bodies of the heroes toward it—Patroclus, Hector, and eventually Achilles.[10] It thereby not only suggests mortality but also exerts its own narrative drive. By falling on cue, these figures mark out the successive stages of the plot.[11] Until the first death to occur in the poem (that of Echepolus at 4.461–62), the verb πίπτω, including compounds,

8. On the variety of formulas and repeated patterns associated with Homeric battle, see Fenik 1968.

9. On the geography and role of Tartarus in the *Theogony*, see Clay 1992; Johnson 1999. Although the Homeric underworld is understood to be located in a general downward direction (Hector's spirit flees downward at death, 22.362; cf. 22.425–26) and although *Il.* 8.15–16 closely parallels Hes. *Th.* 811 and 720, the *Theogony* is much more interested than the *Iliad* in constructing an underground geography. It is noteworthy that in *Odyssey* 11, Odysseus does not actually appear to go underground. In Homer, the geography of death is horizontal rather than vertical. On horizontal and vertical space in Homer, see Wohl 1993; Nakassis 2004; in Hesiod, Purves 2004.

10. On Patroclus' role as a surrogate (*therapōn*) for Achilles, and on his connection—through Achilles' armor—to Hector (all three are described as "equal to Ares"), see Nagy [1979] 1999: 32–34, 292–95. See also Thalmann 1984: 50: "Against the background of the other heroes' deaths that are its forerunners, Achilles' death takes on coherence."

11. λῦσε δὲ γυῖα; λύντο δὲ γυῖα; γούνατ᾽ ἔλυσε(ν); δούπησεν δὲ πεσών, ἀράβησε δὲ τεύχε᾽ ἐπ᾽ αὐτῷ (translated previously); ἤριπε δ᾽ ἐξ ὀχέων ("he fell from his chariot"); ἤριπε δ᾽ ἐν κονίῃ ("he fell in the dust"); θάνατος δέ μιν ἀμφεκάλυψε ("death covered him over"); ἕλε γαῖαν ἀγοστῷ ("he grasped the earth with the flat of his hand"); λίπε δ᾽ ὀστέα θυμός ("his life left his bones"); ἀμφὶ δέ μιν θάνατος χύτο θυμοραϊστής ("life-destroying death poured over him"); ῥέε δ᾽ αἵματι γαῖα ("the earth was running with blood"). On the variations in phraseology used to describe a victim's collapse, see Kirk 1985 ad 5.58; Fenik 1968; Lowenstam 1981. The bibliography on the topic of formulaic repetition in oral epic is too vast to list in detail here. See, among others, Lord [1960] 2000; Hainsworth 1968; Nagy 1996b; Russo 1997: 238–60; Edwards 1997: 261–83 and my discussion in the Introduction. For instances of falling by book of the *Iliad*—counted as occurrences of the following words in any form: πίπτω, ἀναπίπτω, ἀποπίπτω, καταπίπτω, ἐκπίπτω, ἐμπίπτω, aorist of ἐρείπω, including ὑπήριπε and ἐξερίπουσα, except when used in the figurative sense of to have an emotion "fall upon" the *thumos* (9.436; 14.207, 306; 16.206; 17.625), to have *eris* fall upon the gods (21.385), or to "fall" from favor (23.595)—see my notes that follow; *LfgrE* s.v. ἐρείπω, πίπτω; *DELG* ad loc.

and the aorist of ἐρείπω occur only ten times.[12] Unsurprisingly, the use of verbs meaning "to fall" increases after that, in the books where the fighting is heaviest (5, 8, 11, 13, 15, 16, and 17).[13] After a period of mourning for Patroclus in Books 18 and 19, instances of falling rise again with Achilles' *aristeia* and the gods' engagement on the battlefield in Books 20 and 21.[14] In Book 22, each of the five instances of falling corresponds to the death of Hector. The first three narrate his fall on the battlefield (266, 330, 384), and the remaining two figuratively reenact it, as Andromache lets fall first her shuttle (448) and then her body (467) in response to his death.[15] In Book 23, the instances of falling are high but none of them occurs on the battlefield.[16] In Book 24, as the *Iliad* draws to a close, there are no falls at all.

The Homeric body usually falls as a whole, but it can also fall in pieces. Weapons, armor, and a general assortment of body parts complement, or sometimes replace, the fall of the warrior on the field. Apart from the instances in which πίπτω means to "rush or throw oneself bodily upon,"[17] falling in battle always indicates loss or misdirection: a spear fallen short, a helmet pulled from the head, a fallen sword, the dropped leg of a corpse almost pulled clear of the fighting. In the thick of battle, instances of falling pile up, with these minor falls anticipating or echoing the capsizing of the body itself.

If this preliminary introduction to the treatment of falling in the poem indicates anything, it is that falling in the *Iliad* marks the temporality of death. It is extremely unusual for a warrior ever to stand up again after falling all the

12. 1.243, 593, 594; 2.175, 266; 3.289, 363; 4.108, 134, 217, 462 (death of Echepolus).

13. Garland 1981: 43 notes that the greatest number of deaths occur in bks. 5, 11, and 16 (also some of the longest books in the poem). Bk. 5 (nineteen times): 42, 47, 58, 68, 75, 82, 92, 288, 294, 309, 357, 370, 540, 560, 561, 583, 585, 610, 617; bk. 6 (three times): 82, 307, 453; bk. 7 (twice): 16, 256; bk. 8 (eleven times): 67, 122, 260, 270, 314, 329 (twice), 330, 380, 476, 485; bk. 9 (once): 235; bk. 10 (once): 200; bk. 11 (nineteen times): 69, 85, 155, 157, 158, 179, 241, 250, 297, 311, 325, 355, 425, 449, 500, 676, 743, 745, 824; bk. 12 (eight times): 23, 107, 126, 156, 278, 386, 395, 459; bk. 13 (twenty-one times): 178, 181, 187, 205, 207, 289, 373, 389, 389, 399, 442, 508, 520, 522, 530, 549, 578, 617, 618, 742, 832; bk. 14 (six times): 351, 414, 418, 452, 460, 468; bk. 15 (nineteen times): 63, 280, 319, 421, 421, 423, 428, 435, 451, 452, 465, 524, 538, 578, 624, 624, 647, 648, 714; bk. 16 (twenty-four times): 81, 113, 118, 276, 290, 319, 325, 344, 378, 401, 410, 414, 469, 482, 482, 500, 580, 599, 600, 662, 741, 778, 803, 822; bk. 17 (seventeen times): 10, 50, 300, 311, 315, 346, 352, 361, 428, 440, 522, 523, 580, 619, 633, 639, 760.

14. Bk. 18 (twice): 395, 552; bk. 19 (three times): 110, 227, 406; bk. 20 (five times): 388, 417, 441, 456, 487; bk. 21 (seven times): 9, 241, 243, 246, 387, 407, 492.

15. On further parallels between Andromache's fall and that of a warrior on the battlefield, see Segal 1971b: 43–51; Schein 1984: 175–76; Morrison 1999: 141–42.

16. Bk. 23 (ten times): 120, 216, 251, 437, 467, 687, 691, 728, 731, 881.

17. 2.175; 7.256; 9.235; 11.297, 325; 12.107; 13.742; 15.624 (twice), 16.81, 276; 17.639; 21.241, 387; 23.687.

way down to the earth.[18] Usually, the fall signals a turn toward the end—a ges-
ture of finality and closure for the individual who experiences it. As a moment
of closure, though, the movement of turning toward death is startling for its
seriality, as each fall ensures that the battle—and the poem—will go on.[19] Four
times in the *Iliad*, Homer describes the fall of bodies on the field as a repetitive
motion that fills a continuous stretch of time, as warriors fall one after another
("For as long as it was early morning and the sacred daylight increasing / so long
the weapons of both held fast and the people fell [πῖπτε δὲ λαός]," 8.66–67).[20]
The effect is compounded by Achilles' lament in Book 19 that "Too many fall
every day, one after another, / how could anyone take a breath from the labor?"
(19.226–27). In his words, the repetitive falling of bodies fills time so incessantly
that it even appears to clog it up, leaving no room to breathe (ἀναπνέω). This is
not unlike the experience of reading (or listening to) the poem during certain
stretches of the narrative, wherein the space of the text is itself cluttered with the
descriptions of toppling bodies.[21]

The movement of death drives the narrative pace of the poem forward, giving
it its own kind of regenerative energy. Yet, because bodies must always come to
rest, eventually, on the surface of the earth, the Trojan plain turns at times into
a space that is so overloaded with fallen men that it impedes the flow of the
action and the progress of the narrative. So, in Book 7, the battle briefly has to
be stopped in order to catch up with the backlog of corpses that fill the battle-
field (7.375–409). Similarly, in Book 8, Hector has to lead his troops away from
the ships in order to call a meeting in a place free of fallen warriors (8.491). At
the same time, just as too many falls can clutter the limited area of the plain,

18. Those warriors who do manage to regain their footing often fall only to their knees: ἔστη γνὺξ
ἐριπὼν καὶ ἐρείσατο χειρὶ παχείῃ / γαίης ("he stood on bent knee having fallen, and leaned against
the earth with his stout hand"), 5.309–10 (Aeneas), 11.355–56 (Hector); στῆ δὲ γνὺξ ἐριπών, τόξον δέ
οἱ ἔκπεσε χειρός ("he stood on bent knee having fallen, and his bow dropped from his hand"), 8.329
(Teucer). See further Fenik 1968: 34–35. This in itself is only a half-fall—in a true fall, the knees should
release completely (γούνατ᾽ ἔλυσε[ν]). The connection between getting up again and escaping death is
explicit enough for it to be particularly noteworthy when Hector revives after having fallen all the way to
the ground at 14.418–20. After being rescued by his friends, he gets up on one knee at 14.437–39, vomits
blood, and then sinks back down again, before reappearing "sitting up" at 15.239–40, where he says that
he was sure he had died. See also 15.286–89, when Thoas is surprised and disappointed that Hector has
"got to his feet once more and eluded the death spirits," and Diomedes' similarly surprised observation
that Hector has escaped death at 11.362. That Hector keeps getting up like this is evidently a measure of
his greatness. See Morrison 1999: 141.

19. Thalmann 1984: 50: "These deaths are finally the same. Each hero, as he kills and is killed, ad-
vances a process and falls victim to it."

20. =11.84–85; 15.318–19; 16.777–78.

21. See here the notion of enactivist reading, as discussed in Troscianko 2013, and Grethlein and
Huitink 2017.

preventing the battle from moving forward, so, conversely, can too few falls slow the action of the poem down.

The very first death in the poem, that of Echepolus, has a domino effect on the narrative, causing the end of Book 4 and the beginning of Book 5 to pile up with fallen bodies. In the sequence between the death of Echepolus at 4.462 and the end of the book (4.544), which consists of just over eighty verses, seven warriors fall in quick succession. As these falls are connected to one another by a causal (narrative) sequence,[22] so are they also connected to a variety of other falls in the larger scope of the epic by means of the repeated use of formula, language, and theme. In this way, every fall in the poem is both analeptic and proleptic—it cannot help reminding us of falls that have already taken place in the battle and warning of falls that are yet to come.[23] This has an interesting effect on the narrative, though, for if each fall draws the reader either backward or forward to another point in the poem, then the narrative itself is in danger of becoming caught in a loop and never reaching an endpoint. With each fall, the end is technically closer but narratologically further from sight. These analeptic and proleptic characteristics also mirror something of the *Iliad*'s structure, as a poem whose own themes and patterns of action circle out beyond the last line of the work to encompass the death of Achilles and the returns of the Achaeans.

In the larger scheme of things, the repetitive sequence of falling partakes in the concept of cyclical time, best expressed by Glaucus' famous comparison of humankind to leaves (6.146–49):[24]

οἵη περ φύλλων γενεή, τοίη δὲ καὶ ἀνδρῶν.
φύλλα τὰ μέν τ᾽ ἄνεμος χαμάδις χέει, ἄλλα δέ θ᾽ ὕλη
τηλεθόωσα φύει, ἔαρος δ᾽ ἐπιγίγνεται ὥρη·
ὣς ἀνδρῶν γενεὴ ἣ μὲν φύει ἣ δ᾽ ἀπολήγει.

Just as the generation of leaves, so is the generation of men.
For the wind scatters the leaves to the ground, while the wood
flourishes and produces more when the season of spring comes on.
So the generation of men both flourishes and declines.

---

22. 4.462, 463, 482, 493 (twice), 504, 523. Classified by Fenik as a typical example of a "chain reaction" battle motif ("in which Greeks and Trojans slay each other alternately, each man avenging himself, or trying to, on the slayer of the previous victim," 1968: 10).

23. Genette 1980: 33–85. See also Bergren 1983: 38–73; de Jong 1987; Lynn-George 1988: 270.

24. On the notion of "cyclical time" in archaic Greek poetry, see Vidal-Naquet [1981] 1986: 39–60; Vernant [1974] 1990: 1–33. On this passage and its relation to man's growth and decline, see Clay 1982: 113–14.

Like the seasonal recycling of leaves to the ground, the motif of falling creates its own self-perpetuating structure within the narrative logic of the poem. So, all the way through from Echepolus to Rhigmus or from Sarpedon to Patroclus, one fall generates another in the *Iliad* until the final cumulative fall of Hector.[25] It is only with Hector's death that the movement of falling is diverted into other, less grievous contexts, and finally stilled through the reconciliation of Achilles and Priam.[26]

The action of falling is "generative," too, in its association not only with death but also the other cycles of human life, including birth and descent through the family line. In a society in which women typically gave birth in a vertical position, humans enter as well as leave the world by falling.[27] In the *Iliad*, the birth of Heracles is described as a "fall between the feet of a woman," and it is this action, more than any other, that ensures his mortal life of hardship. As the account is given in Book 19, Hera tricks Zeus into granting power to whichever child of his own blood "falls" in birth on a particular day and then prematurely advances the birth of a distant cousin, Eurystheus, while holding back the birth of Heracles (19.106–13):

> τὸν δὲ δολοφρονέουσα προσηύδα πότνια Ἥρη·
> "ψευστήσεις, οὐδ᾽ αὖτε τέλος μύθῳ ἐπιθήσεις.
> εἰ δ᾽ ἄγε νῦν μοι ὄμοσσον, Ὀλύμπιε, καρτερὸν ὅρκον,
> ἦ μὲν τὸν πάντεσσι περικτιόνεσσιν ἀνάξειν,
> ὅς κεν ἐπ᾽ ἤματι τῷδε πέσῃ μετὰ ποσσὶ γυναικὸς
> τῶν ἀνδρῶν οἳ σῆς ἐξ αἵματός εἰσι γενέθλης."
> ὣς ἔφατο· Ζεὺς δ᾽ οὔ τι δολοφροσύνην ἐνόησεν,
> ἀλλ᾽ ὄμοσεν μέγαν ὅρκον, ἔπειτα δὲ πολλὸν ἀάσθη.

> Then weaving tricks the revered Hera addressed him,
> "You will lie, nor will you accomplish what you said.
> Come now swear to me, lord of Olympus, a strong oath

---

25. Echepolus and Rhigmus are the first and last minor Homeric warriors to "fall" in the poem (4.462; 20.487).

26. After the monumental fall of Hector, the motif of falling begins to wind down in the poem. Despite Achilles' best efforts, Hector's body remains impervious to the earth across which it is dragged, again and again, while Achilles, although still alive, takes on the role of fallen victim as mourner for Patroclus (24.10–11; Seaford 1994: 166–70; Morrison 1999: 141 n.58, with references). The motif of falling shifts in direction and emphasis as the poem draws toward closure—consider Ajax's humorous fall in the dung or how falling's significance briefly short-circuits in the repetitive rising and falling of the combatants in the wrestling match (23.725–34, 774–77). The poem does not suggest, however, that the repetitive nature of falling will not start up again in the story of the Trojan War that continues beyond the borders of the poem (most obviously, we know that Achilles will soon fall).

27. Hes., *Th.* 460; Hom. *Hymn Ap.* 117–18.

that he will rule over all of those living around him,
he who falls on this day between the feet of a woman,
whoever of men is born from the blood of your generation."
So Hera spoke. Zeus did not perceive at all her trickery,
swore a great oath, and was then greatly misled.

By an "accident" of the timing of his birth, Heracles falls into a life marked by suffering. Murnaghan has discussed the close connection between birth and death in Greek thought, particularly through the connection between maternity and mortality and the earth.[28] She has shown how the fall of Demophoon's body to the earth in the *Homeric Hymn to Demeter*, for example, which is instigated by the cry of his mother, ensures the child's mortality through a return to the ground.[29]

The correspondence between birth, death, and the gesture of falling to the ground naturally adheres, in the account of the death of Patroclus in Book 16, to the idea of generation and descent. Here, the toppling of Achilles' helmet and its muddying in the earth seals Patroclus' fate and, through a causal chain, Hector's as well (16.793–800):

τοῦ δ᾽ ἀπὸ μὲν κρατὸς κυνέην βάλε Φοῖβος Ἀπόλλων·
ἡ δὲ κυλινδομένη καναχὴν ἔχε ποσσὶν ὑφ᾽ ἵππων
αὐλῶπις τρυφάλεια, μιάνθησαν δὲ ἔθειραι
αἵματι καὶ κονίῃσι· πάρος γε μὲν οὐ θέμις ἦεν
ἱππόκομον πήληκα μιαίνεσθαι κονίῃσιν,
ἀλλ᾽ ἀνδρὸς θείοιο κάρη χαρίεν τε μέτωπον
ῥύετ᾽ Ἀχιλλῆος· τότε δὲ Ζεὺς Ἕκτορι δῶκεν
ᾗ κεφαλῇ φορέειν, σχεδόθεν δέ οἱ ἦεν ὄλεθρος.

Phoebus Apollo knocked the helmet from his head,
which, rolling away, clattered under the hooves of the horses—
a four-horned helmet, its plumes now defiled
with blood and dust. Never before then was it allowed
for the horsehaired helmet to be defiled in the dust,
but it protected the head and beautiful face of a godlike man,
Achilles. But at that time Zeus granted it to Hector
to wear on his head, for his own destruction was nearby.

---

28. Murnaghan 1992: 243–44.

29. *Hom. Hymn Dem.* 253–54. Murnaghan 1992: 245–46. Contrast Demophoon's fall with the ascension of Ganymede, which, as Andrew Ford suggested to me, works as a kind of "reverse fall" by freeing a human being from the trappings of mortality, aging, and death.

The importance of Patroclus' death is symbolically heightened by the fall of the divine helmet and the defilement of its plume in the blood and dust of the ground (795–97). The horsehair plume, the highest part of the helmet, should not touch the ground, and it is significant that later, in Book 17, Achilles' immortal horses let their manes fall to the ground and become sullied (using the same verb, μιαίνεσθαι) in the dust as they mourn Patroclus' death (17.439–40; cf. 19.405–6):

θαλερὴ δ᾽ ἐμιαίνετο χαίτη
ζεύγλης ἐξεριποῦσα παρὰ ζυγὸν ἀμφοτέρωθεν.

their thick manes were sullied
falling down from the harness on each side of the yoke.

The touching of the divine helmet and horsehair to the ground signifies a fall from the immortal realm toward the realm of death and mortality, especially since Achilles' horses stand motionless in this posture like "a grave monument that stands over / the tomb of a dead man or woman" (17.434–35). Only after Zeus breathes immortal strength back into them do they raise their manes from the ground (456–57) and return with divine swiftness to the ships.

But, besides marking death, the fall of Patroclus' arms also tells the story of lineage, of descending from one generation to the next. Achilles' pristine helmet started with the gods and was then passed on from Peleus to Achilles, to Patroclus, and finally to Hector. The death of Patroclus significantly alters the sequence of exchange, because it is only then that the helmet falls to the ground for the first time. As one of the last of the race of heroes to marry an immortal, Peleus received the armor from the gods before passing it on to his son (17.194–97):

ὁ δ᾽ ἄμβροτα τεύχεα δῦνε
Πηλεΐδεω Ἀχιλῆος, ἅ οἱ θεοὶ Οὐρανίωνες
πατρὶ φίλῳ ἔπορον· ὁ δ᾽ ἄρα ᾧ παιδὶ ὄπασσε
γηράς· ἀλλ᾽ οὐχ υἱὸς ἐν ἔντεσι πατρὸς ἐγήρα.

[Hector] put on the immortal armor
of Achilles son of Peleus, which the Ouranian gods had bestowed
on his dear father; and he in turn, in his old age, had passed them on
to his son—
but the son was not to grow old in the armor of his father.

Although the armor protects Peleus from death, in doing so it also commits him to the time-bound process of aging. Achilles, on the other hand, will avoid old age, yet he must suffer the consequences of what it means for his armor to fall.

The transition of the armor from Peleus, who married an immortal, to Achilles, as he embarks on a war that will mark the final separation between gods and men, is drawn out further to include its transition between the bodies of Patroclus (who has just fallen) and Hector (who will fall sooner than he realizes). As it comes into increasingly close contact with falling and mortality, the armor underscores the acceleration with which the *Iliad* marks the movement, in Zeus' overall plan, toward the transition from (and separation between) a time that is purely mortal and a time that is purely divine. In other words, as long as gods are involved in the cycle of human genealogy and its connection to human birth and death, they will always, by implication, be involved in humankind's repetitive sequence of falling from one generation to the next.

The plot of the *Iliad* has been understood as an attempt to mark the separation between those two kinds of time; to separate immortals once and for all from human genealogy and generation.[30] I have suggested that one of the ways in which the poem marks this separation is through the act of falling, whose movement in the direction of the earth (ἔραζε, χαμάδις, χαμαί) indicates a time that is bound up with the vegetative processes of death, regeneration, and the mortal condition. Even if we narrow our focus to consider mortal time only within the lifespan of a human being, it can still be imagined as working in a cycle that differs markedly from the divine experience of time, as Apollo explains to Ares in his famous rephrasing of Glaucus' simile (21.464–66):

οἳ φύλλοισιν ἐοικότες ἄλλοτε μέν τε
ζαφλεγέες τελέθουσιν, ἀρούρης καρπὸν ἔδοντες,
ἄλλοτε δὲ φθινύθουσιν ἀκήριοι.

(mortals) who, like leaves, sometimes
flourish in their brightness, feeding on the fruit of the earth,
but at other times dwindle into lifelessness.

As mortals experience the movement of cycling through time, they also *feel* the effect of time upon their bodies, and this effect is marked by the action of falling. Gods are perpetually "bright" (ζαφλεγέες), but mortal moments of brilliance can last only so long. Eventually, time will catch up with men and they will die,

---

30. The armor traces a genealogy that goes back to the marriage of Peleus and Thetis, when immortals, through the parenting of the race of heroes or "demigods," were still involved in the complicated human processes of birth and death. The *Iliad*, as a poem set in the penultimate year of the Trojan War, marks the end of the race of heroes and the end of the gods' familial involvement in mortal affairs (Clay 1990). As Slatkin 1991 has shown, the difficulties of that familial bond between god and man are represented most strongly in the relationship between Thetis and Achilles, but they are also marked by the suffering that several of the gods experience in trying to protect their sons on the battlefield.

grow old, or at the very least feel the physical effects of fatigue. Thus, although Diomedes claims that his strength is *empedos*—steady or continuous—during his *aristeia* in Book 5 (ἔτι μοι μένος ἔμπεδόν ἐστιν, 5.254), less than fifty verses later he will already have tired, worn out (ἔτειρεν; τείρετο; κάμνε) by the physical effects of sweat and blood upon his body and by the weight of the shield upon his arm ("For the sweat was wearing at him underneath the broad strap / of the well-circled shield; it wore him down, and his arm was tired," 5.796–97).[31] The adjective *empedos* literally means "standing firmly on (in?) the ground" (*LfgrE*), with a sense that developed to mean unchanged or continuous.[32] Scholars have observed that the young Diomedes' claim to have a strength that is *empedos* calls to mind the counterexample of the aged Nestor and his weak knees.[33] Agamemnon's comments in Book 4 are part of a larger refrain, made more than once in the *Iliad*, that Nestor's strength was *empedos* in his youth but has now been wracked by old age (4.313–15):[34]

ὦ γέρον, εἴθ᾽, ὡς θυμὸς ἐνὶ στήθεσσι φίλοισιν,
ὥς τοι γούναθ᾽ ἔποιτο, βίη δέ τοι ἔμπεδος εἴη,
ἀλλά σε γῆρας τείρει ὁμοίϊον ...

Old man, if only, as the spirit is in your chest,
so might your knees follow, and your strength be steady;
but impartial old age wears you down ...

Here and at 11.668–70, being *empedos* translates to having strength specifically in one's knees (γούνατα) and limbs (μέλεα) (11.668–70):

οὐ γὰρ ἐμὴ ἲς
ἔσθ᾽ οἵη πάρος ἔσκεν ἐνὶ γναμπτοῖσι μέλεσσιν.
εἴθ᾽ ὡς ἡβώοιμι βίη δέ μοι ἔμπεδος εἴη ...

My force is not
as it was before in my bent limbs.
If only I were at the peak of my youth, and my strength still lasting ...

---

31. Note also the physical weariness of Ajax at 16.106–11, where the words κάμνω and ἀναπνέω describe his body, although his shield remains *empedos* (Purves 2015). In the Introduction and Chapter 6, I discuss the concept of gesture as a kind of burden that wears on the body.

32. *LfgrE* s.v. "from the lit. meaning 'standing firmly on (in?) the ground' (πέδον) developed on the one hand to *unchanged, undisturbed,* (still) *present* (1a), on the other to (metaph.) *firm, reliable* (1b); sometimes w. a temp. connot.: *continuous* (1c). ... The adv. 2x (*P* 434, ρ 464) applied in the lit. sense to standing (upright and immovably) *in* the ground."

33. Redfield 1975: 172–73, 180; Vernant [1986] 1991: 39–41.

34. Cf. 7.157; 11.669; 23.627, 629.

Aging, then, is just another way of being unstrung and losing the grounded, upright position of being *empedos*. It simply draws out into a process of slow time what the act of falling can accomplish in a half-line with the words λῦσε δὲ γυῖα or γούνατ᾽ ἔλυσε(ν). It parallels, in other words, the process of falling to the ground.[35]

In this way, falling can be seen to telescope the moment of aging, to show in fast forward the body's inevitable loosening and movement toward the horizontal that is brought about with the passage of time. So Thetis complains that her aged husband, Peleus, now "worn out (ἀρημένος) by baneful old age," can do nothing but lie prone (κεῖται) in the house (18.434–35).[36] Knees are of considerable importance in the *Iliad* because they hold a person upright (*empedos*), and in several cases they represent a prime site of strength and vigor for the body. At *Iliad* 15.262–70, for example, Apollo breathes strength back into Hector's weakened legs and knees in order to revive him, and at 19.354, Athena feeds Achilles with nectar "so that miserable hunger not reach his knees." To be *empedos* is thus briefly to achieve an ideal of the human body that cannot be attained in practice—to be secure on one's feet and lasting through time.[37]

Appropriately, therefore, the quality of being *empedos* is linked to the human gravestone, or *sēma* (where the body is symbolically turned upright again), rather than to the body itself.[38] The *sēma* is grounded by a strong connection to the earth in which it stands, and its perdurant quality specifically suggests a length of time that extends beyond the limited lifespan of the human body. Achilles' choice of *kleos aphthiton* (unwithering fame) over a long life reflects on this role of the *sēma*, for the upright and enduring status of the grave marker attaches more closely to the idea of a divine, transcendent time than it does to a vegetative, mortal cycle of time that blazes and fades as it alternates through the seasons via its contact with the earth.

35. On "being released in the knees" as a euphemism for dying, see, e.g., 5.176; 13.360; 15.291. See also Lowenstam 1981: 85 n.29.

36. Cf. 11.1–2. The myth is explained at Hom. *Hymn Aph.* 218–38 (cf. Clay 1982: 112–17). On both Thetis and Eos' special relationship to time, see Slatkin 1991: 28–33.

37. In this way, to be *empedos* can be considered diametrically opposed to the "ephemeral" state of mankind. Fränkel 1946 has argued that the adjective *ephēmeros*, which the Greeks employed to describe the mortal condition, "was used as an equivalent to 'unstable' ... the idea is not that our condition is shifting constantly, but rather that there is no certainty of permanence" (134). On vigor in the knees, see also Snell 1953:8 (quoted in my Introduction, 33); Onians 1951: 174–86.

38. Vernant [1982] 1991: 69; Zeitlin 1996: 31, 42. In the description of Achilles' horses immobilized in their grief for Patroclus (17.434–35), discussed previously, note that they stand *empedos* "like a *stēlē*" or grave marker (ὥς τε στήλη μένει ἔμπεδον). On the *sēma*'s role as a marker that exists indefinitely through time, outlasting the lifespan of the mortal body but attaching to the concept of undying *kleos*, see Redfield 1975: 180; Vernant [1982] 1991: 50–74, esp. 69; Nagy [1979] 1990: 202–22.

Through the gesture of falling, then, mortals undo any claim to being *empedos*, or continuous through time, in their experience of life. Yet, just as the cycle of fall upon fall can be so repetitive as even to become tedious for the reader of the *Iliad*, a different kind of temporal experience, one that is attached to the idea of "long time," is also fundamental to the experience of the Homeric characters on the ground. The last aspect of human time that I discuss in this section is speed: not only the speed at which warriors move across the plain, but also the rate at which they experience time in their daily lives. Speed, as we will see, bears a close relation to the contact of the feet with the earth, which in turn has important associations with the movement of falling. Humans' connection to the ground slows them down and causes them to suffer through time at a laborious rate.[39] Although the life of a Homeric hero may be short, his experience of time is often quite long. The Greeks' effort at Troy is described by Odysseus as an ἔργον / αὔτως ἀκράαντον, a "task / always unfulfilled" (2.137–38), and the arguments about returning home in Book 2 are framed around the ability to endure the extended length of the war. Who better than Odysseus to repeatedly emphasize the motifs of patience (μένων, μιμνόντεσσι, δηρόν τε μένειν, μείνατ'), impatience (ἀσχαλάᾳ, ἀσχαλάαν) and endurance (τλῆτε) in his rallying of the troops in Book 2 (291–300), in a speech that is set against the backdrop of ships whose timbers have rotted with the passing years (2.135)?[40]

In a poem that presents the tragedy of men who die so young, especially as the idea is emblematized by the "untimely" and "short-lived" lifespan of Achilles (1.352; 1.416; 24.540), it is somewhat paradoxical that the passage of time is unbearably slow for the warriors at Troy. The idea of time being "slow" or "long" in quality is accentuated by the extended stretch of time that Achilles stays out of the battle, twice described as δηρόν in the poem (18.125; 19.46).[41] It may also serve us well here to remember Fränkel on the subject of archaic time, who argued that *chronos* in Homer always equals a duration, never a point; and that a state of affairs described with the word *chronos* in early Greek poetry typically suggests a negative evaluation.[42]

---

39. On the dramatic alteration brought about in the pace of modern life with the invention of the bicycle and motor vehicles, see Kern [1983] 2003: 109–30. The Homeric equivalent would be the horse, whose speed brought it close to divine status, and which the immortals themselves often used in their passage between Olympus and the ground (5.752=8.396). Cf. Achilles' immortal horses at *Il.* 17.434–57 and 19.404–17, and my previous discussion. See also Chapter 3.

40. On which, see also Garcia 2013: 51–55.

41. Contrast with the phrase οὔ τι μάλα δήν ("not long at all"), used to describe Achilles' lifespan at 1.416.

42. Fränkel [1931] 1955: 1–2.

The famously long "third day" of fighting, which extends all the way from 11.1 to 18.242, dramatizes the sense of endurance through time that combat requires. Midway through this third day, Hector uses the verb στρεύγεσθαι (*to be slowly hemmed in or choked*) to describe the experience of fighting in battle (15.512). The word primarily conveys a sense of exhaustion, and elsewhere in Homer it refers to the slow experience of dying by starvation (*Od.* 12.351). In both of these cases, man's labored relationship to time is mediated through a connection to the earth. His groundedness commits him to enduring the slow progress of human time, for he can move only as quickly as it takes for his feet to make contact with the earth. In Homeric language, humans are differentiated from gods as beings who "walk upon the earth" (5.442), and, perhaps unsurprisingly, walking—that quintessentially iterative and human gesture, as I discussed in the Introduction—is the one activity that gods have a particular difficulty getting quite right. Commentators have often noted the strangeness of Athena and Hera's "shivering-dove" walk across the plain (5.778–79), and, in Book 13, it is the unusual nature of Poseidon's feet and legs as he walks away from men that reveals him to be a god in human form (13.70–72).[43] Perhaps it is their own particular weightiness that fixes humans in time, enabling them to secure the kind of contact with the ground that gods can never quite replicate. The heaviness of mankind is such that the earth thunders beneath the feet of marching warriors (2.465–66; 20.157) and even motivates, according to at least two accounts, Zeus' instigation of the Trojan War.[44]

The correspondence between walking (or running) and falling is impossible to avoid for the mortal characters of the *Iliad*, who are bound, more than anything else, to a pair of feet that carry them back and forth across a single stretch of earth.[45] On rare occasions mortals do escape the slow, weighty rate of their bodies and achieve brief superhuman moments of speed and brilliance. Achilles and Diomedes, in their respective *aristeias*, are chastised by Apollo for trying to keep pace with the gods (5.440–42; 22.8–9).[46] But, although in such

---

43. Fenik 1968: 75; Dietrich 1983: 73 n.39; Sissa and Detienne 2000: 29; Platt 2011: 58–59. Janko 1992 ad loc. mentions the scholiasts' suggestion of replacing ἴχνια (*footsteps*) with ἴθματα (*movement, gait*) in order to make better sense of this passage (Erbse vol. 3:413).

44. *Cypria* fr. 1 West claims that the weight of the human population was becoming too much for Gaia to bear. A similar explanation for the *Dios Boulē* at *Il.* 1.5 is offered by the D-scholium (Scodel 1982: 39). In Book 18, Achilles appears to register this fact by describing himself as a useless burden on the earth (ἐτώσιον ἄχθος ἀρούρης, 18.104; Murnaghan 1997: 28; Garcia 2013: 185).

45. On walking as a form of "controlled falling," see, e.g., Virilio 1994: 35–60; Gilpin 1994: 50–55: 52; Solnit 2000: 33, and the Laurie Anderson song "Walking and Falling" (1982).

46. On running in the *Iliad*, see Chapter 3. The phenomenon of superhuman speed among mortals is nevertheless severely restricted in the *Iliad*, especially in relation to its treatment in the Epic Cycle; Griffin 1977: 40 and n.16b.

moments mortals might feel themselves to be invincible and unstoppable, it would be more accurate to describe them as simply accelerating toward death, as Dione makes all too clear in her judgment of Diomedes (5.407), and as is also proved by the speed of Patroclus (16.582–83), Hector (5.689–91), and of course Achilles—the most swift footed of humans (πόδας ὠκὺς Ἀχιλλεύς, thirty times, *Iliad*), who is also the most swift fated (ὠκυμορώτατος).[47]

By contrast, the feet of the immortals need not touch the ground even when they step. The tree and mountain tops tremble beneath Poseidon's feet as he completes his journey between Olympus and his underwater home in just four strides (13.18–19). In Book 14, Hera crosses over Pieria, Emathia, and the Thracian hills without her feet once touching the ground (14.224–28), and on her journey with Sleep to Mount Ida, their feet touch the tops of the trees, not the earth (285). Even in sex, the immortals avoid the ground—as Zeus and Hera lie down together, a soft, thick grass of clovers and flowers breaks out, which "which held them up high from the ground" (ὃς ἀπὸ χθονὸς ὑψόσ᾽ ἔεργε, 14.349).

Homer focuses on the point of the gods' departure from Olympus when they descend to the plain at Troy (e.g., βῆ δὲ κατ᾽ Οὐλύμποιο καρήνων: "[s]he came down from the peaks of Olympus," 24.121, cf. 1.44), rather than on their landing on the earth. The movement itself is often described using the verbs ἀΐσσω, to dart, or πέτομαι, to fly, especially with reference to the swift passage of Thetis, Athena, and Hera.[48] When the gods travel, as Scott has observed, Homer attempts to describe a sense of speed that is, in itself, outside the realm of human possibility, by nevertheless drawing analogies with human points of reference.[49] Thus the gods will travel between Olympus and earth as fast as birds, "like a meteor," "as swift as thought," "as rapidly as snow or hail," and so forth.[50] Hera's return from Ida to Olympus in Book 15 is described by using a simile that draws attention to the inherent differences between mortal and immortal experiences of space and time (15.80–83):

ὡς δ᾽ ὅτ᾽ ἂν ἀΐξῃ νόος ἀνέρος, ὅς τ᾽ ἐπὶ πολλὴν
γαῖαν ἐληλουθὼς φρεσὶ πευκαλίμῃσι νοήσῃ,
"ἔνθ᾽ εἴην, ἢ ἔνθα," μενοινήῃσί τε πολλά,
ὣς κραιπνῶς μεμαυῖα διέπτατο πότνια Ἥρη·

---

47. *Il.* 1.505. Cf. 1.417; 18.95, 458; Lynn-George 1988: 162.

48. The adverb καρπαλίμως and adjective ὠκύς are frequently used to describe the flight of the gods. Some common epithets of Iris, whose primary purpose is crossing the space between Olympus and earth, are ποδήνεμος (wind-swift), ὠκέα (swift), and ταχεῖα (fast). On Thetis' rapid traversal and the *Iliad*'s scene change between the sea and Olympus in Book 18, which caused some consternation among the scholiasts, see Porter 2015: 196–97.

49. Scott 1974: 19–22. See also Lloyd [1966] 1987: 185–87.

50. 13.62 and 15.237 with Lloyd [1966] 1987: 187 n.1; 4.75–77; 15.80, with Janko 1982 ad loc.; 15.170–73.

Just as when the mind of a man darts—a man who, having
journeyed far along the land thinks in his deep thought,
"If only I were there, or there!" and he thinks longingly on many
   things—
just so swiftly did the revered Hera eagerly speed in flight.

The simile draws a comparison between the flight of the god and the rapid manner in which the human mind is able to jump from one thought to another. But the simile is also set in context by the slow progress of the man crossing a large stretch of land (ἐπὶ πολλὴν γαῖαν ἐληλουθώς), in contrast to the airborne flight of the goddess, whose body is not bound to the gestural or somatic sequences of movement through time. Their relationship to the ground leads mortals to experience a sense of duration and time that is mediated by their bodies, while the gods, who exist far above what we might call the gravitational or temporal force of the earth, experience a different register of time, in which movement through space can be almost instantaneous.

The simile illustrates how time on Olympus is of a different quality than time on the ground, and is also experienced in a different way. Gods understand the movement of human time and use some of the same temporal markers as humans do (e.g., sunset) to determine it. However, just as gods sometimes fumble when attempting ordinary human movement, such as walking, they do not typically know what it means to *experience* time or—because they live forever—what it means for time to have *length*. While humans age, decay, and die in their passage through time, gods remain fixed and unchanging; they are always still in time and do not move with it.[51] Put differently, gods do not have their "own" time. Instead, from a position outside time, they are able to observe and monitor the time of mortals. In the *Iliad*, Zeus underscores the gods' spatial separation from human time by never descending lower than the peaks of Mount Ida.[52] The distance this affords him allows him to keep his own being at a remove from the mortal experience of time.

---

51. See Clay 1982 on the immortals' securing of agelessness through ambrosia and nectar. As she argues, immortality does not naturally confer agelessness, but the infusion of ambrosia and nectar works to hold back the passage of time that brings with it aging and decay. See further Householder and Nagy 1972: 52–53; Schein 1984: 52–53; Garcia 2013: 161–63. On the description of a god as "immortal and ageless all their days" (ἀθάνατος καὶ ἀγήρως ἤματα πάντα, 8.539; 12.323; 17.444; *Od.* 5.136, 218; 7.95, 257; 23.336) see further Griffin 1980: 144–78; Edwards 1987: 138; Sissa and Detienne 2000: 13–27.

52. The one exception is telling: Zeus lets tears of blood drop toward the ground (ἔραζε) in sorrow at Sarpedon's death (16.459). This is the only time that he physically interacts with the human landscape at Troy, and—as Lateiner 2002 has shown—it is the closest Zeus comes to crossing the line between the immortal and mortal condition.

IMMORTAL FALLS

I have suggested that the mortal experience of time, as it is experienced by the Iliadic warrior on the battlefield, can be characterized by a tendency toward the movement of falling, which in itself represents the pull not only toward death, but also toward time that is lived or embodied. I now want to reconsider the notion that the gods—who are undying and ageless and who, as far as humans can tell, live easily (ῥεῖα ζώοντες, 6.138) and without cares (ἀκηδέες, 24.526)—should be completely immune to these temporal effects. The mark of a god is to experience speed without exhaustion, time without wear upon the body, and descent without feeling either the weight of one's body or its contact with the earth. In his essay on the body of the divine, Vernant has categorized the body of the god as one that is complete, a "super-body" against which the sub-body of the human should be measured ([1986] 1991: 27–49). The super-body of the gods differs from that of mortals in that it possesses the ability to be "here and there at the same time" (46). In his words ([1986] 1991: 46),

> by traveling at a speed as swift as thought, the constraints imposed by the externality of the divisions of space are child's play to [the gods], just as, through the independence they enjoy from natural cycles and their successive phases, they do not know the externality of the divisions of time as they relate to one another. In a single impulse, the gods' corporeal vitality extends across past, present, and future, in the same way that its energy is deployed to the ends of the universe.

Vernant's statements apply to the divine body in general, but in the *Iliad* the case is considerably more complex. On the one hand, it is true that while gods perceive and monitor time, they do not have to go to the trouble of physically experiencing it. According to this logic, gods should also resist the temporal implications of falling. There is a problem, though, in that the passage between Olympus and earth is a vertical one, and that the path of the gods' movement is downward, toward the plain at Troy. If both mortals and immortals ultimately move in the same direction (that is, toward earth), and if, once they are on the ground, both share the same space and act in the same plot, how is it possible to keep the separate mortal and immortal registers of time apart? Although the divinities, who live in the seasonless, unchanging world of Olympus, are set apart from the vicissitudes of time, when they enter into the human space of the earth it follows that they will at least run the risk of falling. Furthermore, without the clear, structural delineation of time separated into the different spatial categories of earth and Olympus, there is always a danger that the figure of the descending god will overlap with the figure of the man who falls at the moment of death or becomes immobilized, and thereby falls, with old age. In turn, the falling of the god may itself be understood figuratively—leading to what can be described, more simply, as a fall into human time.[53]

Vernant's statement that "the gods are here and there at the same time" does not take into account that immortals, because they have bodies, can be *only* in one place at one time. Their bodies bind them to time in the sense that they can only be now here, and *then* there, just as the formulas used to describe their gestures necessarily embed them in a human sphere of experience.[54] Even if they can transport themselves from here to there in the fraction of a second (as we have seen in the previous example of Hera), they can never physically exist in two places simultaneously. Our understanding of divine movement through time will always be complicated by the body of the god, and the way in which it both imitates and differs from the death-bound, aging, and tiring body of mankind.

Through certain devices, such as the simile comparing immortal speed to the process of human time, or the gates of the Hōrai (Hours or Seasons) that explicitly mark the crossing over into a different temporal register (5.749; 8.393), Homer attempts to smooth over the transition between the time of the immortals and the time of men. And yet, written into the background of the gods' effortless descents is another kind of movement, one in which the body of the god is forced into an engagement with lived or experienced time via the process of moving downward toward the ground. Our first example comes from the end of Book 1, when Hephaestus tells of how he was once hurled out of Olympus by Zeus and left to free fall through the air until he came crashing down to earth (1.590–94):

ἤδη γάρ με καὶ ἄλλοτ' ἀλεξέμεναι μεμαῶτα
ῥῖψε ποδὸς τεταγὼν ἀπὸ βηλοῦ θεσπεσίοιο,
πᾶν δ' ἦμαρ φερόμην, ἅμα δ' ἠελίῳ καταδύντι
κάππεσον ἐν Λήμνῳ, ὀλίγος δ' ἔτι θυμὸς ἐνῆεν·
ἔνθα με Σίντιες ἄνδρες ἄφαρ κομίσαντο πεσόντα.

For at another time before now I was eager to protect you,
but he, having seized me by my foot, threw me from the
threshold of Olympus,
and all day I was borne until together with the setting sun
I fell down onto Lemnos, and there was little life left in me.
Thereafter the Sintian men took care of me, having fallen.

---

53. On the figurative aspects of the falling figure, see especially de Man's reading of Keats's *The Fall of Hyperion* (de Man 1986: 3–20) and Caruth's reading of de Man (Caruth 1995: 92–105).

54. Cf. Dietrich 1983: 53: "[Individual gods] had to move from place to place like men, and it was unusual for one to be seen in two places at once." Dietrich's analysis gets to the heart of many of the questions and problems that revolve around the gods' human form. The extent to which the Homeric gods were limited by their position in space is also discussed in Kearns 2004: 63; Garcia 2013: 159–229.

This story appears to explain the origins of Hephaestus' limp, which the Olympians proceed to laugh at in the passage directly following this one. Unlike the other gods whom we have looked at so far, Hephaestus not only falls helter-skelter (that is, tossed out by his foot), but he also falls according to the effects of his own weight. His limp testifies to this, for the injury (if it is sustained from the fall) must be the result of being crushed by his own heaviness. Unusually, too, Hephaestus falls for an entire day (1.592), not because he is lighter than other gods who drop through space almost instantaneously but rather because he alone has taken on the qualities of corporeality in the process of free fall.[55] The gods can certainly make the impact of their body weight felt when they want to, but as "super-bodies" they should ordinarily not be subject to the effects of their own weight.

A passage from Hesiod's *Theogony* provides some illumination on the rates at which objects were expected to fall through space. In his description of Tartarus, Hesiod accounts for the distance between earth and Ouranus by relating how long it would take for a bronze anvil to fall through it (*Th.* 722–23). His claim that the anvil would drop for nine days and come to earth on the tenth implies that there is a fixed relation between the weight of an object and the time that it would take to fall.[56] The nine-day period that it takes for Hesiod's anvil to reach the earth underscores the immense distance that separates the regions of gods and men.[57] According to the physics of the human world, it is a distance that takes a long time to traverse. In Book 1 of the *Iliad*, the weighty body of Hephaestus appears to be bound by the same laws of physics, causing him also to fall over a period of "long time." The scholiasts were understandably concerned by the phrase πᾶν δ᾽ ἦμαρ φερόμην ("I was borne [I fell] all day," 1.592), but eventually concluded that it should be understood to mean no more than that Hephaestus arrived at night, on the grounds that it was inconceivable that a god should fall for an entire day.[58] The discomfort of the scholiast here is important, for it exposes a glitch in the transition from divine to human time frames in the poem.

---

55. At 24.80–82 Iris drops *like* a lead weight, but that is not the same as her embodying the weight herself.

56. As West 1966: ad loc. observes, we can assume that Hesiod chose the anvil because it is the heaviest moveable object that comes to mind: "The simplest explanation of the choice of an anvil in this connection is that, like the anvil which Zeus tied to each of Hera's feet to increase her pain when he strung her up (*Il.* 15.19), it is the first example that comes to mind of a movable object of great weight. Aristotle believed that the heavier an object is, the faster it falls (*Phys.* 216a13), and this was no doubt generally assumed to be the case in antiquity." See n.5, this chapter.

57. One might argue that Hesiod is simply describing a cosmos of different proportions. But see *Il.* 8.15–16 and *Th.* 720, 811 for the overlap between these two descriptions of the geography of the universe. Some indication of the vast distance between the mortal and immortal regions in Homer can be found in the story of Otus and Ephialtes, who, having attained the height of nine fathoms within nine years, attempted to pile mountain upon mountain to reach Olympus (*Od.* 11.307–20), and in the description of the terrifying Eris, whose divine body spans the distance between heaven and earth (*Il.* 4.442–45).

58. Erbse vol. 1: 157–58.

When Hephaestus falls at the end of Book 1, he not only falls according to a human time scheme, but he also adopts a human posture on the ground. Like so many Homeric warriors whose legs have given way beneath them, Hephaestus lies "fallen" (πεσόντα), a word that, like καταπίπτω, which describes his fall just a line earlier, is used in the *Iliad* to refer to men who have died in battle.[59] Through his phraseology, therefore, Hephaestus' account of his fall from Olympus inevitably overlaps, both conceptually and linguistically, with the Iliadic fall of men.

The *Iliad* registers its own anxiety about what it means to fall in such human terms by having the god claim ὀλίγος δ᾽ ἔτι θυμὸς ἐνῆεν—that there was "little life left in me" by the time he reached the ground. In several ways, then, Hephaestus, pitched from Olympus to Lemnos, figuratively represents the Homeric hero gasping out his last breath on the battlefield. The suggestion that an immortal might come close to death occurs elsewhere in the *Iliad*, but usually in connection with binding rather than falling.[60] The best-known example in this category is Ares, who lay bound in a bronze jar for thirteen months (5.385–91):[61]

τλῆ μὲν Ἄρης, ὅτε μιν Ὦτος κρατερός τ᾽ Ἐφιάλτης,
παῖδες Ἀλωῆος, δῆσαν κρατερῷ ἐνὶ δεσμῷ·
χαλκέῳ δ᾽ ἐν κεράμῳ δέδετο τρισκαίδεκα μῆνας·
καί νύ κεν ἔνθ᾽ ἀπόλοιτο Ἄρης ἄτος πολέμοιο,
εἰ μὴ μητρυιή, περικαλλὴς Ἠερίβοια,
Ἑρμέᾳ ἐξήγγειλεν· ὁ δ᾽ ἐξέκλεψεν Ἄρεα
ἤδη τειρόμενον, χαλεπὸς δέ ἑ δεσμὸς ἐδάμνα.

Ares endured, when Otus and mighty Ephialtes,
the sons of Aloeus, bound him in strong chains,
and in a bronze jar he was bound for thirteen months.
Then Ares unwearying of battle would indeed have died,
had not his stepmother, very beautiful Aeriboia,
sent message to Hermes. He stole Ares away,
already worn down, for the harsh bondage was overcoming him.

---

59. πεσόντα (1.594) conforms to the majority of cases by appearing in the final position in the line (1.594; 5.288; 11.745; 15.428; 16.500; 18.395; 22.266). One might also draw a tentative comparison between the use of the verb κομίζω at 1.594 to describe the rescue of Hephaestus by the Sintians and at 13.195–96, where it denotes the retrieval of fallen bodies on the battlefield.

60. Detienne and Vernant [1974] 1991: 115–16. On the differences between binding and falling, see Aesch., *Eum.* 640–46.

61. For a reading of this passage within the context of binding in apotropaic ritual, see Faraone 1992: 74ff. Also important in this context (and much discussed in the scholarship) is the supposed binding of Zeus, alluded to in the *Iliad* by Achilles in conversation with his mother (1.396–400). On which, see Braswell 1971: 16–26; Willcock 1977: 41–53; Lang 1983: 140–64; Slatkin 1991: 66–69; Alden 2000: 38–39; Garcia 2013: 221–29.

Just as Hephaestus' spirit is almost defeated after falling for a day, Ares is almost destroyed by the time he spends entrapped in the jar. It is not clear where the jar was located, but the most likely place for a large jar in the archaic period is beneath or partially submerged in the earth. As binding restricts the god's physical range, preventing him from moving through space "as swift as thought," so too does it restrict him to the confines of human, grounded time. Through the physical location of his body in the earth, the god finds himself engaged in time.[62] Like the human characters in the *Iliad*, Ares, in almost dying, is forced to endure (τλῆ) time and to experience what it is for time to be thirteen months long.[63] Both gods, in this way, either fall into or are trapped within a temporality where the passing of months and days is not simply an empty category to be filled up with pleasant and quotidian pursuits, but rather a kind of time, inasmuch as the god physically experiences it, where every hour or minute counts.

The fall of Hephaestus thereby marks several temporalities at once, and all of them are connected with the idea of human time. It marks the time of death but also the long, slow process of enduring time, before the moment of death itself. As the legs of the god crumple beneath him, the figure of divine time loses a status that I earlier compared to being *empedos*: sure of foot and everlasting. But Hephaestus' act of falling also associates him with human time (and the narrative tempo of the *Iliad*) by setting him within a cycle of seriality and repetition. For, after Hephaestus has fallen once, he is doomed to fall again, re-enacting with his own, singular body the sequence of fall upon fall that drives the plot of the *Iliad*. In Book 18, he explains that his limp so embarrassed Hera that she herself threw him a long way from the heavens. Having fallen (πεσόντα) into the Ocean, he was rescued by Thetis and Eurynome, and lived with them for nine years before returning to Olympus (18.394–405).

Hephaestus is twice caught up in the cycle of falling, and he comes close to suffering, like mortals, through the process of his fall. As an aftereffect of falling, Hephaestus displays his strained relationship to time through his body. The dragging of his foot lingers on as a physical trace of his encounter with human temporality. Through his limp, the god will always carry with him the sign of a specific event that took place in his past. In a way that is not generally applicable to the other gods, moreover, Hephaestus' movement—even on Olympus—is always connected to the passage of time. He is described in Books

---

62. Similarly, in the *Theogony*, gods who have transgressed are punished by being placed beneath the earth, in Tartarus, and are forced to endure a specific length of time away from the gods (one year in a breathless sleep, followed by nine in isolation), *Th.* 795–804.

63. Cf. Detienne and Vernant [1974] 1991: 115–16. On the frequent appearance of the motif of endurance in archaic poetry, see Thalmann 1984: 82–92. On the unusual long suffering of the immortal Thetis, see Slatkin 1991: 17–52, esp. 27. On gesture as a form of endurance, see my Introduction and Chapter 6.

1 and 18 as hurrying and bustling with his crooked feet.[64] While Thetis' nature as "silver-footed" and Iris' as "wind-footed" make it easy for them to move virtually instantaneously, Hephaestus feels the burden of time: his "nimbleness" is energetic, rather than effortless, and he, like a tired Homeric warrior, sweats in his workshop.[65] Like Odysseus (*Od.* 8.321), Hephaestus carries the experience of his suffering through time in his legs.[66]

Scholarship on the *Iliad* has sought to account both for this "second fall" of Hephaestus and for the phenomenon of "immortal death" in general. This work has drawn on, among other approaches, that of neoanalysis, mythological innovation, Homeric religion, and the use of the precedent or paradigm.[67] Many of these approaches are based on solving the problem of how to make the passages I have been discussing either "fit" or "not fit" into the formal structure of the poem or the religious structure of Homer's world. I would argue, on the other hand, that their disjointedness is important to the make-up of the epic as a whole, precisely because it thematizes the awkward transition that is in play in the *Iliad* between the time of gods and the time of men.[68] Pucci has argued that, despite the temporal framing of the plan of Zeus upon the structure of the narrative, the relation between the time of men and the time of the gods in the *Iliad* is always indeterminate, and sometimes incoherent.[69] The jolt in the formal structure of the poem that occurs in descriptions of Hephaestus' fall is important, because it registers the corresponding jolt that takes place within the

---

64. 18.369–74, 410–17. Note the attention paid to Hephaestus' gait at 18.371, 372, 373, 393, 411, 417. On Hephaestus' status as a craftsman that connects him, "doomed in his legs," to a lower social stratum, see Thalmann 1988: 24. On his associations with the half-land, half-sea creatures of the seal and especially the crab, see Detienne and Vernant [1974] 1991: 259–75.

65. 18.372, 414–15. The only other god to sweat in the *Iliad* is Hera, who describes how she has expended a great deal of sweat and energy in bringing the Trojans to ruin (4.27). Cf. Zeus' comment about immortal sweat at 15.228.

66. The parallels between Odysseus and Hephaestus were first explored fully by Braswell 1982. For other instances of Odysseus' weak legs (*Il.* 3.191–224; *Od.* 8.230–33; *Od.* 17.196–338), see Newton 1987: 13–14 and n.8, as well as my Chapter 3.

67. Willcock 1964: 141–54, 1977: 41–53; Braswell 1971: 16–26; Willcock 1977; Griffin 1978: 1–22; Dietrich 1979: 129–51; Levy 1979: 215–18; Anderson 1981: 323–27; Lynn-George 1982: 239–45; Lang 1983: 140–64; Alden 2000.

68. For scholars who have celebrated these moments of disjuncture, see, e.g., Dietrich 1979: 145–46 (on the "rough joins" in the treatment of the different religious elements in Homer); Slatkin 1991 (on Thetis); Pucci 2000: 33–48.

69. Pucci seeks to establish "dans quelle mesure le récit [de l'*Iliade*] renferme et articule dans ses plis le temps divin, et le rapport qu'il établit entre le temps divin et le temps humain" (2000: 35). As he concludes, "[o]n verra que l'encadrement que le temps divin fournit à l'action humaine est toujours, dans une certaine mesure, indéterminé, parfois incohérent et même bafoué par l'action réelle." But cf. Murnaghan, who sees the "plan of Zeus" and the "plan of Achilles" as operating essentially in concert, yet without Achilles' full understanding of events (1997: 23–42).

overall logic of a narrative that seamlessly attempts to insert the gods "who are immortal and ageless" into the human time on the ground at Troy.

Nowhere is this jolt more explicit than in the wounding of the gods in Books 5 and 21. The associations that I have been tracing between the falling body of the god Hephaestus and the falling body of the Homeric warrior finally converge in the figure of Ares. Struck by a spear in Book 5, Ares, enraged and in pain, follows Aphrodite up to Olympus. Once there, he complains to Zeus that only the swiftness of his feet enabled him to escape the fate of either lying on the battlefield among the corpses "for a long time" (δηρόν), suffering pains, or living without strength (5.885–87):

> ἀλλά μ᾽ ὑπήνεικαν ταχέες πόδες· ἦ τέ κε δηρὸν
> αὐτοῦ πήματ᾽ ἔπασχον ἐν αἰνῇσιν νεκάδεσσιν,
> ἤ κε ζὼς ἀμενηνὸς ἔα χαλκοῖο τυπῇσι.

> But my swift feet carried me away. Otherwise for a long time
> I would have suffered pains there among the dread corpses,
> or I would still be barely alive due to the blows of the bronze spear.

Ares' speed, the celebrated swiftness of his feet, saves him from the human predicament of falling, which—as we have seen in the case of Hephaestus and humans whose limbs eventually tire—is often associated with weakness in the feet or legs. Even so, Ares does not seem to be able to shake the image of his own body lying strewn on the battlefield. Later in the poem, he claims that he will disobey Zeus' instructions and fight among the men, even if doing so means that he will end up lying among the corpses "in the blood and the dust" (15.117–18):

> εἴ πέρ μοι καὶ μοῖρα Διὸς πληγέντι κεραυνῷ
> κεῖσθαι ὁμοῦ νεκύεσσι μεθ᾽ αἵματι καὶ κονίῃσιν.

> even if it is my fate to lie stricken under the blow of a thunderbolt
>   from Zeus,
> along with the corpses in the blood and dust.

Like Hephaestus, Ares appears to be unable to fall just once in the poem. As it turns out, these two imaginary or virtual deaths are just trial runs for his actual fall in Book 21. Here, Ares does finally fall in battle, toppling under the weight of a stone thrown by Athena (21.403–9):

> ἡ δ᾽ ἀναχασσαμένη λίθον εἵλετο χειρὶ παχείῃ
> κείμενον ἐν πεδίῳ μέλανα τρηχύν τε μέγαν τε,
> τόν ῥ᾽ ἄνδρες πρότεροι θέσαν ἔμμεναι οὖρον ἀρούρης·
> τῷ βάλε θοῦρον Ἄρηα κατ᾽ αὐχένα, λῦσε δὲ γυῖα.
> ἑπτὰ δ᾽ ἐπέσχε πέλεθρα πεσών, ἐκόνισε δὲ χαίτας,

τεύχεά τ᾽ ἀμφαράβησε· γέλασσε δὲ Παλλὰς Ἀθήνη,
καί οἱ ἐπευχομένη ἔπεα πτερόεντα προσηύδα·

She, drawing back, took up in her stout hand a stone
lying in the plain—black, rough, and huge,
that men from before set up to be a boundary-stone of a field—
this she threw at bold Ares in the neck, and she let loose his limbs.
He covered seven acres having fallen, his hair full of dust,
and his armor rang about him. Pallas Athena laughed,
and vaunting she addressed him with winged words.

As Loraux has observed in her reading of these three passages from the *Iliad* and of a similar scene depicting the fall of Ares in the *Shield of Heracles* (359–67), the virtual deaths of Ares here are made both real and symbolic by what she calls a "textual ruse." In her words, "Ainsi, toutes les formules qui, inlassablement, donnent le mort aux combattants sont là, mais parfois affectées d'une légère modification, unique dans l'œuvre" (1986: 341). This textual strategy must take place, according to Loraux, because Ares' is not an ordinary death, and the modification to the formulaic language of death goes to show that he is not really dead.[70] Like the oversize body of Ares, then, that fills seven *plethra* of the battlefield,[71] the fall of the god does not fit exactly into the language of Homeric death, but—importantly—the diction of falling is both typical and modified just enough to let the poem succeed in having it both ways. The body of Ares falls into the kinetic practice of human gesture just as it falls into the poetic practice of formula, but in each case body and formula fail to slot completely into the pattern of what men in the *Iliad* actually do and suffer.

70. Loraux here follows Lowenstam 1981, who describes this phenomenon as a "mock scene" (a scene that "suggest(s) unrealized possibilities by means of transformations of commonly attested formulae," 84). See also Morrison 1999: 138. The following words and phrases used to describe the fall of Ares (21.403–9) employ typical battle-scene language (the one anomaly is the feminine gender of the participles denoting Athena as the assailant): ἀναχασσαμένη λίθον εἵλετο χειρὶ παχείῃ / κείμενον ἐν πεδίῳ μέλανα τρηχύν τε μέγαν τε (21.403–4); κατ᾽ αὐχένα (406); λῦσε δὲ γυῖα (406); πεσών (407); καί οἱ ἐπευχομένη ἔπεα πτερόεντα προσηύδα (409). The formula is modified in the following places: ἐκόνισε δὲ χαίτας (407); τεύχεά τ᾽ ἀμφαράβησε (408). For a detailed reading of these passages, see Lowenstam 1981: 84–87.

71. On the problem of the gods' size in relation to both the human world on the ground and the cosmic world of Olympus, see, e.g., 5.838–39 (where Diomedes' chariot groans under Athena's weight); 18.516–19 (on the relative size of Athena and Ares as they are depicted on Achilles' shield). Gordon 1979 is illuminating on this topic in reference to Pheidias' colossal statue of Zeus at Olympia (inspired, according to tradition, by *Il.* 1.528–30). In reference to Strabo's complaint (8.3.30) that the god was so tall that, if he had stood up, he would have broken through the ceiling of the temple, he observes (1979: 14), "I take it that Pheidias incorporated a deliberate allusion to the puzzle over the gods' ability to transcend human polarities into his design: Zeus is in the temple, but also not—he does not 'fit.'"

Concerning Ares' "second fall" (15.115–16), moreover, we might add to Loraux's observation about the substitution of ὁμοῦ for the usual ἐν with νεκύεσσι at 15.118 (κεῖσθαι ὁμοῦ νεκύεσσι, which is usually translated as "lie among the dead").[72] In Ares' case, it is important to note that he lies not only among (ἐν) or *in the same place as* the corpses on the battlefield, but also—if we expand our reading of ὁμοῦ to include all its definitions—*at the same time* as they do. By uniting with mortals in the act of having fallen, Ares enters into a relationship with them that he imagines might even exist on the same temporal register.

Like Ares and Hephaestus, Aphrodite's knees collapse beneath her as she is struck by Athena in Book 21.[73] This is potentially a dangerous moment for the narrative, as the gods' bodies start to topple on the battlefield in a wave that comes close to imitating the endless cycle of human falls. Lowenstam has observed that this scene resembles the pattern of death and fighting among humans on the battlefield.[74] But it is a potential that is never realized in the *Iliad*, a poem in which gods do not, in the end, lose their immortality on any count. It is important to the foundation of Zeus' rule, however, that the potential to fall be kept alive among the gods. The fall from Olympus hangs as an ominous threat over the immortals throughout the poem, underscored by Zeus' tossing of Atē out of the heavens by her hair (19.130–31) and by his attempt to throw out Sleep (14.258).[75] In Book 8, Zeus imitates the actions of his Hesiodic counterpart by threatening to hurl those gods who disobey him "far into murky Tartarus" (8.13). In his threats, Zeus makes it clear that he can subject the bodies of the gods to the human physics of falling, but that he will always escape this particular form of "gravity" himself. A few lines later (19–27), he claims that even if all the gods tied a golden cord to Olympus and attempted to pull him down from the sky, they would never succeed in toppling him. He goes on to threaten, however, that—if he wished—he might easily drag all the gods along with the earth and sea up by that same golden cord, and securing it around the horn of Olympus, leave all of them suspended there, dangling in midair (8.18–27):

εἰ δ᾽ ἄγε πειρήσασθε, θεοί, ἵνα εἴδετε πάντες·
σειρὴν χρυσείην ἐξ οὐρανόθεν κρεμάσαντες
πάντες τ᾽ ἐξάπτεσθε θεοὶ πᾶσαί τε θέαιναι·   20

---

72. Loraux 1986: 340 nn.15–16. For ἐν + νεκύεσσι, see 5.397; 10.349; cf. 5.886.
73. *Il.* 21.425, felled by Athena: τῆς δ᾽ αὐτοῦ λύτο γούνατα καὶ φίλον ἦτορ ("her knees and her dear heart went slack on the spot."
74. Lowentsam 1981: 84–87.
75. Cf. 5.897–98; 8.402–05; 15.21–24.

ἀλλ' οὐκ ἂν ἐρύσαιτ' ἐξ οὐρανόθεν πεδίονδε
Ζῆν' ὕπατον μήστωρ', οὐδ' εἰ μάλα πολλὰ κάμοιτε.
ἀλλ' ὅτε δὴ καὶ ἐγὼ πρόφρων ἐθέλοιμι ἐρύσσαι,
αὐτῇ κεν γαίῃ ἐρύσαιμ' αὐτῇ τε θαλάσσῃ·
σειρὴν μέν κεν ἔπειτα περὶ ῥίον Οὐλύμποιο   25
δησαίμην, τὰ δέ κ' αὖτε μετήορα πάντα γένοιτο.
τόσσον ἐγὼ περί τ' εἰμὶ θεῶν περί τ' εἴμ' ἀνθρώπων.

Come, make the attempt, gods, so that you all may know.
Hang from the heavens a golden chain
and all of you gods and goddesses take hold of it.   20
But you would not drag me down from heaven to the ground,
me—Zeus the highest ruler—not even if you labored hard over it.
But when I should eagerly desire to drag you,
I would draw you up with earth and sea as well.
Then the golden chain I would bind around the peak of Olympus,   25
so that all would again be held aloft in the air.
So much greater am I than gods and than men.

It is notable in this passage that Zeus distances himself from the other gods
by emphasizing that he cannot be pulled downward (πεδίονδε) toward the con-
dition of mortality. At the same time he is careful to remark on the physical
strain such exertion would wear upon the bodies of the other gods (οὐδ' εἰ μάλα
πολλὰ κάμοιτε, 8.22), although he himself, he suggests, would be able to lift the
entire cosmos without any effort at all. But what is perhaps most interesting
about Zeus' bizarre threat is that it culminates in an image of the entire earth,
and the gods along with it, suspended in the moment of free fall. As scholars
have noted, the image is reminiscent of the punishment of Hera, whom Zeus
recalls having once suspended from the heavens with anvils tied to her ankles
(15.18–21):

ἦ οὐ μέμνῃ ὅτε τ' ἐκρέμω ὑψόθεν, ἐκ δὲ ποδοῖιν
ἄκμονας ἧκα δύω, περὶ χερσὶ δὲ δεσμὸν ἴηλα
χρύσεον ἄρρηκτον; σὺ δ' ἐν αἰθέρι καὶ νεφέλῃσιν
ἐκρέμω·

Don't you remember when I hung you from on high, and from your feet
I let down two anvils, and around your hands I threw a golden,
unbreakable bond? You were hanging there in the aether and the clouds.

In both examples, the gods are explicitly bound (δησαίμην, δεσμόν), con-
forming to the traditional means that scholars have argued brings immortals

closest to the human state of death. But now there is something more that we can say about these particular forms of punishment. In both, the gods are pulled downward by a physical weight (the earth or the anvils) that keeps them poised in a permanent state of almost-falling. Scholars have long drawn a connection between the anvils that pull Hera down from the heavens and the anvil used by Hesiod to illustrate the distance between the heavens and earth.[76] The connection helps us to understand the hanging of Hera as the beginning of a fall, especially if we consider that Hephaestus, the Olympian who falls most memorably in the *Iliad*, bears the anvil as one of his trademark tools (18.476; *Od.* 8.274). Indeed, it may well be the association that Hephaestus shares with anvils and that Ares shares with bronze that causes them to be attracted, through the weight of their particular metals, to the concept of heaviness that I have traced in this history of falling.[77] In my final chapter, I explicitly connect this notion of heaviness with the human experience of gesture.

What is the particular effect of Zeus' punishment of Hera by hanging her with anvils attached to her ankles, or his threatening of the Olympians with the story of the golden cord? In both cases, the suspension of the gods in space, dangling in midair, puts them in a position of also being suspended in time. If the end result of falling, for humans, is death, then it is most appropriate that the supreme punishment for the gods should be always to be kept on the brink of the moment before death—the moment of the fall—because, for the gods, the full (human) implications of falling can never be realized. By forcing the Olympians to engage with weight and falling, Zeus also forces them to come as close as possible to death and the human experience of suffering through time.

Although similar sets of anxieties and questions have clustered around those moments in the *Iliad* when the immortal status of Ares and Hephaestus is compromised, scholars have not put their "quasi-deaths" side by side and considered their significance as a paired set of falls.[78] Nor has falling itself been recognized as a sustained motif, which extends far beyond its primary role as a formulaic marker of death for the Homeric warrior on the battlefield. I hope to have shown here that the shared diction and expression between the long falls of Hephaestus, from Olympus to earth, and the warrior-falls of Ares on

76. *Th.* 722–23; Beckwith 1998: 92 n.3.

77. Hesiod describes his anvil as being made of bronze (*Th.* 722), but it is hard to determine whether Homer's anvils are made of bronze or iron (Gray 1954). On Ares' connection with bronze, cf. Loraux 1986: 347; Nagy [1970] 1999: 156§9 n.1, with references. James Ker first suggested to me that Hephaestus' connection to the human activity of falling might be tied to his role as a god of technology, especially given that he uses the anvil, Hesiod's measure of falling.

78. For a notable exception, appearing since this argument was first published, see Garcia 2013: 159–229.

the Trojan plain illustrate different versions of the same thing. In each case, a god falls victim to the weight of his own body and, in turn, experiences time—through his body—in a way that is similar to how humans experience time on the ground. In attempting to "fit" the gods into a narrative that is told to human scale and with human points of reference, Homer places the divine body at the intersection between mortal and immortal worlds. I have explored here some of what happens when that body falls out of place and consequently finds itself caught up in a gesture that is quintessentially human.

3

Running

δεύτερος δ᾽ ὁ καλούμενος Ἀχιλλεύς· ἔστι δ᾽ οὗτος, ὅτι τὸ βραδύτατον
οὐδέποτε καταληφθήσεται θέον ὑπὸ τοῦ ταχίστου· ἔμπροσθεν γὰρ
ἀναγκαῖον ἐλθεῖν τὸ διῶκον ὅθεν ὥρμησεν τὸ φεῦγον, ὥστε ἀεί τι προέχειν
ἀναγκαῖον τὸ βραδύτερον.

The second [of Zeno's arguments] is the one called "Achilles." It is this: what
is slowest, when running, will never be caught by what is fastest. For it is
necessary for the pursuer to first reach that point from where the pursued set
out, with the result that the slower one must always be ahead to some degree.
—Aristotle, *Physics* 6.9.239b14–18

IF MY SECOND CHAPTER UNCOVERED A NARRATIVE LOGIC CONNECTED
to the falling of bodies vertically to the ground, my third moves horizontally
in an attempt to uncover the different speeds and temporal vectors in Homeric
epic. I use the positionality of running to show how the plots of the *Iliad* and
Odyssey both are in motion and frustrate motion (often at the same time),
arguing that the triple scheme of chasing, fleeing, and catching (διώκω, φεύγω,
and καταλαμβάνω in Zeno's Paradox) is particularly suggestive for its ability to
illuminate the complexities of Homer's narrative technique. This chapter, there-
fore, collects under the heading of "running" a number of different stances and
positionalities for the body in motion, including walking, catching up with one's
opponent, overtaking in a race and—finally—the trajectory (or "running") of
thrown objects. I take as my premise a claim that holds for other chapters in this
book as well (particularly those on leaping and standing, but also evident in my
discussion of walking in Chapter 2), namely that the plot takes its direction and
especially its progress or momentum from the actions of its bodies. Following
this premise, I attempt to show how a reading of gestures and stances can reveal
a complex underlying time structure for the Homeric plot that resembles in
many ways the paradoxical logic of Zeno's Achilles.

The world of the *Iliad* is one in which, to use the words of Sarpedon, one
must always strive to be "among the first" (μετὰ πρώτοισι), and the kinaesthetic
dynamics of that poem foreground the problems and strategies involved in
getting ahead.[1] The *Odyssey*, on the other hand, presents a different picture, a
world where the positioning of oneself as first or last is central to the problem
of achieving one's nostos. In that epic, away from the charged space and specific

1. *Il.* 12.315, 321, cf. 324. Hector says the same at 6.445.

rules of the battlefield, running might also transfer to other competitive categories and other ways of coming in "first" or "last." It is clear in both poems that—while being still on one's feet may provide ideal starting positions for epic plots (as with *Iliad* 1.6, discussed in Chapter 5)—legs need to move in order for a narrative to progress. The point may seem overly obvious, but a careful examination of an ordinary gesture like running in both poems can in fact bring new aspects of Homeric epic to light. In this chapter, I examine the complementary actions of catching up and overtaking in order to argue that the way in which characters in the *Iliad* and the *Odyssey* engage in running reveals important distinctions between the two poems.

Catching up and overtaking are similar actions in that they depend on two figures running—one ahead and one behind the other—yet the power dynamics embedded in the meaning of being "first" or "last" are notably altered at the moment of the transition from attaining to overtaking.[2] The small passage from the one to the other draws out the distinction between running in war and running in a race, as it is marked out in the shift from battleground to running track.[3] In this chapter, I set my reading of Homeric running within two primary frames of inquiry, arguing that speed of foot can have as much to do with the organization and timing of the poem as with the strategy of a particular character on the battlefield or during his return home. On the one hand, therefore, I look at how various temporalities in the poem affect or are manipulated by the actors in the epics, and, on the other, at how they can be strategized by the poet himself in the organization of his narrative. These two approaches are complementary to each other, for they both reveal how running and its attendant actions open up new ways of reading time and technique in Homer. The *Iliad,* as I show, is a poem that is particularly associated with the thematics of catching up. Yet, in both epics, Homer counters the overall validity of that concept through the various manifestations of overtaking initiated by the figure of Odysseus.

2. The verbs that describe the acts of running (θέω, τρέχω) and reaching or catching up with (αἱρέω, ἱκάνω, ἱκνέομαι, καταμάρπτω, κιχάνω, μάρπτω, τέτμον) in Homer are varied, as are the verbs that describe chasing (δίεμαι, διώκω, ἐπείγω, ἐπιτρέχω, μεθάλλομαι) and running ahead or fleeing (ἐκφέρω, προθέω, προφεύγω, τιταίνω, ὑπεκπροθέω, ὑποφεύγω, φεύγω, φοβέομαι), but the movement of the pursuing figure toward his target is motivated largely by the same impulses and physical actions. See Létoublon's detailed study of verbs of running (1985: 181–99). The verbs that denote overtaking in Homer are παραδύω, παρατρέχω, παραφθάνω, παρελαύνω, παρεξελαύνω, παρεξέρχομαι, παρέρχομαι, φθάνω.

3. Depending on the kind of running that takes place, the one who runs first is either quarry or victor, either fleeing in desperation or surging ahead in jubilation. The associations between games and battle have been well discussed in the scholarship. See, for example, Dickie 1984; Thalmann 1998: 133–40; Kyle 2007: 54–71, and further references in the following notes.

As a guiding thread for this inquiry, I use a selection of passages from the *Iliad* and the *Odyssey* to examine the significance of the difference between catching up and overtaking as it pertains to Achilles and Odysseus. The distinction that I am suggesting in their running styles and abilities fits securely within the broader rubric of the *biē* (force) / *mētis* (cunning) divide by which these two heroes are often evaluated. But I wish here to rethink those categories by setting them within a kinaesthetic frame. What the actions of Odysseus in the *Odyssey* teach us is that it is not necessarily how fast the body moves that is important, but rather that sometimes the best way to move forward is by a complex rearrangement of the categories of being first and last, fast or slow, as they are played out on the battlefield or in the athletic arena. The weary-legged and possibly also thin- and short-legged Odysseus' unique understanding and manipulation of that fact are key elements in Homer's articulation of the disparity between Odysseus and his swift-footed, Iliadic counterpart.[4]

Before we can fully understand how overtaking works in Homer we must spend some time with the kind of running that is so important to the *Iliad*, and that is the notion of running in order to catch up with somebody. To this end, I begin by rehearsing some familiar material, by analyzing a series of "catching ups" that are coordinated around the bodies of Hector and Achilles, culminating in the famous unsuccessful chase of *Iliad* 22. In the second part of the chapter, I look at how Odysseus positions himself in relation to an "Achilles" or Iliadic (formulaic) style of running, primarily in Books 8 and 9 of the *Odyssey*. I analyze as a bridge between the two parts the various acts of running that take place within the funeral games for Patroclus. The races there will serve as a transition in the movement from attaining to overtaking that this chapter seeks to chart.

RUNNING AND CATCHING UP IN THE *ILIAD*

Achilles is the fastest of all the warriors at Troy and the hero who runs with the most intensity, and he is paradigmatic of the notion that success, especially on the battlefield, comes through speed.[5] He embodies the principle that a good warrior will not only run far out in front in battle, but will also outstrip his

---

4. *Od.* 8.233; *Il.* 3.196–97, 211, and n.54 in this chapter; see also *Od.* 18.68, where Odysseus' thighs are described as beautiful and strong (καλούς τε μεγάλους τε). On Achilles' swift-footed epithet (n.66, this chapter) and its ironic resonances in the *Iliad*, see Graziosi and Haubold 2005: 48–56.

5. Men, animals such as dogs and horses (e.g., 10.437; 19.415; 22.162–63; Griffith 2006b), and gods (e.g., Ares 5.430; 8.215; Nagy [1979] 1999: 327) are all celebrated for the speed at which they move in the *Iliad*, in ascending order of velocity; the gods themselves can move "as swift as thought" (Vernant 1991: 27–49). Achilles' swiftness was legendary (see further Edwards 1985: 15; Burgess 2009: 13–15), and he in fact runs more slowly in the *Iliad* than elsewhere (Pi., *Nem.* 3.51–52; Griffin 1977: 40).

opponent, and in reaching him, cut him down.[6] Not until Achilles reenters the battlefield in Book 20, however, do we see his famous feet at last move into action. Then they travel with the speed of a wind-driven fire (20.490–93) in pursuit of Hector, Aeneas, Polydorus (the fastest of Priam's sons), and numerous other Trojans, a large number of whom escape by fleeing back into the citadel and some of whom are chased down and killed on the plain or trapped and killed within the river Scamander. A fairly standard vocabulary of chasing, fleeing, and catching occurs frequently through Achilles' *aristeia* in Books 20 and 21. Even when he stands in one place to fight in traditional Homeric combat (as against Aeneas), the vocabulary of speed energizes both Achilles' rhetoric and that of his opponent.[7] Everywhere in these two books, therefore, we find bodies fleeing, springing, darting, running, pouncing, chasing, and rushing, with a recurrent emphasis on the feet and legs.[8]

As Achilles continues to progress through this section of the poem, the description of his actions becomes increasingly associated with the language of chasing. At the end of Book 21, as the Trojans flee en masse toward the city gates, Achilles runs so fast that he is even able to keep pace with Apollo (21.600–605):

αὐτῷ γὰρ ἑκάεργος Ἀγήνορι πάντα ἐοικὼς
ἔστη πρόσθε ποδῶν, ὁ δ' ἐπέσσυτο ποσσὶ διώκειν·
ἧος ὁ τὸν πεδίοιο διώκετο πυροφόροιο,

6. Catching up happens frequently on the *Iliad*'s battlefield in the sequence of combat whereby a warrior pursues, reaches, and most likely kills his opponent (e.g., 5.65–66). There are exceptions to this order, of course (e.g., 16.597–98). It was a mark of honor to run out in the forefront of battle as a *promachos* (e.g., 22.459, where Andromache states that Hector used to run far ahead [πολὺ προθέεσκε] in battle; Odysseus says the same about Neoptolemus at *Od.* 11.515. See further.Fenik 1968; van Wees 1988: 1–24, 1994: 1–14.

7. 20.89–93, 187–94 (Aeneas' previous flight from Achilles down the slopes of Mount Ida), and 20.226–29 (the twelve foals of Boreas, which run so fast that their feet do not break the tips of the grain). In this way, chasing annuls the standard constraints of a formal duel, one of the most important forms of heroic fighting. See further Tsagalis (2012: 28–43) on how the Iliadic duel operates in a markedly different kind of space from that of the running of two heroes across the field.

8. E.g., ἀΐσσω (20.277, 401; 21.247, 254, 303); ἅλλομαι (20.353; 21.174, 536); ἀπαΐσσω (21.234); ἀποτρέπω (20.109, 119); διώκω (21.3, 601, 602); ἐκθρῴσκω (21.539); ἐκφεύγω (21.66); ἐνθρῴσκω (21.233); ἔπομαι (21.256); ἐπορούω (20.284, 442, 445; 21.33, 144, 392); ἐπισσεύω (20.288, 447; 21.227, 234, 601); ἐφάλλομαι (21.140); ἐφέπω (20.337, 357, 359, 494; 21.100); ἐφίημι (20.454; 21.424, 524); ἐφορμάω (20.461); θέω (20.53); θρῴσκω (20.381, 21.126); θύ[ν]ω (20.412, 493, 21.234); κιχάνω (20.454, 21.128, 263, 605); κλονέω (20.492; 21.528, 533, 554); μάρπτω (21.489, 564); μεθορμάω (20.192); μεταΐσσω (21.564); μετατροπαλίζομαι (20.190); οἰμάω (21.252 [see also my Chapter 4]); ὁρμάω (20.265, 572, 595); παραΐσσω (20.414); πηδάω (21.269, 302); σεύω (20.148, 189, 325); τρέπω (21.349, 603); ὑπεκπροθέω (21.604); ὑπεκφεύγω (20.191); ὑπεράλλομαι (20.327); ὑποτρέχω (21.68); φεύγω (20.190, 350, 402, 449; 21.6, 13, 23, 35, 52, 57, 93, 129, 256, 296, 472, 493, 496, 528, 532, 542, 554, 558, 580, 609); φθάνω (21.262, 576); φοβέω (20.90, 187; 21.4, 206, 267, 575, 606); γούνατα (20.435; 21.52, 114, 270, 302, 425, 506, 611); πόδες (20.59, 157, 189, 324, 410, 411, 441, 456; 21.241, 269, 271, 453, 557, 564, 601 [twice], 605, 611).

τρέψας πὰρ ποταμὸν βαθυδινήεντα Σκάμανδρον,
τυτθὸν ὑπεκπροθέοντα· δόλῳ δ’ ἄρ’ ἔθελγεν Ἀπόλλων,
ὡς αἰεὶ ἔλποιτο κιχήσεσθαι ποσὶν οἷσι·

The far-shooter, having likened himself in all respects to Agenor,
stood before his feet, and [Achilles] rushed (ἐπέσσυτο) to chase
    (διώκειν) him on foot.
For so long he chased him across the grain-giving plain,
having turned him toward Scamander the deep-whirling river,
him running just a little ahead (ὑπεκπροθέοντα). With this trick Apollo
    enticed him
so that he was constantly expecting to catch up (κιχήσεσθαι) with
    him with his feet.

Three of the four running verbs in this short passage preview the running that is about to occur in the following book between Achilles and Hector.[9] Thus ἐπισσεύω occurs again at the beginning of Book 22 to describe Achilles' swift advance upon Hector (22.26); διώκω a further eight times in Book 22, with Achilles always in the chasing role (22.8, 157, 158, 168, 173, 199, 200, 230); and κιχάνω one more time, to describe how Hector's fate has now caught him up (22.303).[10] In fact, the prominence of διώκω (*to chase*) at the very end of Book 21 and on into Book 22 suggests a narrowing in on the final pursuit of Hector by Achilles. In the frenetic movement from *Iliad* 20.1 to 21.599, by contrast, we encounter several verbs denoting rushing, leaping, whirling, and running, but διώκω occurs only once (21.3).

While Achilles runs on with his remarkable speed and intensity, Hector awaits him at the beginning of Book 22 in a posture of such stillness that Homer calls him "shackled" by fate (Ἕκτορα δ’ αὐτοῦ μεῖναι ὀλοιὴ μοῖρα πέδησεν, 22.5). The other significant instance in the poem when Homer places Hector at the city gate occurs during his meeting with Andromache (6.390–502), in a section of the *Iliad* that rehearses the concept of Hector being "caught up with" in precisely this location.[11] That section is worth drawing on now for the light it sheds on Hector's stance as Achilles approaches the city walls. In the second half of Book 6, Hector's visit to the city brings him for a time into Paris and Helen's bedroom, where he urges Paris to come out and fight. Paris agrees and tells

---

9. Cf. Fenik 1968: 214 on this scene as an example of an anticipatory device.

10. The fourth running verb, ὑπεκπροθέω (*to run just a little ahead of, outstrip*), does not occur in Book 22. Note, however, its use at 9.506 (Atē ahead of the Litai, discussed later in this chapter) and *Od.* 8.125 (the running race on Scheria).

11. At 16.712 Hector pauses at the Scaean gates and decides whether to take an offensive or defensive move against Patroclus.

Hector that he will follow and catch him up (κιχήσεσθαι) on his way out of the city after he has put on his armor (6.341). Hector immediately afterward stresses the importance of the timing of this meeting upon Helen, asking her to hurry Paris along, "so he may catch up (καταμάρψῃ) with me while I am still in the city" (6.363–64).

Following that conversation, Hector goes looking for Andromache and learns that she has left for the city wall (6.388). This sets him hurrying back along the same path through which he had entered the city, hoping to reach his wife before she leaves. At the Scaean gates, instead of meeting Paris as planned, he unexpectedly meets Andromache, who catches up with him much as we had been prepared to expect Paris would (6.392–94):

εὖτε πύλας ἵκανε διερχόμενος μέγα ἄστυ
Σκαιάς, τῇ ἄρ' ἔμελλε διεξίμεναι πεδίονδε,
ἔνθ' ἄλοχος πολύδωρος ἐναντίη ἦλθε θέουσα

when he reached the gates, having made his way through the great city—
the Scaean gates, where he would exit to the plain—
there his richly dowered wife approached him, running.

After the conversation between Hector, Andromache, and their son, Andromache turns away from Hector and follows the path back to the city, looking back (ἐντροπαλιζομένη, 496) at her husband as she goes. Once home, she weeps with her servants because she does not expect to ever see him returning to her again (Hector had foreseen the same thing of himself at 6.367). He will not, she believes, be one of those "fleeing ahead" (προφύγοντα, 502) of the strength and hands of the Achaeans.

The scene that Andromache envisions in Book 6 and the one that takes place at the beginning of Book 22 (as the other Trojans "flee like fawns" within the gates and Hector stands still) thereby quietly mirror each other. Hector's position in front of the Scaean gates in both of these scenes places him at an interesting temporal crossroads, as in the first case Andromache imagines her husband's future as she retreats and continually looks back at him, while in the second that imagined future appears running at full speed toward him. In both instances, Hector stands still at the intersection.

At the same time, at the very moment when Andromache is retreating from Hector at the gates, Paris is also running to meet him, and he catches up with his brother just when Hector is about to turn away for the battlefield. Although so elaborately prepared for earlier, their meeting almost does not happen, for Paris had been lingering in his bedroom and now reaches Hector only at the very last moment (6.514–16):

αἶψα δ' ἔπειτα
Ἕκτορα δῖον ἔτετμεν ἀδελφεόν, εὖτ' ἄρ' ἔμελλε
στρέψεσθ' ἐκ χώρης ὅθι ᾗ ὀάριζε γυναικί.

suddenly then
he met his brother, glorious Hector, when he was about
to turn away from the spot where he had been conversing with his wife.

Through these lines and the long description of Paris running through the city
that preceded them (6.503–14), we are invited to measure Paris' speed in relative
terms: it took exactly as long for Paris to be left by Hector and then eventually
catch up with him as it did for Hector to walk farther into the city, look for his
wife, go back to the Scaean gates, and then hold a conversation with her. The
act of catching up thereby works, as Lorenzo Garcia has observed,[12] to channel
the separate temporal threads of each character's activity within the city into a
single, organized timeline. Andromache herself catches up (κιχάνω) with the
handmaids she had left behind after leaving Hector at the gates (6.498), thereby
further refining the overall effects of symmetry and timing in this scene.

As for Paris, his own actions are held at bay in the narrative in the second half
of Book 6 until it is time for Hector to meet with him. Then, like a horse that
has been stalled in the manger and suddenly breaks free (6.506–11), he is given
thirteen lines to bound from his bedroom to the spot that Andromache has just
vacated. Through the motif of the running figure, in other words, Homer allows
one thread of his narrative to "catch up" with another.[13] By slowing down or
accelerating the speed of his characters as they travel on foot, he is able to en-
gineer two perfectly coordinated moments of coincidence and narrative timing.
Hector's presence at the gate thereby draws various timelines toward and away
from him along so many spokes, organizing the various temporalities of the
poem into a coherent system. It is not that those timelines *themselves* run at dif-
ferent speeds; it is that they act as paths along which Homer can choose to have
his characters move either quickly or slowly. The discrepancy between Hector's,
Paris' and Andromache's relative speeds makes this system dynamic, enabling
those characters who have been temporarily "left behind" to catch up with the
main part of the story. The careful management of the running in the second

12. Garcia 2007: 54–61, 2013: 25.

13. See especially the charts denoting different timelines for the *Iliad* in Zielinski 1889–1901. This
method of reading a narrative according to a separate strand of time for each character is outlined well
in Shklovsky 1965: 25–57. See also, for Homer, Whitman and Scodel 1981: 1–15; Scodel 2008: 115–16, with
further bibliography throughout. Much of this scholarship deals with the question of whether events
presented sequentially in Homeric epic should be understood as occurring simultaneously.

half of Book 6 shows that speed of foot can have as much to do with the organization and timing of the poem as with strategy on the battlefield. As I continue to explore, the gesture of "catching up" that is at work on a narratorial level in Book 6 underpins the catching up that takes place on a more strictly actorial plane in Books 20–22. In this way, the two levels reinforce each other, drawing our attention to the dynamic nature of the exchange between Achilles and Hector.

As Hector waits at the Scaean gates at the beginning of Book 22 there is a sense, as we have now seen, in which he is re-enacting an earlier moment in the epic. Later in the book his fate (μοῖρα, the same fate that shackled him at 22.5) will catch him up (κιχάνω, 22.303). But here we are invited to imagine the past storylines that previewed this scene catching up with him, too. Instead of Paris, it is now Achilles who speeds toward Hector in a simile that compares the runner to a horse (22.21–24). Indeed, if the simile here triggers a recollection of Paris as a horse that runs free, having suddenly broken loose from its shackles (6.506–11), so does it remind us that Paris' simile was also applied to Hector running forward in battle at 15.263–70, in a posture that is quite opposite to his shackled position as he awaits Achilles in Book 22.[14]

The similarities between the scenes in Books 6 and 22 may also gesture toward a third point in time, for Achilles' own impending death will take place at the same Scaean gates before which Hector now stands.[15] After Hector's death, Paris and Achilles will meet at the site toward which both, in their respective scenes, now run. We can imagine the scene played three times, in other words, with Paris, Achilles, and Hector each appearing twice, in each possible combination of pairs but never all together. The different temporalities that converge in Hector's still posture at the beginning of Book 22 are bound up with the recurrent placement of certain figures in the same point in space at key moments in the poem, but also with the speed and the timing with which those figures keep reaching him.

---

14. *Il.* 6.506–11 (=15.263–68): ὡς δ' ὅτε τις στατὸς ἵππος, ἀκοστήσας ἐπὶ φάτνῃ / δεσμὸν ἀπορρήξας θείη πεδίοιο κροαίνων, / εἰωθὼς λούεσθαι ἐϋρρεῖος ποταμοῖο, / κυδιόων· ὑψοῦ δὲ κάρη ἔχει, ἀμφὶ δὲ χαῖται / ὤμοις ἀΐσσονται· ὁ δ' ἀγλαΐηφι πεποιθώς, / ῥίμφα ἑ γοῦνα φέρει μετά τ' ἤθεα καὶ νομὸν ἵππων· ("Just as when some-stalled horse, fed on barley in the stable, / breaks out of his bonds and runs across the plain, striking it with his hooves, / being accustomed to wash in the well-flowing river, / exalting. And he holds his head high, and his hair on both sides glances over his shoulders. Trusting in his brilliance, / nimbly his knees bear him to the haunts and pasture of horses"). On this simile looking ahead to the later simile comparing the running of Achilles and Hector to racehorses, see the perceptive analysis of Tsagalis 2008: 279–81.

15. Achilles' death and its location are prophesied later in the book (22.359–60), as well as elsewhere in the poem (sometimes the site is specified as the Scaean gates, at other times as under the walls of Troy). See further Burgess 2009: 38–39, 43–55.

To read these scenes as anticipatory of a later, key moment beyond the end of the epic is also to consider what never in fact happens in the *Iliad*: the running toward each other of Achilles and Paris. The parallelism between Paris and Achilles extends beyond the symmetrical placement of their movement in these two scenes toward the Scaean gates. For Paris runs through the city toward Hector "trusting in his quick feet" (ποσὶ κραιπνοῖσι πεποιθώς, 6.505), a phrase that occurs at only one other time in Homer, to describe Achilles as he sets out after Hector at the start of the chase in Book 22: Πηλεΐδης δ᾽ ἐπόρουσε ποσὶ κραιπνοῖσι πεποιθώς ("the son of Peleus sprang forward, trusting in his quick feet," 138).[16] The correspondence between Paris and Achilles, who sit out the battle for certain spells of the poem, is thus briefly illuminated by the speed of their feet as they run toward Hector from opposite directions and from opposite parts of the text.[17]

Before Achilles is able to catch up with Hector, the latter starts to run. So begins the final, cumulative chase of the poem, in which the two famously enter a dreamlike vortex with neither able to outpace the other and where the words in the line similarly start to chase and circle one another.[18] This circling can be seen in the fourfold repetition of οὐ and οὔτε, and the repetition of φεύγω, δύναμαι, and διώκω in the following lines (22.199–201):[19]

ὡς δ᾽ ἐν ὀνείρῳ οὐ δύναται φεύγοντα διώκειν·
οὔτ᾽ ἄρ᾽ ὁ τὸν δύναται ὑποφεύγειν οὔθ᾽ ὁ διώκειν·
ὡς ὁ τὸν οὐ δύνατο μάρψαι ποσίν, οὐδ᾽ ὃς ἀλύξαι.

Just as in a dream it is not possible to catch the one fleeing,
for it is neither possible for the one to run away nor the other to pursue,
so was the one not able to catch up with his feet, nor the other to escape.

The runners, like the scene, become temporarily frozen in time, as Achilles, despite the careful foreshadowing of the exquisitely timed acts of "meeting" and "catching up" in Book 6, never manages to reach his opponent on foot. His

---

16. I thank Mario Telò for this observation.

17. As an anonymous reader points out, the convergence of Paris, Achilles, and Hector at this spot may symbolize a complementary distribution within the wider matrix of the epic tradition. Thus we might think not only of Achilles and Paris vying in the *Aethiopis* as Achilles and Hector do here, but also of the racing of Paris against his own brothers in the funeral games that Priam had set up for him, before it is known that Paris is still alive. Hyginus tells us that the games included a race (Fab. 273.12: *cursu*), in which Paris defeated his own brothers (Fab. 91.5: *fratres suos superavit*), although Hector is not listed in the group of competitors. In Euripides' fragmentary *Alexander*, however, which featured the event as a major plot element, Hector is defeated by Paris in the race (fr. 62aK).

18. Clay 2002a.

19. See also Tsagalis 2008: 284.

pursuit of Hector is compared to a chariot race in which a great prize lies in sight (22.162–66), but "they were not trying to win an animal for sacrifice, nor an ox-hide ... they were running for the life of Hector, breaker of horses" (22.159–61). The simile is important because it underscores a fleeting point of contact between the two arenas of battle and athletics, as the thematics of running converge and draw apart in the difference between catching up and overtaking.[20]

In Book 22, however, the runners are too well matched and the chase ends without conclusion. There is speed, certainly, but none of the timing that we found in Book 6.[21] Without the connective spark that comes from one character catching up with another, the plot cannot move forward clearly from one action to the next.[22] The speed at which the two men run instead compares to scenes of endless running that can be found in ekphrastic descriptions.[23] It is only when Athena tricks Hector into stopping that Achilles is able to approach and kill him. One consequence of that shift from running to standing is that Hector's death affords Achilles none of the satisfaction of catching up with his opponent. Perhaps this frustration explains in part his decision to drag Hector behind his chariot around Patroclus' tomb, as if it could reactivate the motion and momentum of their earlier chase. Even in death, Hector is made to run with Achilles, albeit with his feet as bound (22.396) as they were when he first stood his ground at the beginning of the book.[24]

The theme of running evolves through *Iliad* 20–22, and then again into 23, in the movement from combat, to chase, to race. During the funeral games for

---

20. See further Ziogas 2011: 258–61 and Ormand's chapter on Atalanta (2014a: 137–60). Both demonstrate several ways in which Atalanta's chasing of Hippomenes (Frr. 73, 75, 76 M–W) forecasts the chasing of Hector by Achilles, especially insofar as Hippomenes is racing in a competition for his life (Ormand) and in Hesiod's use of the word φεύγω following its role in Homer (Ziogas).

21. In this way, their pace compares to what Jameson has written of the continuously-running action in de Bont's film *Speed*: "contrary to expectation, its title does not designate temporality or velocity, nor change in time, nor even repetition any longer, but rather the absence of temporality altogether" (2003: 714–15).

22. As examples of how catching up can act as a narrative device, we might consider that Plato's *Republic* is set in motion by a boy catching up with Socrates, or that the stories in Ovid's *Metamorphoses*, such as the chase of Daphne by Apollo, reach their climax and point of transformation into a new narrative at the exact moment when one figure reaches another. See further Knox 1990: 183–202, 385–86; Hardie 1999: 89–107; Lovatt 2005.

23. On the Shield of Achilles, for example, Homer likens the movement of dancing boys to the "running" of a potter's wheel, where the word for the wheel, τροχός, comes from τρέχω, to run (18.599–601). The circular movement of the potter's wheel suggests timelessness and the absence of an endpoint, just as the running of Achilles and Hector (ῥίμφα μάλα τρωχῶσι, 22.163) in a series of circles around the walls of Troy takes on the timeless and aimless quality of a dream (Purves 2010: 55–59). On the Hesiodic Shield of Heracles, a tripod lies before charioteers as a prize that is never awarded because the end of the race will never be seen by the observer ([*Scut.*] 310–11).

24. For further discussion of this scene, see my Chapter 6 (154–58).

Patroclus, the seemingly endless whirling around the walls of Troy of Book 22 is translated into the ordered structure of turning, once, and then returning.[25] The two races that the Achaeans compete in during the games, first on chariot and then on foot, are plotted on a track with a single turning point (τέρμα[τα]) that the competitors run out to, turn around (ἑλίσσω, 23.309, 320, 466), and then come back from.[26] By running away from the ships and back again, instead of— like Achilles and Hector—around and around the walls of Troy, the athletes in these races symbolically remedy Patroclus' mistake, who ran on without turning back despite Achilles' instructions.[27]

But the most significant way in which these races, especially the chariot race, reconfigure and remember the pursuit of Hector by Achilles in *Iliad* 22 is that, here, the men competing not only catch up with but also overtake one another. By doing so, the competitors subvert the expected order of positions in the race, leading to the famously complicated allotment of prizes.[28] The risky act of over-taking performed by Antilochus in the chariot race (23.417–34) demonstrates this point particularly clearly. This is a scene that has received considerable scholarly attention and its details can be rehearsed quickly here.[29] Before the chariot race, Nestor coaches his son on the details of the track (23.306–48), but the son modifies his father's advice by choosing to overtake at a slightly different place than instructed (23.418–24).[30] This decision allows Antilochus, who has slower horses, to overtake Menelaus and finish slightly ahead. Antilochus makes his move at a spot where the road is narrow, thus forcing Menelaus, who had been in front, to pull back (23.431–34). Once he has been overtaken, however, Menelaus steadily regains his ground, so that by the very end of the race he has

25. So too is Achilles' dragging of Hector's corpse around Patroclus' tomb (which also seems endless), resolved by the return of the body to Priam. There, as with the race out to the post and back, the repetitive figure of circular movement is replaced by Priam's journey out and back, mirroring the structure of the *diaulos* (see following note).

26. They are both examples of the *diaulos* race. Note that the same formula is used to describe both races at 23.373 and 768 (Gagarin 1983: 38).

27. Achilles tells Patroclus, "After you have driven [the Trojans] from the ships, come back (ἰέναι πάλιν, 16.87)" and "But turn back (πάλιν τρωπᾶσθαι) once you set salvation on the ships" (16.95–96). The point is elaborated in Frame 2009: 161–62.

28. Achilles attempts to award the second prize to Eumelus simply because his horses are the fastest (23.536–8), even though, because of divine intervention and a crash, he places last in the race. The spectators, too, have trouble accepting that the final ordering of positions in the chariot race does not reflect the natural order of the competitors' abilities (480). See further (with bibliography) Thalmann 1998: 136–37.

29. Gernet 1948: 177–88; Willcock 1973: 1–11; Detienne and Vernant [1974] 1991: 11–26; Gagarin 1983: 35–39; Dunkle 1987: 1–17; Roisman 1988: 114–20; Nagy 1990: 208–10; Scott 1997: 213–27; Kitchell 1998: 159–71; Frame 2009: 131–72; Elmer 2015.

30. Although scholars dispute the exact details of where on the track the overtaking happens, there is no mention of a turning post. See Gagarin 1983: 35–39; Roisman 1988: 114–20; Richardson 1993: 218; Frame 2009: 136.

reduced almost entirely the distance between himself and Antilochus (516–22). Homer even tells us that Menelaus would have passed Antilochus if the course had been any longer (526–27).

Antilochus' skill in overtaking is a classic manifestation—perhaps *the* classic manifestation in the *Iliad*—of *mētis* (cunning) winning out over *biē* (force).[31] The cleverer man with slow horses is able to bring a series of calculations into play about the length of the running track and the timing of events in order to surpass a competitor who relies on the speed of his horses alone. Indeed, the only "overtaking" (φθάνω) that Menelaus can admit for Antilochus is ironic, in that the latter's horses will precede his own in the tiring of their knees and feet (φθήσονται τούτοισι πόδες καὶ γοῦνα καμόντα / ἢ ὑμῖν, 23.444–45). It is hardly surprising, therefore, that the other character who performs a significant act of overtaking in this book is Odysseus, who wins the footrace by overtaking the lesser Ajax (ἦλθε φθάμενος, 23.779) thanks to the intervention of the goddess of *mētis* herself, Athena (23.758–79).

An interesting complication arises when we consider that in both the *Iliad* and the *Odyssey* those who are swiftest on their feet are sometimes also the younger members of their community. This is true of Polydorus, the youngest son of Priam (20.407–10), and of Antilochus, as we hear elsewhere in Homer (*Od.* 3.112, 4.202).[32] If young men run more swiftly than those elders who are nevertheless still in their prime, then it is not surprising that racing by foot is given less prominence than racing by chariot in Homeric epic.[33] At the same time, however, the idea that the swifter man may be younger sits uncomfortably alongside the Homeric convention that those of an earlier generation are

31. As Kyle 2007: 60 notes, *mētis* appears five times in the passage and starts the line three times. See further Detienne and Vernant [1974] 1991: 11–26, 49–47; Dunkle 1987; Roisman 1988: 114–20; Nagy 1990: 202–22. Elmer 2015 makes the ingenious argument that the formula is forced into a paradoxical usage in this scene within the "narrow road" of the turn, only to be reinforced and corrected to its proper use after the race. His argument, which branches out into a discussion of the different ethical frameworks of the *Iliad* and *Odyssey,* dovetails with this chapter in interesting ways. See Nagy [1979] 1999: 326–28 on the connections between swiftness and *biē.*

32. It also accounts for the swiftness of Achilles, who is stronger than Odysseus in battle but whom Odysseus overtakes in wisdom and age (ἐγὼ δέ κε σεῖο νοήματί γε προβαλοίμην / πολλόν, ἐπεὶ πρότερος γενόμην καὶ πλείονα οἶδα, "but I would far overtake you in intelligence, since I was born ahead of you and know more," *Il.* 19.218–19). On Achilles' speed relative to Odysseus', cf. 23.792. Note also that Patroclus, who is older than Achilles (11.787), catches up with him in a simile in Book 16 that also reverses their ages. There, Patroclus is likened to a small girl who runs after her mother (Achilles), slowing her down, and catching hold of her dress (16.7–10).

33. As Pavlovskis (1976: 201) has written of the youths who participate in the footrace in *Aeneid* 5, "these boys have no future before them, and the rapidity with which they run their course seems to prophesy the brevity of their lives." From the opposite end of the spectrum, that Nestor is given a prize in the funeral games without competing (23.615–24) explains the necessity of privileging those who were born before, even if they are now too old to compete. See also Thalmann 1998: 136–37.

superior in every way to those who come after them, for to be πρότερος is to be further ahead not only in age but also in space.

Thus, when Antilochus offers to Menelaus the prize he won by overtaking him, he claims, "For I, my lord Menelaus, am younger / by far than you, and you are the greater and go before (πρότερος) me" (23.587–88). Later in the book Antilochus loses the footrace to Odysseus and Ajax and afterward claims (23.787–92),[34]

> εἰδόσιν ὔμμ' ἐρέω πᾶσιν, φίλοι, ὡς ἔτι καὶ νῦν
> ἀθάνατοι τιμῶσι παλαιοτέρους ἀνθρώπους.
> Αἴας μὲν γὰρ ἐμεῖ' ὀλίγον προγενέστερός ἐστιν,
> οὗτος δὲ προτέρης γενεῆς προτέρων τ' ἀνθρώπων·
> ὠμογέροντα δέ μίν φασ' ἔμμεναι· ἀργαλέον δὲ
> ποσσὶν ἐριδήσασθαι Ἀχαιοῖς, εἰ μὴ Ἀχιλλεῖ.

> Friends, I will tell you what you all already know, that still even now
> the immortals honor older men.
> For Ajax is older (προγενέστερος) than I by a little,
> but this man is from a prior (προτέρης) generation, from men who
>   came before us (προτέρων).
> They say he is green in old age. For it is difficult
> for the Achaeans to challenge (ἐριδήσασθαι) him with their feet,
>   except for Achilles.

Odysseus is placed in the curious position of belonging to the πρότεροι generation and also of being ὠμογέρων, an adjective that appears only here in Homer and that translates as something like "green" or "unripe" old age. The oxymoron suggests that Odysseus is both old and young; that he can have it both ways.[35] From this position of being πρότερος twice—further ahead in age, as an older man, and farther ahead in running, as if he were a younger man—nobody can challenge him in the speed of his feet, except, that is, Achilles. Here, toward the very end of the epic, the suggestion of competition (ἐριδήσασθαι) between Achilles and Odysseus serves as a subtle, even reconciliatory, counterpoint to the vying of Achilles and Agamemnon in the poem's opening lines.

34. Kyle 2007: 62 states, "The younger men, Antilochus or Ajax, son of Oileus, should win."

35. Odysseus' status as simultaneously "old" and "young" also mirrors his status on Ithaca when he returns in the persona of an old beggar, prompting Irus to ask him how he can fight against a younger man (*Od.* 18.31)—I thank Craig Russell for this observation. Frame 2009: 151 makes a related argument about the combination of youthful and old elements in the characterization of Antilochus in *Iliad* 23. He argues that Antilochus, although young in age, resembles an older man (specifically, the older Nestor) in terms of his knowledge and skill, and a younger man in terms of his reckless actions in the race.

Whereas there the two heroes "stood apart in strife" (διαστήτην ἐρίσαντε, 1.6, chap. 5), leading to an immobilizing of Achilles' famous feet for the first two-thirds of the poem, in Book 23 the difference between Achilles and Odysseus is figured instead as a closing of the gap between two competitors in a race.

I have tried to show so far that running and catching up in the *Iliad* are note-worthy not merely as an important battle strategy but also for the way in which they point to the combined significance of timing and speed in the poem. In particular, I have pointed to the thematic resonance of catching up for the poem as a whole, seeing it as a key gesture within the *Iliad*'s poetics. I have also suggested that, at the end of the epic, this gesture is co-opted by Antilochus and Odysseus and transformed—within the athletic context of *Iliad* 23—into the art of overtaking. In the second half of this chapter, I consider the consequences of moving from a poetics of catching up to a poetics of overtaking.

Overtaking Odysseus

In Book 8 of the *Odyssey*, while Odysseus is being entertained by the Phaeacians on the final stage of his journey home, a scene of feasting and athletic competition is interspersed by the three songs of Demodocus (Odysseus at Troy; Ares and Aphrodite; the Trojan horse).[36] After the first song, in response to the taunting of Euryalus at his initial refusal to participate in the games, Odysseus angrily defends his status before throwing a discus far beyond those already scattered in the field (*Od.* 8.179–98). We will return to this discus throw later on. For now, however, I want to consider Odysseus' words after that throw, when he continues to defend his prowess as an athlete ("I stand far out ahead of all others," 8.221), but draws attention to his legs (8.230–33):

> οἵοισιν δείδοικα ποσὶν μή τίς με παρέλθῃ
> Φαιήκων· λίην γὰρ ἀεικελίως ἐδαμάσθην
> κύμασιν ἐν πολλοῖς, ἐπεὶ οὐ κομιδὴ κατὰ νῆα
> ἦεν ἐπηετανός· τῷ μοι φίλα γυῖα λέλυνται.

> I fear that someone of the Phaeacians could overtake me
> only on foot, for I was all too beaten down in a bad way
> amidst the many waves, since there was no sufficient
> provision on the ship. And so my limbs are slack.

Although Odysseus outdistanced men younger than himself in the footrace during Patroclus' funeral games, he will not run now against the younger but

---

36. On the Phaeacian games, especially in relation to the martial *aethloi* (contests) and the funeral games of the *Iliad*, see Thalmann 1998: 134–53; in relation to movement and dance, see Olsen 2017b.

less warlike Phaeacians, on the grounds that he has prematurely lost his runner's physique on board ship.[37] Specifically, his limbs are slackened (γυῖα λέλυνται), a seafaring modulation of the Iliadic formula for death. We might compare them to Nestor's limbs and knees in the *Iliad*, which are no longer firm, as they used to be.[38]

What, then, are the consequences of Odysseus' transformation into a "slow" hero by this point in his life, a competitor who hints that he might come in last? Do these lines cast an anxious look back to the *Iliad*, where men were constantly running in battle and where it was a point of honor to run out in front and challenge an opponent? Certainly, the lines draw our attention to Odysseus' need to prove his heroic worth in a setting in which there has been little opportunity to engage in running. More specifically, how should we understand Odysseus' words in relation to the end of the *Iliad*, where Odysseus not only won the running race but where Antilochus afterward claimed that only Achilles could challenge Odysseus in the speed of his feet? Was Antilochus only being conciliatory there, or can we detect behind his words hints of a rivalry between Achilles and Odysseus?

I would not press the latter point were it not that Demodocus had alluded to precisely such a rivalry in the first of his three songs (8.72–82), before the games began.[39] Not two hundred lines later (8.223–33), Odysseus picks up that thread by overturning several of the points in Antilochus' speech from the *Iliad*. He first makes himself "young," by telling the Phaeacians he will compete with anyone except the men of the generation ahead (πρότεροι) of him, such as Heracles or Eurytus, famed for their skill in archery (8.221–25).[40] But he then says that he will not compete on foot, because he no longer has the strength in his legs, as we saw previously. He thus undermines both of the points that Antilochus made about him in *Iliad* 23, reversing the terms by which he had previously appeared both "young" and "old."

---

37. As Felson 1999: 94 notes, Odysseus calls the Phaeacians νέοι (in her words, "you young pups") when he challenges them to compete with him in the discus throw (8.202).

38. Cf. *Il.* 4.313–15; 11.668–70; my Chapter 2.

39. On the poetic tradition of the rivalry between Achilles and Odysseus, see esp. Nagy [1979] 1999: 45–58, who discusses passages such as *Il.* 9.308–429, where Achilles expresses a dislike of Odysseus; Edwards 1985; Martin 1989: 62–65; Danek 1998: 142–50 (with further bibliography). The quarrel between Achilles and Odysseus is an event that is said to make Agamemnon glad in his heart because "the best of the Achaeans were contending" (*Od.* 8.78), alluding to a prophecy concerning the capture of Troy. See further Braswell 1982: 130 n.5; Heubeck et al. 1998: ad 8.75.

40. See further Schein 2002b: 193–205; Buchan 2004a: 97–98. The reference to archery here looks forward to Odysseus' stringing of the bow in *Odyssey* 22 (Thalmann 1998: 140–41 [with further bibliography], 171–237), and to his successful hitting of his target there (compare the attempts of Polyphemus to hit Odysseus' ship with a rock, discussed later in the chapter [88–89]).

Odysseus' apology for his feet at this particular moment in the poem is carefully placed, moreover, between the first and second of Demodocus' songs. In the first song, as I have discussed, the mention of a rivalry between Achilles and Odysseus recalls, however subtly, Antilochus' speech after Odysseus' victory in the running race during the funeral games for Patroclus.[41] Now, in Demodocus' second song, the theme of running, overtaking, and speed is given prominence through the story of Ares and Aphrodite (8.266–367), in which the slow god, Hephaestus, manages to "catch up" with the swift-footed Ares. As scholars have noted, Hephaestus' slowness of foot echoes Odysseus' comments about his weak legs just a little earlier, and it is one of the many means by which Homer draws an association between Odysseus and Hephaestus.[42] In the song, Ares is described as swift footed (ἀρτίπος, 8.310) and fastest of all the gods (8.331), while Hephaestus is lame (χωλός, 8.308) and weak on his feet (ἠπεδανός, 8.311).[43]

Hephaestus' capture of Ares—by setting out from home as if on a journey and then turning back once his wife and Ares have gone to bed together—incorporates vocabulary (κιχάνω, αἱρέω) that is familiar from the *Iliad*'s lexicon of running. Yet it is not the fastest one who wins, but rather the one who bides his time, taking a detour out and back. The moral of the story is clear (8.329–31):

οὐκ ἀρετᾷ κακὰ ἔργα· κιχάνει τοι βραδὺς ὠκύν,
ὡς καὶ νῦν Ἥφαιστος ἐὼν βραδὺς εἷλεν Ἄρηα,
ὠκύτατόν περ ἐόντα θεῶν, οἳ Ὄλυμπον ἔχουσι

He who performs bad deeds does not fare well. For the slow catches
    up with the swift,
just as now even Hephaestus, being slow, caught hold of Ares,
even though Ares is the fastest of the gods who live on Olympus.

Placed within the larger frame of Demodocus' first song and Odysseus' comment about his legs, Hephaestus' clever plot allows us to see more clearly the strategy behind some of the overtaking that Odysseus maneuvers both on the Homeric plain and in the second quarter of the *Odyssey* (particularly Books 8 and 9). In *Iliad* 10, for example, Odysseus captures Dolon by allowing him to overtake (παρεξέρχομαι, παραφθάνω, παρατρέχω) him by just a little (τυτθόν, 10.344–50) and then by deliberately expanding the distance between them,

41. This observation is also made by Buchan (2004a: 98–102), whose work on these passages has had an important influence on my own.

42. See further Burkert 1960: 130–44; Newton 1987: 12–20; Braswell 1982: 129–37; Olson 1989: 135–45; Zeitlin 1996: 19–52; Buchan 2004a: 100–101. On the self-deprecatory stance of the trickster, see Rosen 1990: 11–25.

43. Ares is frequently described as fast (θοός) in the *Iliad* (see n.5, this chapter). See further Braswell 1982: 134, and, on Hephaestus' gait, my Chapter 2 (58–59).

countering the normal practice in which one tries to close the gap with one's rival in a race or on the battlefield (10.350–54). Meanwhile, Athena ensures that none of the other Achaeans get ahead (φθάνω) of Odysseus and Diomedes in capturing Dolon.[44] Yet Odysseus' plan works by confining Dolon in the space before the ships, where the two Achaeans are then able to reach him.[45] Odysseus' premeditated approach to both setting out and returning, in other words, is founded on a backward and forward tracking method that diverges from the way that other heroes pursue their targets.[46] He uses a strategy opposite to Dolon's, who promised Hector that he would run "straight through" (διαμπερές) to the Achaean ships (10.325). By contrast, Odysseus—like Hephaestus—stops, waits, and allows himself to be overtaken. He understands, in other words, that the slow and indirect path is sometimes the better one.

In Book 11 of the *Odyssey*, upon unexpectedly coming across Elpenor in the Underworld, Odysseus again finds himself "overtaken" to his own advantage. His first words to Elpenor, "you have come faster (ἔφθης) on foot than I could in my black ship" (11.58), play on the association he made on Scheria between traveling by ship and losing a race.[47] Elpenor, significantly the very youngest (νεώτατος, 10.552) of Odysseus' crew, both wins the race to the underworld and also loses it, since—in coming first—he finds himself left behind (καταλείπω) by the rest.[48] Indeed, the presence of φθάνω (*to anticipate, overtake*) in Odysseus' little joke signals not only the practice of overtaking on the battlefield but also how death can "overtake" a warrior in that context, too.[49]

The ploy of winning by coming last (and vice versa) is further illustrated in the scenes between Odysseus and Polyphemus. First, Odysseus elicits from the

---

44. Diomedes is especially concerned, since the plan leaves open the possibility that he might "come in second" (ὃ δὲ δεύτερος ἔλθοι, 10.368). Achilles worries about coming in second, using the same phrase, when chasing Hector around the walls of Troy (22.206–7).

45. The verbs used for catching up are κιχάνω and ἅπτομαι (10.376–77).

46. In this Odysseus adopts the same kind of strategy as Hermes, to whom he has often been compared. In the Homeric Hymn, Hermes walked backward, erasing his tracks, rather than in a forward line. As scholars have noted, Odysseus' epithet *polutropos* ("many-pathed") is applied also (and only also) to Hermes (*Hom. Hymn Herm.* 13, 439). See further Pucci 1982: 53, who connects the epithet with Odysseus' "zigzagging" strategy for survival, drawing a contrast with Achilles and the *Iliad*; Clay 1983: 29; Buchan 2004a: 102.

47. Ahl and Roisman 1996: 123–25. The verb φθάνω (*to anticipate, get ahead of*) has precisely the sense of "overtake" here. Cf. *Il.* 21.262, where φθάνω is applied to the running ahead of water in a simile describing the river Scamander's pursuit of Achilles, and its use at 10.368 (discussed earlier).

48. *Od.* 11.53: σῶμα γὰρ ἐν Κίρκης μεγάρῳ κατελείπομεν ἡμεῖς ("we left behind his body in Circe's halls"). For the use of the verb λείπω to denote leaving a contender behind in a race, see *Il.* 23.407, 522–23 (discussed earlier); *Od.* 8.125.

49. *Il.* 11.451: φθῆ σε τέλος θανάτοιο κιχήμενον, οὐδ' ὑπάλυξας ("the endpoint of death caught you up and overtook you, nor did you escape"). Death is figured as a runner fairly often in the *Iliad* (see, e.g., 20.449). Cf. Steiner 2010: ad 17.476.

Cyclops the promise that he will be eaten "last," using a word, πύματος, that also refers to coming in at the back (*Od.* 9.369; cf. *Il.* 4.253–54; 11.65). He thereby puts Polyphemus in the position of competing with a contender who, although coming from the back, beats him at his own game.[50] Even the verb, μάρπτω, that describes Polyphemus' action in snatching up the men to eat (9.289, 311, 344) is also used of catching up in the scenes depicting the running of Achilles in the *Iliad* (21.564; 22.201).

Over the course of the Cyclops episode, Homer increasingly introduces and makes use of the vocabulary of competing and games in order to give Odysseus a Hephaestian advantage of *mētis* over *biē*. It was just this kind of advantage that he had in winning the race against the faster Ajax in the games of *Iliad* 23.[51] This advantage is especially evident, too, in Odysseus' escape from Polyphemus' cave (9.444–52):

> ὕστατος ἀρνειὸς μήλων ἔστειχε θύραζε,
> λάχνῳ στεινόμενος καὶ ἐμοὶ πυκινὰ φρονέοντι.   445
> τὸν δ' ἐπιμασσάμενος προσέφη κρατερὸς Πολύφημος·
> "κριὲ πέπον, τί μοι ὧδε διὰ σπέος ἔσσυο μήλων
> ὕστατος; οὔ τι πάρος γε λελειμμένος ἔρχεαι οἰῶν,
> ἀλλὰ πολὺ πρῶτος νέμεαι τέρεν' ἄνθεα ποίης
> μακρὰ βιβάς, πρῶτος δὲ ῥοὰς ποταμῶν ἀφικάνεις,   450
> πρῶτος δὲ σταθμόνδε λιλαίεαι ἀπονέεσθαι
> ἑσπέριος· νῦν αὖτε πανύστατος."

> The ram was coming last of the flock to the doorway,
> constrained by his fleece and me thinking close-packed thoughts,   445
> and feeling him mighty Polyphemus spoke:
> "Dear ram, why do you hurry through the cave like this,
> last of the flock? In the past, you were never left behind when you went
>   with the sheep,
> but you were always first by far to graze on the soft flowers of the grass,
> striding magnificently, and first you reached the streams
>   of the rivers,   450
> first you longed to return to the pen
> in the evening. But now you are last of all."

---

50. The golden-age aspects of the Cyclops' world would make him unused to competition. On competition in relation to the Phaeacians, see Dickie 1984: 237–76; Thalmann 1998: 141–53; Buchan 2004a: 36–49.

51. On the themes of *mētis* and *biē* in the Cyclops episode, see (among others) Schein 1970: 73–83; Clay 1983: 112–25; Pucci 1998: 113–30.

The repetition of the words for first (πρῶτος) and last (ὕστατος) in this passage makes clear the rearrangement that Odysseus' presence beneath the ram has set in play.[52] The animal, which is earlier called the best of all the flock by far (μήλων ὄχ᾽ ἄριστος ἁπάντων, 9.432), and which is accustomed to walk out to pasture with giant strides (μακρὰ βιβάς, 9.450) like a great Homeric warrior,[53] is now in very last position, left behind (λελειμμένος, 9.448) as if in a race.

Odysseus may not have the strongest or sturdiest of legs, but—just as in the passage from Book 3 of the *Iliad* where his ram-like appearance causes others to underestimate him—he is able to use his physique to his advantage when escaping from the cave.[54] The weight of Odysseus and his "close-packed thoughts" counters the lightness and youth of men who, like the dancing Phaeacians, move quickly on their feet.[55] Only by these means, however, is Odysseus able to slip by Polyphemus.[56]

This aspect of overtaking is skillful and subtle, inasmuch as Homer manipulates strategies and overturns a clearly coded set of positions that had been plotted so carefully on the battlefields and athletic grounds of the *Iliad*. We can see in the figure of the great ram who carries him a reference back to the Odysseus of *Iliad* 3, but in recasting that identity by taking a position at the back, he also overturns the *Iliad*'s value system precisely because he prevents the ram from stepping out in respectable Iliadic style.

As he turns to leave the Cyclopes' island, Odysseus shouts back to Polyphemus, καὶ λίην σέ γ᾽ ἔμελλε κιχήσεσθαι κακὰ ἔργα ("your bad deeds were well past due to catch up with you," 9.477). His use of κιχάνω and κακὰ ἔργα recalls the moral of the Ares and Aphrodite story: οὐκ ἀρετᾷ κακὰ ἔργα· κιχάνει τοι βραδὺς ὠκύν ("He who performs bad deeds does not fare well, for the slow catches up with the swift," 8.329). In his own words, therefore, Odysseus indicates that he clearly believes himself to have come in first after all.

There is a final coda to Odysseus' and Polyphemus' alternate restaging of who is ahead and who behind in a reweaving of motifs from *Odyssey* 8 and the *Iliad*.

---

52. πρῶτος (23.265, 275, 538), ὕστατος (23.536), and πανύστατος (23.532) are all used of the positions in a race in the funeral games of *Iliad* 23.

53. The formula occurs in the *Iliad* to describe a warrior striding out to battle (7.213; 15.307, 686. Cf. 3.22; 13.809; 15.676; 16.534; *Od.* 11.539).

54. Odysseus' legs are described as—possibly—short and thin and he is likened to a deep-fleeced ram at *Il.* 3.191–224; Clay 1983: 121, 1999: 363–67; Newton 1987: 13 n.8.

55. Being light on one's feet and swift are usually synonymous. Cf. Hes. *Fr.* 62 M–W, where Iphicles runs so fast over the asphodel that he does not bend or break it, and *Il.* 20.226–29, for the same motif in relation to the foals of Boreas.

56. It is relevant to note here that the word "slip by" in Homeric Greek does in fact indicate to deceive as well as to pass by (e.g., παρεξέρχομαι, *Il.* 10.344 [run past]; *Od.* 5.103–4 [deceive]). It is not surprising to see that the language of speed has crossed over to the realm of thought in the *Odyssey*; in that poem, swiftness is no longer just a physical process. At *Od.* 13.291–92, Athena says to Odysseus, "He would be shrewd and crafty, whoever could get by (παρέρχομαι) you in all your trickery." Cf. *Il.* 1.132.

For Odysseus does not escape the Cyclopes' island without being almost struck by two huge stones thrown by Polyphemus after his ship. These stones, like the vocabulary of racing that occurs in Odysseus' escape from the cave, look back to Odysseus' experiences at the Phaeacian games in Book 8 and help us to reevaluate that act of throwing within the conceptual frame of overtaking. When Odysseus reluctantly competes in those games with a discus throw, he chooses a discus that is bigger, thicker, and heavier than the Phaeacians had thrown before him and easily wins the competition. His throw engages with the language of overtaking (ὑπερπέτομαι, ὑπερίημι) in a way we have not so far considered (8.186–98):

> Ἦ ῥα καὶ αὐτῷ φάρει ἀναΐξας λάβε δίσκον
> μείζονα καὶ πάχετον, στιβαρώτερον οὐκ ὀλίγον περ
> ἢ οἵῳ Φαίηκες ἐδίσκεον ἀλλήλοισι.
> τόν ῥα περιστρέψας ἧκε στιβαρῆς ἀπὸ χειρός,
> βόμβησεν δὲ λίθος· κατὰ δ' ἔπτηξαν ποτὶ γαίῃ   190
> Φαίηκες δολιχήρετμοι, ναυσίκλυτοι ἄνδρες,
> λᾶος ὑπὸ ῥιπῆς· ὁ δ' ὑπέρπτατο σήματα πάντων
> ῥίμφα θέων ἀπὸ χειρός· ἔθηκε δὲ τέρματ' Ἀθήνη
> ἀνδρὶ δέμας εἰκυῖα, ἔπος τ' ἔφατ' ἔκ τ' ὀνόμαζε·
> "καί κ' ἀλαός τοι, ξεῖνε, διακρίνειε τὸ σῆμα   195
> ἀμφαφόων· ἐπεὶ οὔ τι μεμιγμένον ἐστὶν ὁμίλῳ,
> ἀλλὰ πολὺ πρῶτον· σὺ δὲ θάρσει τόνδε γ' ἄεθλον·
> οὔ τις Φαιήκων τόδε γ' ἵξεται οὐδ' ὑπερήσει."

He spoke, and darting up with his cloak still on he grabbed hold of a
   discus,
bigger than the others and thick, stouter not by a little
than the kind the Phaeacians had been throwing between themselves.
Spinning around he released it from his stout hand,
and the stone flew with a great humming, and they crouched
   down toward   190
the earth, the long-oared Phaeacians, men famous for their ships,
under the cast of the stone. For it flew beyond (ὑπέρπτατο)
   the marks of all the others,
running (θέων) nimbly from his hand. Athena marked its limit,
having likened herself to the form of a man, and she spoke out a word:
"Even a blind man, stranger, could distinguish your mark,   195
by feeling it. For it is not mixed in with the group,
but is first by far (πολὺ πρῶτον). Be confident in this contest,
no one of the Phaeacians will reach (ἵξεται) this mark nor
   overthrow (ὑπερήσει) it."

The discus "runs" (θέων) lightly from Odysseus' hand, and the mark of its distance is τέρματα, a word that is used elsewhere in Homer only for the turning posts in a chariot or running race.[57] Thus, although Odysseus refuses to participate on foot, Homer nevertheless appropriates the language of the running track in order to have him win this contest at the Phaeacian games.[58] Odysseus' stone falls "first by far" of the rest (πολὺ πρῶτον), just as the ram and the best charioteer are accustomed to run "first by far" (πολὺ πρῶτος) of the pack (*Od.* 9.449; *Il.* 23.288). Even the "feeling" performed by the blind man in Athena's hypothetical example is strikingly reminiscent, as Mark Buchan has observed (2004: 41–42), of the blind Polyphemus' feeling of his sheep when he determines their positions exiting the cave (*Od.* 9.446). The throw of the discus, although it has nothing ostensibly to do with running, is also phrased in this passage to connect with the idea of a race, with the order of the stones from first to last standing in for the order of runners. Twice, Homer hints that the discus has found a position in a field of other men instead of other inanimate objects. First, there is a pun on λᾶος, the genitive form of the word denoting the stone discus that Odysseus throws at line 192, and λαός, the word for men.[59] Second, there is the unusual usage of ὅμιλος at line 196 to denote the "throng" of the other stones in the competition, a term used elsewhere in Homer only of people.[60]

Finally, by picking up and throwing a stone discus that is heavier than the ones the Phaeacians use, Odysseus in effect reaches back to the tradition of the earlier men he had just refused to engage with, the πρότεροι who were able to lift much heavier stones than the men of later generations. Odysseus thereby registers a kind of chronological separation from the Phaeacians by his refusal to engage in games to do with speed and synchronicity. He will run neither alongside them nor "at the same time" as they do. Instead, he is able to participate via the discus in a diachronic way, for stones and the marks of stones lie in the field for a long time across the span of generations.[61] Again, therefore, Odysseus "overtakes," ending up "by far the first," although he is one of the last to throw; he wins without ever moving himself from the starting point. This

---

57. *Il.* 22.162; 23.309, 333, 358, 462, 466, 757. The adverb ῥίμφα is paired with θέων frequently in Homer to describe the act of running. On the application of verbs for running to projectiles in Homer, see Létoublon 1985: 183–84.

58. As Thalmann (1998: 140) observes, Odysseus' superiority as an athlete is in fact evident from the very beginning of the *Odyssey* (1.11–19), which "points to Odysseus as surpassingly the man of ἄεθλοι (*aethloi*) in comparison with the other warriors at Troy, and so in this way as in others it implicitly claims its own superiority to other heroic narratives."

59. Buchan 2004a: 72–88.

60. Martin 1984: 47.

61. *Il.* 21.403–5. Cf. 5.302–4[=]20.285–87; 12.380–83, 445–50. Homer refers to the men of the age preceding the heroes at Troy using πρότεροι at *Il.* 4.308; 5.637; 11.691; 21.405; 23.332, [790]; *Od.* 8.223.

kind of overtaking is very different from the exquisitely timed acts of catching up that we saw taking place outside the gates of Troy in *Iliad* 6, as it is also different from Achilles' single-minded pursuits in Books 20–22.

As Odysseus leaves on his ship, Polyphemus does one better in the trope of picking up the kind of rock that only men of old could handle, this time by breaking off part of a mountain crag and throwing it after Odysseus. But he finds himself participating in a mixed number of competitive arenas, and his throw does not hit its mark. The rock lands just a little (τυτθόν) in front of the ship on first try (κὰδ δ' ἔβαλε προπάροιθε νεὸς κυανοπρῴροιο / τυτθόν, ἐδεύησεν δ' οἰήϊον ἄκρον ἱκέσθαι, "he cast it down in front of the blue-prowed ship / by a little, and failed to reach the tip of the prow," 9.482–82), and just a little (τυτθόν) behind it on the second (9.537–40):

αὐτὰρ ὅ γ' ἐξαῦτις πολὺ μείζονα λᾶαν ἀείρας
ἧκ' ἐπιδινήσας, ἐπέρεισε δὲ ἶν' ἀπέλεθρον,
κὰδ δ' ἔβαλεν μετόπισθε νεὸς κυανοπρῴροιο
τυτθόν, ἐδεύησεν δ' οἰήϊον ἄκρον ἱκέσθαι.

Then again lifting a stone much larger
he let it go, whirling it, and put immeasurable strength into it.
But he cast it down behind the blue-prowed ship,
by a little, and failed to reach the tip of the rudder.

Polyphemus' cast co-opts both the physicality of Odysseus' discus throw and the language of fighting on the battlefield, specifically that of Ajax making a throw in the *Iliad* (7.268–69).[62] Indeed, it makes perfect sense that we would find a correspondence between Ajax and Polyphemus here, since both are exemplars of *biē*, or force. Ajax throws a stone again (and again incompletely, although it at first looks successful) at Hector in Book 14.[63] But even here, as with the lesser Ajax in the running race and as in his own competition with Odysseus for the arms of Achilles, he still comes in second. While Ajax always seems to be trapped in his ranking of "second to Achilles," Odysseus—whether he is overtaking or being overtaken—always manages to win.[64]

---

62. δεύτερος αὖτ' Αἴας πολὺ μείζονα λᾶαν ἀείρας / ἧκ' ἐπιδινήσας, ἐπέρεισε δὲ ἶν' ἀπέλεθρον. . . ("Then again Ajax, lifting a stone much larger, / let it go, whirling, and put immeasurable strength into it"). Like Ajax, Polyphemus and Odysseus "whirl around" to make their throws, although the verbs used are different, and in both examples the stones they hurl are greater than the one previously thrown.

63. *Il.* 14.409–13. He also hurls an iron weight in the funeral games for Patroclus, where it "overtakes" (ὑπέρβαλε) the marks of all the others (23.842–43). But Polypoites' throw, after Ajax's, goes much farther.

64. *Il.* 2.768–70; 17.279–80 (Ajax is "best of the Achaeans" after Achilles). On the triangulation of Achilles, Ajax, and Odysseus (where Ajax always comes in second or last), see Hinckley 1986: 209–21,

A surprising number of connective threads link Polyphemus' final two throws in *Odyssey* 9, by way of the games and songs in *Odyssey* 8 and the battle scenes of the *Iliad*, back to the overtaking of Ajax by Odysseus in the footrace in *Iliad* 23. In Book 8 of the *Odyssey*, Odysseus' throw is successful because it overtakes all the others, yet Polyphemus' throw fails for precisely that reason: it falls always just too far ahead or behind the target it is aiming to catch up with. The ship moves, just as a runner in a race does, and is always just out of reach. When Achilles chases Apollo at the end of *Iliad* 21, the god always runs just a little too far in front (τυτθὸν ὑπεκπροθέοντα) to be caught (604).[65] To throw the stone beyond its mark is, for the Cyclops, as useless as the act of overtaking is for Achilles. Both characters rely on their physical prowess alone to obtain their target (strength in the former's case, speed in the latter's); they are not interested in bypassing or overtaking it in order ultimately to achieve their goals.

By shouting out his name to the Cyclops and engaging him in competition, and by skillfully alternating between the categories of pursuer and pursued, Odysseus is able to come in first by coming in last (in the order of being eaten and in his exit from the cave). Polyphemus' parting curse ties in to the theme of their encounter, since there he requests that, if Odysseus must reach his homeland, he come in late (ὀψέ, 534). The runner most renowned for his speed in the *Iliad* runs fast and early, but with a fate that moves in tandem with his feet and that will not turn him back from Troy.[66] Odysseus, on the other hand, understands that the *Iliad*'s running should best be seen as part of a *diaulos* race, the second half of which is comprised of the return home.[67] He is also shown

who also discusses the wrestling match between Odysseus and Ajax in the games. On Athena as a supporter of winners, see Willcock 1970: 6–7.

65. By throwing at a moving target, Polyphemus can gain no satisfaction in throwing his stone ahead (*pro*) or behind (*meta*). Instead, like Achilles chasing Hector, he finds himself in a race against an opponent whom he cannot catch up with. Cf. Žižek 1991: 4 on the fable of Achilles and the tortoise and Zeno's Paradox, cited as an epigraph to this chapter: "The crucial feature of this inaccessibility of the object was nicely indicated by Lacan when he stressed that the point is not that Achilles could not overtake Hector (or the tortoise)—since he is faster than Hector, he can easily leave him behind—but rather that he cannot attain him: Hector is always too fast or too slow" (with thanks to Mark Buchan for this reference). Note that in Greek myth, when Cephalus' hound (which no animal could escape) was sent after the uncatchable Teumessian fox, Zeus was forced to resolve the paradox by turning them both to stone (Apollod., *Bibl.* 2.57–59; Aristodemus, fr. 5; Tzetzes, *Chiliades* 1.20.542–72). A version of the story is attributed to the Epic Cycle (Photius, *Lexicon*: Τευμήσια).

66. Achilles is variously described in the *Iliad* as ὠκύς ("swift," e.g., 19.295), πόδας ὠκύς ("swift footed," e.g., 1.58), ὠκύμορος ("swift fated," e.g., 1.417), and ὠκυμορώτατος ἄλλων ("the most swift fated of all," 1.505). In Book 19, his horse tells him that speed will never be enough to save him ("we too might run with the blast of Zephyr, who, they say, is the nimblest of all. But it is fated that you will be destroyed by the force of a god and a man," 415–17).

67. As Aeschylus' Clytemnestra put it: δεῖ γὰρ πρὸς οἴκους νοστίμου σωτηρίας, / κάμψαι διαύλου θάτερον κῶλον πάλιν ("In order to retain their homecoming [the Achaeans] must turn the other leg

throughout the poem to be particularly fortunate not to have been the first in arriving home.

The quarrel between Agamemnon and Achilles that sets the *Iliad* in motion is sparked, Agamemnon claims (*Il.* 19.270–75), by Atē, a goddess whom it is impossible to catch up with or overtake, but whom the Litai (Prayers) run in pursuit of nonetheless (*Il.* 9.502–7):

καὶ γάρ τε Λιταί εἰσι Διὸς κοῦραι μεγάλοιο,
χωλαί τε ῥυσαί τε παραβλῶπές τ' ὀφθαλμώ,
αἵ ῥά τε καὶ μετόπισθ' Ἄτης ἀλέγουσι κιοῦσαι.
ἡ δ' Ἄτη σθεναρή τε καὶ ἀρτίπος, οὕνεκα πάσας
πολλὸν ὑπεκπροθέει, φθάνει δέ τε πᾶσαν ἐπ' αἶαν
βλάπτουσ' ἀνθρώπους· αἱ δ' ἐξακέονται ὀπίσσω.

For the Litai (Prayers) are the daughters of great Zeus,
lame and shriveled and squinting,
who go with good heed behind Atē (Ruin).
But Atē is strong and swift footed, and she runs far ahead of
all of the Litai and outstrips them all across the earth,
harming men. They, the Litai, come as healers behind her.

To run ever ahead like this, or, conversely, to run ever in pursuit, constitutes one of the tragic strains of the *Iliad*, where the running of characters in battle so often leads to their own deaths and sometimes denotes a kind of impossible striving (Apollo outran Achilles at *Il.* 21.604, using the same verb as the one here: ὑπεκπροθέω). A parallel between this passage and another from the *Odyssey* is especially telling for the difference it reveals about the two poems' approaches to running. The epithet ἀρτίπος (sound or swift of foot) that here describes Atē occurs in only one other place in Homer, to describe Ares in precisely the context when he is being caught up with by the slower but more cunning Hephaestus (*Od.* 8.310) in Demodocus' song.

In the *Odyssey*, especially in the section tracing Odysseus' journey home, coming from behind takes a special prominence as a means of avoiding and subverting the *Iliad*'s heroic model.[68] The gesture of running thereby exposes a

of the *diaulos* back toward home," *Ag.* 343–44). It is this turn of the *diaulos* leg that reminds us, finally, that all running requires turns of some kind or another, and that the act of doing so–whether the turn is like Hector's, Antilochus', or Hephaestus'–demands our attention just as much as running does. See also Frame 2009: 170 on this passage's relation to *Iliad* 23, and Bonifazi 2009: 481–510, on the multidirectionality of *nostos* (esp. 506).

68. That Odysseus appears prominently as an overtaker in the battle scenes of the *Iliad* only in the Doloneia fits with the prevailing scholarly opinion that Book 10 is late in date and an awkward fit with the rest of the poem (see further Hainsworth 1993: 151–55; Danek 1988).

difference between the two poems in terms of their portrayal of character and their kinetic orientations, for the *Odyssey* is a poem that, rather than attempting to "run forward," loops and reverses according to the topographical and narratorial patternings of its *polutropos* hero, tackling in its own way the same frustrations expressed by Achilles in the *Iliad*.[69] I would not want to suggest that the *Iliad* is only and exclusively about catching up, nor that Odysseus is to be only and always understood as an overtaker; yet an examination of the difference between these two ways of running uncovers larger thematic concerns that serve, in subtle but important ways, to differentiate one epic from the other.

69. Pucci 1982: 39–62 and n.46, this chapter.

4

Leaping

οἴμησεν δὲ ἀλεὶς ὥς τ᾽ αἰετὸς ὑψιπετήεις

he leapt, having crouched, like a high-flying eagle
—*Iliad* 22.308=*Odyssey* 24.538

WE START AT AN END THAT IS ALSO A BEGINNING, WITH THE
soaring, rebellious leap of Odysseus just ten lines before the close of the poem.
Oimaō is not a common Homeric verb but it expresses an insistently Homeric
impulse: to leap forward in attack against one's enemy or prey.[1] Never mind
that Odysseus has no victim to land on—that he is left hanging, or we should
say soaring, at the end of this line, borne aloft by the aerial lengthening of
ὑψιπετήεις at verse end. His gesture expresses an elegant lightness of spirit and
possibility for the poem that the weight of Zeus' thunderbolt and accumulating
stops in the next two lines only partially counter (*Od.* 24.538–40):

οἴμησεν δὲ ἀλεὶς ὥς τ᾽ αἰετὸς ὑψιπετήεις
καὶ τότε δὴ Κρονίδης ἀφίει ψολόεντα κεραυνόν,
κὰδ δ᾽ ἔπεσε πρόσθε γλαυκώπιδος ὀβριμοπάτρης.

he leapt, having crouched, like a high-flying eagle
and then the son of Kronos released a sooty thunderbolt,
which fell down before the gray-eyed daughter of the mighty father.

Although seldom remarked upon,[2] this leap forms the last explicit, vivid, and in-
deed visible gesture of the *Odyssey*, the hero's farewell pose before exiting the poem
forever. Despite Athena's forceful orchestration of an ending, one character breaks
free and tries to resist the drive toward closure. He does so by employing two ac-
tions, a crouch and a leap, which embody, as I go on to argue, the potential for fu-
ture action in the poem. Indeed, the potential nature of Odysseus' movement is all
the more evident because it remains essentially unfinished. His leap is foreshort-
ened both because the poem comes to an end rapidly afterward and because it is
an abbreviated quotation of the extended Iliadic simile that marks Hector's truly

---

1. *DELG* 783. R. Führer writes that οἰμῆσαι is related to οἴμη but perhaps influenced by ὁρμάω
(*LfgrE* s.v.). Führer defines it as rushing ("losstürmen") and pouncing ("sich stürzen"). οἰμάω is also in
the same semantic field as ἀΐσσω, ἰθύω, ὁρμάω, [ἰθὺς] πέτομαι, and σεύομαι.

2. For an important exception see Stanford [1948] 1998: ad loc.

final gesture: his leap toward death in Book 22. These are the only two places in Homer in which this line appears,[3] and in one the occasion is momentous, in the other inconsequential. Yet in both of its occurrences, and in very different ways, the verse marks a potential transition toward an end for the two poems.

Odysseus' story ends ten verses beyond the phrase in question, with Athena establishing peace treaties between Odysseus and the relatives of the suitors and sending both factions home, but only after she has herself initiated the start of a battle (24.516–43):

Τὸν δὲ παρισταμένη προσέφη γλαυκῶπις Ἀθήνη·
"ὦ Ἀρκεισιάδη, πάντων πολὺ φίλταθ' ἑταίρων,
εὐξάμενος κούρῃ γλαυκώπιδι καὶ Διὶ πατρί,
αἶψα μάλ' ἀμπεπαλὼν προΐει δολιχόσκιον ἔγχος."
Ὣς φάτο, καί ῥ' ἔμπνευσε μένος μέγα Παλλὰς Ἀθήνη.   520
εὐξάμενος δ' ἄρ' ἔπειτα Διὸς κούρῃ μεγάλοιο,
αἶψα μάλ' ἀμπεπαλὼν προΐει δολιχόσκιον ἔγχος,
καὶ βάλεν Εὐπείθεα κόρυθος διὰ χαλκοπαρήου.
ἡ δ' οὐκ ἔγχος ἔρυτο, διαπρὸ δὲ εἴσατο χαλκός·
δούπησεν δὲ πεσών, ἀράβησε δὲ τεύχε' ἐπ' αὐτῷ.   525
ἐν δ' ἔπεσον προμάχοις Ὀδυσεὺς καὶ φαίδιμος υἱός,
τύπτον δὲ ξίφεσίν τε καὶ ἔγχεσιν ἀμφιγύοισι.
καὶ νύ κε δὴ πάντας ὄλεσαν καὶ ἔθηκαν ἀνόστους,
εἰ μὴ Ἀθηναίη, κούρη Διὸς αἰγιόχοιο,
ἤϋσεν φωνῇ, κατὰ δ' ἔσχεθε λαὸν ἅπαντα·   530
"ἴσχεσθε πτολέμου, Ἰθακήσιοι, ἀργαλέοιο,
ὥς κεν ἀναιμωτί γε διακρινθῆτε τάχιστα."
Ὣς φάτ' Ἀθηναίη, τοὺς δὲ χλωρὸν δέος εἷλε·
τῶν δ' ἄρα δεισάντων ἐκ χειρῶν ἔπτατο τεύχεα,
πάντα δ' ἐπὶ χθονὶ πῖπτε, θεᾶς ὄπα φωνησάσης·   535
πρὸς δὲ πόλιν τρωπῶντο λιλαιόμενοι βιότοιο·
σμερδαλέον δ' ἐβόησε πολύτλας δῖος Ὀδυσσεύς,
<u>οἴμησεν δὲ ἀλεὶς ὥς τ' αἰετὸς ὑψιπετήεις.</u>
καὶ τότε δὴ Κρονίδης ἀφίει ψολόεντα κεραυνόν,
κὰδ δ' ἔπεσε πρόσθε γλαυκώπιδος ὀβριμοπάτρης.   540

---

3. Bakker argues that less frequent but significantly placed occurrences of repeated phrases can refer to one another in a more directly allusive manner than normal formulas. He categorizes this under his "scale of interformularity" (2013: 158ff.). Janko, who similarly states that "the less frequent a repetition, the more I think we should notice it," discusses the twofold occurrence of a phrase used only at Hector's and Patroclus' deaths (*Il.* 16.856–57=22.362–63; Janko 1998: 9–10). On Homeric intertextuality in general see my discussion in the Introduction (12–13).

δὴ τότ' Ὀδυσσῆα προσέφη γλαυκῶπις Ἀθήνη·
"διογενὲς Λαερτιάδη, πολυμήχαν' Ὀδυσσεῦ,
ἴσχεο, παῦε δὲ νεῖκος ὁμοιΐου πολέμοιο,
μή πώς τοι Κρονίδης κεχολώσεται εὐρύοπα Ζεύς."
  Ὣς φάτ' Ἀθηναίη, ὁ δ' ἐπείθετο, χαῖρε δὲ θυμῷ.   545
ὅρκια δ' αὖ κατόπισθε μετ' ἀμφοτέροισιν ἔθηκε
Παλλὰς Ἀθηναίη, κούρη Διὸς αἰγιόχοιο,
Μέντορι εἰδομένη ἠμὲν δέμας ἠδὲ καὶ αὐδήν.

Gray-eyed Athena [as Mentor] stood next to [Laertes] and
    addressed him,
"Son of Arceisius, most beloved by far of all my companions,
pray to the gray-eyed daughter and to father Zeus,
and quickly, having much brandished it, launch your far-shadowing
    spear!"
So she spoke, and Pallas Athena breathed great strength into him.   520
He then prayed to the daughter of great Zeus
and quickly, having much brandished it, launched his
    far-shadowing spear,
and struck Eupeithes through the bronze-cheeked helmet.
It did not check the spear, but the bronze went through,
and he fell with a thud, and his armor clattered around him.   525
Then Odysseus and his gleaming son fell upon the frontfighters,
striking with their swords and their double-pointed spears,
and they would have killed everyone and deprived each of a
    homecoming,
had not Athena, daughter of aegis-bearing Zeus,
shouted out with her voice and restrained all the people.   530
"Hold back from grim battle, men of Ithaca,
so that with all speed you may be parted without bloodshed!"
So spoke Athena, and a pale fear seized them.
The weapons dropped from their terrified hands,
and fell to the ground, all of them, as the goddess spoke out her
    command.   535
They turned toward the city eager for their lives.
But then much-enduring brilliant Odysseus shouted terribly,
<u>and leapt having crouched like a high-flying eagle.</u>
But the son of Kronos released a sooty thunderbolt,
which fell down before the gray-eyed daughter of the mighty father.   540

Gray-eyed Athena addressed Odysseus then,
"God-born son of Laertes, resourceful Odysseus,
Hold back, stop the strife of destructive battle,
lest somehow the son of Kronos, far-shouting Zeus, become angry
    with you!"
So spoke Athena, and he obeyed, pleased in his heart.   545
Afterward she made oaths on both sides,
Pallas Athena, daughter of aegis-bearing Zeus,
likening herself to Mentor in body and voice.

Odysseus' leap, therefore, occurs just after that moment in the text when
the goddess abruptly turns from initiator (24.517–19) to restrainer through
her repeated use of imperatives and verbs of restriction after line 530.[4] Since
Athena plays both roles frequently, especially in battle situations, these scenes
of initiation and restraint are quite typical. But insofar as they follow very
quickly one upon the other, the ending of the *Odyssey* comes across as espe-
cially compressed. Somewhere in the middle of all this (although not exactly
in the middle) comes Odysseus' swoop, further complicating the dynamics of
the scene.

   Although there is much to admire in these final lines, there is no doubt
that the ending is sudden; attempts to explain or solve it go back at least to
Hellenistic times, when scholars suggested that the *Odyssey* properly ended
midway through Book 23 (with some modern ones following suit).[5] Taking
a different approach, I follow the trajectory that Odysseus launches with his
leap, looking beyond the immediate context of line 538 toward the alternate
plot lines and competing authorial impulses that the gesture invites. As such,
I trace Odysseus' leap through two passages in the *Iliad* (Hector's last leap
in Book 22, as just mentioned, and—as a parallel for a gesture that is left in-
complete in the text—Achilles' partial drawing of his sword in Book 1), using
them to think through the significance of Odysseus' final gesture here. At
the same time, I try to show how this leap falls into a small category of ges-
tures or actions that are somehow misaligned with the stories that their actors
move through, revealing a potential moment of divergence between body and
narrative form.

---

   4. κατὰ δ' ἔσχεθε (530), ἴσχεσθε (531), ἴσχεο, παῦε (543).
   5. Dindorf ad 23.296; Bury 1922; Page 1955: 113 ("the last few events are crammed together most
unHomerically and spurred into a brief and breathless gallop"); Kay 1957; Kirk 1962: 250; Rossi 1968;
Wender 1978: 63 (the ending is "ludicrous in its staccato leaps hither and thither"). On ending beyond
the end of the *Odyssey*, see Roberts 1997; Purves 2010: 65–96.

MAKING THE LEAP

As the last performance of Odysseus' heroic self, his farewell gesture might be thought to make perfect sense. What Homeric hero would not want to be remembered in such a blaze of glory, with actions that appear to leap straight from the *Iliad*, mirroring the jumps, shouts, and conquests of Achilles, for example, in Books 20 and 21?[6] Scholars such as Richard Martin have stressed the hero's awareness of and active participation within a tradition that is evolving beneath his own moving feet; these heroes are, as he puts it, "their own authors; performers in every sense."[7] As a figure "constantly under pressure to convince audiences" both internal and external that he is living up to heroic standards, the hero's role as self-conscious performer of his own story is forged as much through his actions as his words.[8] Leaping is one of the ways a Homeric hero might best express this role. Joseph Nagy has shown something similar for the Ulster Cycle, where the medieval Irish hero performs a kind of hurtling jump that, although it does not always work, allows him to overleap topographical confines or narrative constraints, or indeed to "vault over the record set by his heroic predecessors" (2009: 3–5). The hero's leap "showcases him at his most performative" (17) and this performance is thereby inevitably entangled with the whole complex structure of narrative direction and design; the vibrant self-propulsion of a body through space cannot help carrying the momentum of the plot along with it. It is no surprise, then, that leaping bodies lead both to the starts of stories and to the ends of lives, as such quintessential leapers as Protesilaus and Remus have shown.

As a narrative configuration, then, the crouch-and-leap that Odysseus ends with more typically marks a new beginning or some form of plot acceleration. When Pindar gets stuck partway through the beginning of *Nemean* 5, he stops

---

6. Achilles leaping in Books 20 and 21: Πηλείδης δ᾽ ἑτέρωθεν ἐναντίον <u>ὦρτο</u> λέων ὥς ("the son of Peleus leapt in front of him from the other side like a lion," 20.164); αὐτὰρ Ἀχιλλεὺς / ἐμμεμαὼς <u>ἐπόρουσεν</u> ἐρυσσάμενος ξίφος ὀξύ, / σμερδαλέα ἰάχων ("but Achilles / eagerly leapt having drawn his sharp sword, / shouting terribly," 20.283–85); <u>ἆλτο</u> ("he leapt," 20.353); ἐν δ᾽ Ἀχιλεὺς Τρώεσσι <u>θόρε</u> φρέσιν εἱμένος ἀλκήν, / σμερδαλέα ἰάχων ("Achilles leapt among the Trojans, his heart emboldened, / shouting terribly," 20.381–82); <u>ἀνεπᾶλτο</u> ("he leapt up at," 20.424); αὐτὰρ Ἀχιλλεὺς / ἐμμεμαὼς <u>ἐπόρουσε</u> κατακτάμεναι μενεαίνων / σμερδαλέα ἰάχων ("but Achilles sprang, furiously eager to kill, / shouting terribly," 20.441–43); <u>ἐπόρουσε</u> ("he sprang upon," 20.445); <u>ἐφορμηθείς</u> ("having sprung forward," 20.460); <u>ἔσθορε</u> δαίμονι ἶσος ("he jumped like a god," 21.18); <u>ἐπᾶλτο</u> κατακτάμεναι μενεαίνων ("he leapt up eager to kill," 21.140); <u>ἐπόρουσεν</u> ("he rose up," 21.144); Πηλείδης δ᾽ ἄορ ὀξὺ ἐρυσσάμενος παρὰ μηροῦ / ἆλτ᾽ ἐπί οἱ μεμαώς (the son of Peleus having drawn his sharp sword from his thigh / leapt upon him eagerly," 21.173–74), <u>ὡρμῆσατ᾽</u> ("he leapt," 21.595). At 21.536, Priam says of Achilles: δείδια γὰρ μὴ οὖλος ἀνὴρ ἐς τεῖχος <u>ἅληται</u> ("I am afraid that the destructive man will leap into our enclosure"). Cf. Diomedes in *Il.* 5, who is like a lion leaping over the wall of a sheepfold (138, 142, 161).

7. Martin 1989: 90; cf. 98 on the importance of individual heroic "style."

8. Nagy 2009: 4.

short and then pulls himself into a crouch in order to launch into the main narrative of his song (19–21):

> μακρά μοι
> αὐτόθεν ἅλμαθ᾽ ὑποσκά-
> πτοι τις· ἔχω γονάτων ὁρμὰν ἐλαφράν·
> καὶ πέραν πόντοιο πάλλοντ᾽ αἰετοί.

> may someone mark a
> long jumping-ground for me from here.
> For I have a light spring in my knees
> and eagles leap across the sea.

In these verses, Pindar places himself in the role of athletic victor, a stand-in that ensures that his poem finds its proper direction.[9] Yet when it is the *hero* (rather than the narrator) who exhibits such extraordinary physical abilities, the sheer force of his kinetic energy has the potential to take the narrative off track. Something similar might be said of Odysseus' leap at the end of the *Odyssey*, which does not appear at all aligned with the poem's convergence toward closure. Concerning the phenomenon of the "leaping hero," Joseph Nagy points to "the intriguing danger" of the hero going off script; that he might, "in some alternative narratological universe ... break [. . .] through the delicate surface of [the] text" and, in so doing, reach an altogether different ending (2009: 17). What if Odysseus too had broken through the surface of our *Odyssey* with his jump? We already know of one story, involving Odysseus' walking beyond the end of the text with an oar on his shoulder.[10] What different direction does this airborne leap take us in? Does it suggest the start of some new story or the return of an old one?

As we already saw in the Pindar passage, the crouch that Odysseus pulls himself into before leaping is an important part of the equation. ἀλείς, the aorist passive participle of εἴλω, denotes the drawing of the body together and gathering in of energy. As with the leap, I want to isolate this posture and allow it to stand still in the time of the text, as if it were a single frame in a stop-motion sequence (Figure 4.1). For the crouch represents an important moment

---

9. On the complicated structure of *Nemean* 5, see, e.g., Burnett 2005: 57–76. On jumping in athletic competition and on the question of whether the athlete jumped from a crouch, like the eagle and Odysseus, or from a run-up, see Mouratidis 2012.

10. On Odysseus' journey inland as a rite of initiation to Poseidon, see Eustathius ad loc. and the references in Purves 2010: 65–96, esp. 72.

Figure 4.1. Eadweard Muybridge, *Animal Locomotion,* vol. 1, plate 163, *Jumping, standing broad jump* (excerpt), 1887. *Source:* Boston Public Library. Wikimedia Commons.

of potential that narrative constantly grapples with: the pauses, indecisions, and drawings back that mark the progress of any plot. For both protagonist and reader, crouching gives us a perspective from which to take stock of a situation and prime ourselves in order to react to it.

Henry James' short story "The Beast in the Jungle" thematizes precisely this notion of the crouch as prelude to what the narrator there calls "the *big it*"—some as yet unspecified event located just around the corner.[11] Throughout the story, James plays with the concept of timing, of waiting for the "now" that will define one's life and for the "it" to happen (244). What is particularly important about his story is that the beast that his protagonist, John Marcher, imagines forever waiting in its jungle is drawn into an eternal crouch; a posture that suggests anticipation, uncertainty, and suspense. This too is the way that animals and warriors crouch throughout the *Iliad* and the *Odyssey,* whether in defensive or offensive positions.[12] The bend in the knees marks a drawing in of energy, a looking forward to the spring, in situations that usually indicate fight or flight. Yet Henry James deliberately presses on the figure of the crouching beast to signify anticipation as an end in and of itself. Contrary to Marcher's expectation, nothing exists beyond the crouch in either his story or his life. Despite the "inevitability" of the gesture, the beast never springs (249):

> Something or other lay in wait for him, amid the twists and the turns of the months and the years, like a crouching beast in the jungle. It signified little whether the crouching beast were destined to slay him or to be slain. The definite point was the inevitable spring of the creature ... Such was the image under which he had ended by figuring his life.

11. James [1903] 2004: 245. The protagonist thinks of himself as carrying a "concentrated burden, his perpetual suspense, ever so quietly" (248). Cf. Varro *ling. lat.* 6.77 on gesture as a form of "carrying" (*gerere*), as discussed in my Introduction and Chapter 6. I thank Aaron Kachuk for alerting me to this story.

12. See n.53, this chapter.

Among Homer's ancient critics, this same notion of the "crouching beast" works as a rhetorical figure for how best to organize words in a speech.[13] According to Demetrius, a well-expressed speech should carry the energy and orientation of a kind of "crouch" or "coil" (*On Style* 8):

ὥσπερ ⟨γὰρ⟩ τὰ θηρία συστρέψαντα ἑαυτὰ μάχεται, τοιαύτη τις ἂν εἴη συστροφὴ καὶ λόγου καθάπερ ἐσπειραμένου πρὸς δεινότητα.

Just as beasts, when they fight, gather themselves into a crouch, so should there be such a gathering-in of language, as if in a coil, for the sake of its force.

In doing so Demetrius uses the same verb (συστρέφω: *to gather oneself together in preparing to spring*)[14] that the exegetical scholia use to explain ἀλείς within the formula under discussion (ΣbT *Il.* 22.308b [=*Od.* 24.538]; Erbse vol. 5: 324):

ἀλείς· ἀθρόον ἑαυτὸν συστρέψας· οἱ γὰρ εἰς δρόμον ἑαυτοὺς δόντες οὐκ ἀνειμένως πορεύονται, (bT) ἀλλὰ συστρέφονται (T).

aleis: having gathered himself together all at once. For those who commit to a race do not proceed in a leisurely manner, but they gather themselves together in preparation to spring.

Similarly, in his commentary on the *Odyssey*, Eustathius remarks on these lines,

οἴμησε δὲ ἀλείς, ὅ ἐστι συστραφείς, ὥς τ᾽ αἰετὸς ὑψιπετήεις, ὃ καὶ ἐν Ἰλιάδι ἀπαραλλάκτως κεῖται. Ὀδυσσεὺς δὲ ὁ τοιοῦτος ἀετός.

He leapt having crouched, which is to say having gathered himself in preparation to spring, like a high-flying eagle, which also occurs in exactly the same way in the *Iliad*. Odysseus is just such an eagle.

All of this suggests Odysseus' own articulation of a powerful kinetic and poetic statement, a charging up rather than a releasing of the energy and momentum that passes back and forth between plots and the bodies that animate them. His role as a poet figure perhaps comes back into play at this moment, insofar as his leap—οἶμα—may be cognate with οἴμη, the word for "path of song."[15] The term is a familiar one from the *Odyssey*, and its occurrence there in the plural

---

13. My thanks to James Porter for pointing me to the following passage.

14. See also Demetr., *Eloc.* 10, 20 and the notion of a period "bending back at the end" (10, 16, 17).

15. The connection is likely at the least through folk etymology. See Chantraine (*DELG* 783: "Du point de vue des Grecs, οἶμα 'élan,' οἰμάω 'sélancer' doivent être associés à οἶμος."). οἶμα occurs twice in the *Iliad*. On both occasions, it describes the actions of animals within similes, in comparisons referring to Patroclus (16.752) and Achilles (21.252).

especially indicates that there is always more than one direction that a per-
former can move in.[16]

But it is only the interaction of Odysseus' body with the external environ-
ment of what is happening in the story at the particular moment in which he
jumps that can put this reading into play. If it were not for the fact that Athena
had explicitly called the fighting to a halt, Odysseus' behavior at the end of the
poem would be entirely unremarkable. Left to their own devices, warriors fre-
quently act like birds of prey and the killing of one minor character (Eupeithes
at 523–25) traditionally leads to the killing of another.[17] The attempt to chase
fleeing warriors is standard heroic material, and Odysseus has already been
"warmed up" by the small Iliadic battle scene that preceded his leap at 516–27.
There, in an explicit nod to the way in which the end of the *Odyssey* plays on
Iliadic *schēmata*, Laertes, when instructed by Athena on exactly how to make a
kill, artfully reverts her imperative *proiei* ("send forth your spear") back into its
correct Iliadic formulation as a third person imperfect, resulting in a perfectly
executed Iliadic death:[18]

(519, Athena)   αἶψα μάλ' ἀμπεπαλὼν προΐει δολιχόσκιον ἔγχος

                  straightaway brandish and hurl your far-shadowing spear!

(522, narrator)   αἶψα μάλ' ἀμπεπαλὼν προΐει δολιχόσκιον ἔγχος

                  he straightaway brandished and hurled his far-shadowing
                  spear

Among other Iliadic motifs occurring in this single *androktasia*, the most ob-
vious is the highly formulaic δούπησεν δὲ πεσών, ἀράβησε δὲ τεύχε᾽ ἐπ᾽ αὐτῷ
("he fell with a thud, and his armor clattered around him") that caps the scene at
525 and, as is its nature, invites further fighting.[19]

---

16. *Od.* 8.74, 481; 22.347. See further Becker 1937; Thalmann 1984: 123–24; Ford 1992: 40–48;
Worman 2015.

17. See Fenik 1968 on the chain reaction motif.

18. Προΐει occurs eight times in the *Iliad* within the formula ἀμπεπαλὼν προΐει (and seven times,
as here, with the addition of δολιχόσκιον ἔγχος), but always in the imperfect. See further Erbse [1972]
1997: 263–320, with reference to Page 1955. On *schēma*, the Greek word for gesture, scheme, or figure of
speech, see my Introduction, n.8.

19. For discussion of this formula, see my Chapter 2. On Iliadic motifs at the end of the *Odyssey*,
see especially Pucci 1987, 1996, and 1998. As Eustathius notes, the *Odyssey*'s closing scene lends a nice
symmetry to *Odyssey* 22 and thus to the poem as a whole: καὶ ὅρα θαυμασίαν περιπέτειαν, βάλλονται
γὰρ καὶ πίπτουσι κακοῦργοι χείριστοι, ἔνδον μὲν τῆς πόλεως Ἀντίνοος, ἔξω δὲ Εὐπείθης· ἐκεῖνος μὲν ὑπὸ
τοῦ υἱοῦ, οὗτος δὲ ὑπὸ τοῦ πατρός ("notice the remarkable *peripeteia*, for the very worst of the bad men
fall: Antinoos inside the city, and Eupeithes outside. The former is killed by the son, and the latter by the
father").

The sequencing of instruction (518–19) and action (521–22) at such close quarters in the text, separated here by only a single line ("So Pallas Athena spoke, and breathed into him great strength," 520) leads to a compression that is unusual but not unexpected, given that we are so close to the poem's end. As Don Fowler and Philip Hardie have both suggested, there is often a series of "microcosmic recapitulations" as epic narratives draw toward closure, and most commentators on the end of the *Odyssey* talk of a necessary narrowing of scope and motifs through repetition and abbreviated citation in the *Odyssey*'s final lines.[20] We can also detect in this battle scene what Adrian Kelly (2007b) has described as the "Decreasing Doublet" motif—here the mini battle narrative, comprising a single killing, serves as a decreased doublet of *Odyssey* 22. As he argues, this kind of diminution is a closural strategy that is widespread in early Greek epic. Moreover, since—as Peter Brooks has put it—"repetition is all about finding the right end" we should not have a problem with all of this authorially sanctioned repetition at the close of the poem (1984: 140).

The problem, though, comes when Odysseus keeps going on his Iliadic track, thereby introducing a different kind of repetition, which I will call here "rebellious repetition." What I mean by this is that there are certain moments when the epic body acts according to habit, performing typical actions or gestures, but in doing so it directly challenges the plot's proper course. In this case, it is possible to see a conflict of interests between leaper and narrator; or to put it more generally, between the concerns of the author or plot director and the kinetic potential of the warrior-as-improvisor, whose body is overlaid with the impulses, imprints, and habits of the poetic tradition that created him. As I suggest in the Introduction, there is a kind of *generic* patterning or programming that the Greek epic tradition instills in the heroic figure, an index of oft-repeated gestures and stances.

These normative and usually obedient gestures become rebellious when they start to move on a different trajectory, or when they fail to take into account other strategies that are pushing the plot in a particular direction.[21] Odysseus' leap, as I have noted, is cued by the formulaic δούπησεν δὲ πεσών, which typically occurs as part of a "chain reaction" of killings in Homer.[22] His obedience to

---

20. Fowler 1997: 19; Hardie 1997: 146. On the anticlimactic nature of most ancient endings, see Farron 1982: 136.

21. Bourdieu calls the lag effect when habitus no longer accords with external circumstances "hysteresis" ([1972] 1977: 78, 83). My thanks to Ben Radcliffe for this observation.

22. See also my Chapter 2. The problem, though, is that in Homer death is repetitive. We do not expect single killings of minor characters; we instead expect, as Fenik taught us, "chain reactions." With so much repetition happening elsewhere in this part of the text, it is especially pointed that an *androktasia* should occur in the singular. On reformulated repetition, see Eide 1999.

the norms of Homeric battle scenes is enough to override Athena's command to stop. In this instance, once he has been set on a certain path, Odysseus listens to kinetic impulse first and plot direction second.[23]

DRAWING THE SWORD

Perhaps the most famous example of potential narrative disobedience in Homer, and a gesture that is also left unfinished, is Achilles' attempt to draw his sword and kill Agamemnon in Book 1 of the *Iliad*. This scene provides a clear example of the tension between external authorial control and internal impulsive action in Homer.[24] I want to think about the problem not in terms of free will or double determination but quite differently, by paying attention simply to what Achilles' body does and does not do.[25] The scene in which Achilles debates with himself about whether to kill Agamemnon or "cease his anger and check his spirit" at the very beginning of the poem is well known (1.188–92) and is followed by the hero's decision to pull his sword from its hilt ("As he was pondering these things in his mind and spirit, he was drawing from its scabbard his great sword"). Here is the passage in full (*Il.* 1.188–221):

Ὣς φάτο· Πηλεΐωνι δ' ἄχος γένετ', ἐν δέ οἱ ἦτορ
στήθεσσιν λασίοισι διάνδιχα μερμήριξεν,
ἢ ὅ γε φάσγανον ὀξὺ ἐρυσσάμενος παρὰ μηροῦ   190
τοὺς μὲν ἀναστήσειεν, ὁ δ' Ἀτρεΐδην ἐναρίζοι,
ἠὲ χόλον παύσειεν ἐρητύσειέ τε θυμόν.
ἧος ὁ ταῦθ' ὥρμαινε κατὰ φρένα καὶ κατὰ θυμόν,
ἕλκετο δ' ἐκ κολεοῖο μέγα ξίφος, ἦλθε δ' Ἀθήνη
οὐρανόθεν· πρὸ γὰρ ἧκε θεὰ λευκώλενος Ἥρη,   195
ἄμφω ὁμῶς θυμῷ φιλέουσά τε κηδομένη τε·
στῆ δ' ὄπιθεν, ξανθῆς δὲ κόμης ἕλε Πηλεΐωνα
οἴῳ φαινομένη· τῶν δ' ἄλλων οὔ τις ὁρᾶτο·
θάμβησεν δ' Ἀχιλεύς, μετὰ δ' ἐτράπετ', αὐτίκα δ' ἔγνω
Παλλάδ' Ἀθηναίην· δεινὼ δέ οἱ ὄσσε φάανθεν·   200
καί μιν φωνήσας ἔπεα πτερόεντα προσηύδα·
"τίπτ' αὖτ' αἰγιόχοιο Διὸς τέκος εἰλήλουθας;

---

23. Pelliccia's observation (1995: 267) that sometimes the internal organs can exhibit the kind of "bad timing" that steers characters toward poor choices is a helpful one. There is, in other words, a third kind of "timing" that somatic repetition engenders, and that can occasionally be dyschronic with the timing of the plot (cf. n.21, this chapter).

24. Pucci 1998: 76–77.

25. Lesky 1961 (on double determination); Willcock 1970: 2.

ἦ ἵνα ὕβριν ἴδῃ Ἀγαμέμνονος Ἀτρεΐδαο;
ἀλλ' ἔκ τοι ἐρέω, τὸ δὲ καὶ τελέεσθαι ὀΐω·
ἧς ὑπεροπλίῃσι τάχ' ἄν ποτε θυμὸν ὀλέσσῃ."   205
    Τὸν δ' αὖτε προσέειπε θεὰ γλαυκῶπις Ἀθήνη·
"ἦλθον ἐγὼ παύσουσα τὸ σὸν μένος, αἴ κε πίθηαι,
οὐρανόθεν· πρὸ δέ μ' ἧκε θεὰ λευκώλενος Ἥρη
ἄμφω ὁμῶς θυμῷ φιλέουσά τε κηδομένη τε·
ἀλλ' ἄγε λῆγ' ἔριδος, μηδὲ ξίφος ἕλκεο χειρί·   210
ἀλλ' ἤτοι ἔπεσιν μὲν ὀνείδισον ὡς ἔσεταί περ·
ὧδε γὰρ ἐξερέω, τὸ δὲ καὶ τετελεσμένον ἔσται·
καί ποτέ τοι τρὶς τόσσα παρέσσεται ἀγλαὰ δῶρα
ὕβριος εἵνεκα τῆσδε· σὺ δ' ἴσχεο, πείθεο δ' ἡμῖν."
    Τὴν δ' ἀπαμειβόμενος προσέφη πόδας ὠκὺς Ἀχιλλεύς·   215
"χρὴ μὲν σφωΐτερόν γε θεὰ ἔπος εἰρύσσασθαι
καὶ μάλα περ θυμῷ κεχολωμένον· ὡς γὰρ ἄμεινον·
ὅς κε θεοῖς ἐπιπείθηται μάλα τ' ἔκλυον αὐτοῦ."
    Ἦ καὶ ἐπ' ἀργυρέῃ κώπῃ σχέθε χεῖρα βαρεῖαν,
ἂψ δ' ἐς κουλεὸν ὦσε μέγα ξίφος, οὐδ' ἀπίθησε   220
μύθῳ Ἀθηναίης.

So he spoke. And pain came upon the son of Peleus, and the heart
in his rugged breast pondered in two ways,
whether he should draw his sharp sword from his thigh   190
and cause a commotion among them, and kill the son of Atreus,
or whether he should cease his anger and check his spirit.
As he was pondering these things in his mind and his spirit,
he was drawing from its scabbard his great sword, but then Athena
    arrived
from heaven. For the white-armed goddess Hera had sent her forth,   195
Hera who loved and cared equally for both men in her heart.
She stood behind him and took hold of the blond hair of the son of
    Peleus,
appearing only to him. For none of the others saw.
Achilles was amazed, and turned around, and straightaway he
    recognized
Pallas Athena. Terribly her eyes gleamed.   200
Addressing her with winged words he said,
"Why, child of aegis-bearing Zeus, have you come?
Was it to witness the hubris of Agamemnon, son of Atreus?

But I proclaim this, which I think will indeed come to pass.
Because of his arrogance he will soon one day lose his life." 205
Then the gray-eyed goddess responded,
"I came to quell your anger, if you might be persuaded,
from heaven. The white-armed goddess Hera sent me forth,
since she loves and cares for you both equally in her heart.
But come, let go your strife, do not draw your sword with
    your hand! 210
Reproach him by saying how things will be.
I proclaim thus, and it will also come to pass
One day three times as many shining gifts will be offered to you
to make up for his arrogance. Check yourself, and obey me!"
In response swift-footed Achilles addressed her, 215
"Goddess, I must obey the command of you both,
even though I am so angry in my heart. That is the better way.
Whoever obeys the gods, they listen to him also."
So speaking he checked his heavy hand on the silver hilt
and back into the scabbard he pushed the great sword, nor did he 220
disobey the command of Athena.

As others have shown, scenes in which a hero ponders (μερμήριξεν, 189;
ὥρμαινε, 193) about whether or not to draw his sword and kill form an estab-
lished sequence in the heroic repertoire.[26] Odysseus ponders similarly within
the Cyclops' cave, for example, as well as in *Odyssey* 10 when he wants to cut
off the head of the traitorous Eurylochus, and in both cases he is persuaded by
reason and words not to do so.[27] But Athena's decision in Book 1 to physically
restrain Achilles from acting on his own instincts by standing behind him and
holding him back by the hair (197) pitches his body at an arc, preventing him
from completing a sequence of actions that have already been set in motion.
Caught in a kind of freeze-frame, with the sword half-pulled from its sheath,
Achilles and Athena discuss the options and potential outcomes of the quarrel
(202–14), resulting in Achilles admitting that the goddess must be obeyed
(216–18).

26. Arend [1933] 1975: 106–15; Edwards 1980: 12–13.

27. Pelliccia 1995. *Od.* 9.299–302; 10.249, 321. His men restrain him (ἐρήτυον) with words. The two
instances of sword drawing carried out by the suitors in *Od.* 22 (79–81, 90–91) are not pondered and not
successful.

By checking his hand on the hilt of his sword and pushing it back into its scabbard (219–21), he reverses the gesture he had initiated twenty-five lines earlier. The text works hard to make us think that this is the best option for Achilles, but—as Pietro Pucci has argued—it is not absolutely clear that it is. It is rather the best option for the narrative, as engineered at this point by the gods. By halting the drawing of his sword, Achilles causes countless deaths, including Patroclus', as well as ensuring that he will lose his own nostos and die at Troy. He does, however, also unwittingly ensure that the plot of the *Iliad* can move forward.[28]

Achilles thinks all along that the plot of the *Iliad* is *his* choice, but it is at the cost of his own body becoming increasingly immobilized.[29] When he re-enters the battle on his own now-compromised terms, Achilles repeats with vigor the gesture that he was prevented at the very beginning from performing, drawing his sword and leaping again and again in Books 20 and 21.[30] Whereas in Book 1, Achilles had allowed himself to be persuaded and his hand to be stayed, he now tells Thetis, "Do not, although you love me, hold me back from the fighting (μήδε μ' ἔρυκε), for you will not persuade me (οὐδέ με πείσεις, 18.126)," as if raging still against his initial disciplining by Athena.

Indeed, it is so much the tendency of a hero like Achilles to reach for his sword that there is even a kind of genetic coding to this action. For Neoptolemus, as we learn in the *Odyssey*'s underworld, could not stop feeling for the hilt of his own sword in the wooden horse (*Od.* 11.531: ξίφεος ἐπεμαίετο κώπην), a sign of his own eagerness to jump out and fight while the men around him trembled and wept. What these impulses to reach for the sword and leap suggest is that Homeric poetics can also be understood as a kind of nerve system, along which movement pathways are relayed by the force of repetition and habit.[31]

The language of the struggle between Achilles and Athena in *Iliad* 1 is framed in terms of persuasion, with the verb πείθω occurring four times, sometimes in compound forms (207, 214, 218, 220). But more emphatic is the repeated use of

---

28. This is the only time in Homer when the epic conventions of *mermêrizein* passages are not respected, insofar as the sudden appearance of a god to aid in the formulation of a decision is not necessarily advantageous for the character involved. As Pucci writes, "the goddess intervenes to save Agamemnon at the expense of Achilles' booty, honor and—ultimately—life" (1998: 76) and goes on to surmise that "the gain is the reader's and the reader's only. For from the goddess's solution arises the wrath of Achilles, that is, the poem itself" (77).

29. See further my Chapter 5; Buchan 2012: 45–46; *Il.* 18.104 (ἐτώσιον ἄχθος ἀρούρης). Note that ἐτώσιον is normally used of vainly cast missiles.

30. Achilles draws his sword at *Il.* 20.284; 21.116, 173; For the several instances of him leaping in Books 20–21, see n.6, this chapter.

31. James [1890] 1950: 104–27; Agamben [1992] 2000: 49–60. Further discussed in my Introduction.

verbs that all mean to check, hold back, or leave off: ἐρητύω (192), παύω (192, 207), λήγω (210), ἴσχομαι (214), and ἔχω (219). Indeed, Achilles' initial deliberation is set up as a contrast between ἐρυσσάμενος ("whether to draw his sword," 190) and ἐρητύσειε (". . . or check his spirit," 192), a contrast that is emphasized by their shared first syllable, ἐρ-, falling at the same metrical position in the line each time. This minute repetition accentuates the opposing terms of Achilles' dilemma: to draw or to check. And indeed, the initial syllable of that opposition sounds again (with lengthening) a little later on, with εἰρύσσασθαι at line 216 (χρὴ μὲν σφωίτερόν γε θεὰ ἔπος εἰρύσσασθαι, "Goddess, I must obey the command of you both"). As Michael Lynn-George has noted (1988: 45), although Achilles' choice of whether to "draw" his sword or "obey" Athena's command can be semantically understood only as either one or the other, the two words insist on overlapping—what we have here are the different aorist middle forms of ἐρύω (*to draw*) and ἐρύω (*to save or keep*), which are identical in their first principal parts.[32] In fact, throughout this passage a series of initial *er* sounds can be traced, from ἐρυσσάμενος and ἐρητύσειε (190, 192) through ἐρέω at 204 and ἔριδος at 210, to εἰρύσσασθαι at 216. This glimmering of initial *er*s keeps vivid in our minds the presence of both a word not fully realized and a sword not fully drawn. Indeed, the stalled, incomplete repetition of *eruō* catches in stop motion precisely the long-drawn-out pause of Achilles' hesitation as he tries to decide what to do.

For it is quite clear that Achilles pulls his sword out of the scabbard only partially before he is physically stopped. He begins to do so at line 194, as indicated by the imperfect tense of ἕλκετο ("he was drawing his great sword from the scabbard, but then Athena arrived"), but we can tell from Athena's command at 210 ("do not draw your sword with your hand") that the action is never completed. Indeed, as Mark Edwards observes, we would normally expect ἕλκετο δ' ἐκ κολεοῖο μέγα ξίφος to end with ἀργυρόηλον and, by implication, with the revelation of the sword itself, "silver studded" and bright for action.[33] Instead of a description of the sword, however, we find Athena (ἦλθε δ' Ἀθήνη), whose appearance at the end of the line comes as something of a surprise; the verb ἦλθε interrupts ἕλκετο and leaves the sense of the action curtailed. In a similar way, the repetition of only the first syllable of ἐρυσσάμενος reminds us that the action that it describes is still unfinished—Achilles' hand has managed to get only partway through the gesture it anticipated performing, inasmuch as

---

32. Lynn-George 1988: 45. See further *DELG*: 376–77.
33. As at *Il.* 3.361 (quoted in the following note); 13.610; Edwards 1980: 13, as cited in Pucci 1998: 72.

the sword has been pulled out of its scabbard only for the distance of a single syllable.

This interrupted gesture is enough, however, to create considerable tension in the poem, especially since we are aware that this participle, if it were to be completed, would be paired with a verb marking Agamemnon's death. An example can be found at *Il.* 21.116–17, where Achilles is now very much his own freewheeling and free-willed agent:[34]

Ἀχιλεὺς δὲ ἐρυσσάμενος ξίφος ὀξὺ
τύψε κατὰ κληῖδα παρ' αὐχένα. . . .

Achilles, having drawn his sharp sword,
struck him on the collarbone beside his neck. . . .

By contrast, only the potential force of ἐρυσσάμενος is brought to light in *Iliad* 1. During that split second of indecision the time of the plot is miraculously extended into what we might call, following Erin Manning, "the elasticity of the almost" (2009: 29–42). And indeed the ἄψ that begins verse 220 ("back into the scabbard he pushed the great sword") is definitive, setting in motion a plot that will always look back to, repeat, and try to repair the moment that marks the beginning of Achilles' wrath and isolation.

The discordance that I have tried to trace in this passage from *Iliad* 1 between the ingrained habits and inclinations, the "muscle memory," of the heroic body, on the one hand, and the necessary movement of the plot in a particular direction, on the other, has shown how the hero's sense of self is vitally kinetic—to the extent that his vigor is both a necessary component of, and at the same time a complication for, that other great energy source—the "engine" or "motor" of the plot.[35] For after Book 1, Zeus will be forced to conjure numerous drawings of swords in a sequence of deaths whose main purpose will be to bind the plot through repetition and somehow keep the story rolling during the long period in which Achilles remains inactive. When Achilles pitches his body against Agamemnon, however, extraordinary measures must be taken to correct his movement, including a quite exceptional stilling of narrative time while Achilles turns around and has a conversation with a goddess whom nobody else can see.

The action of *Odyssey* 24 is unfinished in a different way. Instead of a long, slow-motion sequence depicting the micro-gestures of a stalled beginning, the end of the *Odyssey* presents two swift actions (crouching, leaping) in a single line

---

34. See again *Il.* 3.361–62 (Ἀτρείδης δὲ ἐρυσσάμενος ξίφος ἀργυρόηλον / πλῆξεν, "The son of Atreus, having drawn his silver-studded sword, / struck. . . .").

35. Brooks 1984: 37–61.

of verse, allowing us to run together the various stop-motion images of Figure 4.1 into a moving picture.[36] But in both versions, the various ways in which Athena restrains the action of the poem run counter to the hero's adoption of a position that encapsulates the potential for future action. I suggested that in the *Iliad* the stop-motion action of Achilles' partially drawn sword results in an opening stance for the plot that is paradoxically based on the body positioning itself in a backward arc of restraint.[37] This backward arc is not a position that shows up in many other places (unless we want to count the verb αὐερύω, used of the head of an animal when it is drawn back in sacrifice a little later in Book 1).[38] But it is curious that this position provides the starting point for one epic while the gathering in of energy for a leap provides the closing stance of another. In both cases, Athena does a good deal of restraining—and although this is not so unusual for Athena, the parallels are striking, with the same words for persuasion and "holding off" recurring in both passages.[39]

In both cases, too, the contradictory impulses of the heroes' momentarily deviant bodies activate similar moments of possibility and uncertainty within the language of each passage. For in Book 1 Achilles' gesture initiates two predictions for the future (204, 212), while in *Odyssey* 24, Odysseus' leap precedes two hypothetical statements (first a past contrary-to-fact condition: "And now they would have killed them all, and destroyed their homecoming, had not Athena ... cried out" [528–29], and next a negative purpose clause: "in order that Zeus ... not be angry with you," [544]), both suggesting open-endedness a mere number of lines before the end. As Irene de Jong observes, "the if-not situation ... subtly suggests that if not for Athena, Odysseus and his men would have gained full victory" (2001: 586). Yet, as she goes on to note, this is a story that simply cannot end with the "good kind Odysseus, characterized at the poem's opening as a man eager to save the lives of his companions (1.6), killing all his own people" (586).

---

36. As both James O'Maley and Ineke Sluiter have pointed out to me, there may be some significance in the ordering of the verbs in the line. It would seem to fit more naturally with the flow of the movement itself (following the sequence of a Muybridge strip) for the participle *aleis* to appear before *oimēse*, or for crouching to appear in the line before leaping. That it does not (although the sequence is entirely typical for Homeric Greek) helps us to hold back the moment of the leap, even as the simile of the eagle suggests flight.

37. Cf. Agamben ([1992] 2000: 55) discussing Deleuze on film image as a "moving picture," "Every image, in fact, is animated by an antinomic polarity: on the one hand, images are the reification and obliteration of a gesture (it is the *imago* as death mask or symbol); on the other hand, they preserve the *dynamis* intact (as in Muybridge's snapshots or in any sports photograph)."

38. 1.459. Cf. 2.422.

39. πείθω: *Il.* 1.207, 214; *Od.* 24.545; κατέχω: *Od.* 24.530; ἴσχω: *Il.* 1.214; *Od.* 24.531, 543; παύω: *Il.* 1.192, 207; *Od.* 24.543.

But if the opening of the *Iliad* sets up a parallel with the end of the *Odyssey* that can help us to interpret the role of heroic action in the stopping and starting of plots, so too can the *Iliad*'s most important internal "ending" that is not yet its end, the death of Hector, help us to unlock certain aspects of Odysseus' farewell leap. When Hector realizes that his time is up, after having been tricked by Athena and having lost his spear to Achilles, he gathers his energy up for his own last leap (22.300–311):

"νῦν δὲ δὴ ἐγγύθι μοι θάνατος κακός, οὐδ' ἔτ' ἄνευθεν,   300
οὐδ' ἀλέη· ἦ γάρ ῥα πάλαι τό γε φίλτερον ἦεν
Ζηνί τε καὶ Διὸς υἷι ἑκηβόλῳ, οἵ με πάρος γε
πρόφρονες εἰρύατο· νῦν αὖτέ με μοῖρα κιχάνει.
μὴ μὰν ἀσπουδί γε καὶ ἀκλειῶς ἀπολοίμην,
ἀλλὰ μέγα ῥέξας τι καὶ ἐσσομένοισι πυθέσθαι."   305
    Ὣς ἄρα φωνήσας εἰρύσσατο φάσγανον ὀξύ,
τό οἱ ὑπὸ λαπάρην τέτατο μέγα τε στιβαρόν τε,
οἴμησεν δὲ ἀλεὶς ὥς τ' αἰετὸς ὑψιπετήεις,
ὅς τ' εἶσιν πεδίονδε διὰ νεφέων ἐρεβεννῶν
ἁρπάξων ἢ ἄρν' ἀμαλὴν ἢ πτῶκα λαγωόν·   310
ὣς Ἕκτωρ οἴμησε τινάσσων φάσγανον ὀξύ.
ὁμήθη δ' Ἀχιλεύς, μένεος δ' ἐμπλήσατο θυμόν.

"Now evil death is close to me, no longer far off,   300
and there is no escape. So at some point this must have been dear to
Zeus and his far-shooting son, who before now protected me
zealously. But now fate has caught up with me.
May I not die without effort and fame,
but doing something great to be remembered by future generations."   305
So speaking he drew his sharp sword,
which hung by his side, great and heavy,
and he leapt having crouched like a high-flying eagle,
who goes along the plain through the dark clouds
in order to snatch either a soft lamb or crouching hare.   310
So Hector leapt brandishing his sharp sword.
But Achilles set upon him, and he was filled with rage in his heart.

At the moment of his death Hector manages to achieve what neither Achilles nor Odysseus could in the two passages we have been considering. The complete nature of his actions is reflected in the expanded description of the sword, now drawn fully from its scabbard ("which hung by his side, great and heavy," 307) and brandished proudly as he leaps. As Richardson (1993) notes, τινάσσων φάσγανον ὀξύ ("brandishing his sharp sword," 311) invokes φάσγανον ὀξὺ ἐρυσσάμενος ("drawing his sharp sword") from our passage in *Iliad* 1 (190). In fact, the phrase φάσγανον ὀξύ occurs nowhere else in the *Iliad* beside these two passages; it is more typical to find other words for sword—ἄορ or ξίφος— accompanying the adjective ὀξύς (*sharp*) in Homer.

After the drawing of the sword comes Hector's leap, utilizing the same formula that we have been discussing at *Odyssey* 24, but here too we see expansion into a two-lined simile describing the eagle and his prey (308–10). In these lines, therefore, we see Hector completing Achilles' and Odysseus' unfinished actions, drawing out both sword and simile into the space offered by his own unambiguous and determinate end.[40] His acceptance, moreover, that this is the only way his story can now go—that Athena has effectively run him down to this single path from which there is no other way out (οὐδ' ἀλέη, 301)—creates space for him in the text to leap far and long.[41]

Hector, no less a self-conscious performer than any other epic hero, leaves behind the competitive arena forever with a soaring bid for *kleos*.[42] Odysseus' leap can, of course, be seen in a similar way, for instead of turning back toward the city of Ithaca as instructed, he tries to jump into a different narrative space, a competitive arena where he might well lose his life but would also gain glory. But it is clear that there is no room for this kind of open competition, or heroic self-performativity, on the edge of Laertes' farm. Odysseus cannot, at this point, jump back into the *Iliad*, yet his action, if understood as a quotation of Hector's, highlights two very different modes of exiting an epic plot.[43]

Odysseus' shifting at the end of the *Odyssey*, then, as he tries to position himself in relation to the end of his story, shows that the impulses and habits of his body cannot easily separate themselves from both specific intertexts with other epic scenes *and* a kind of general, learned practice of how to move through epic situations. This too can explain something of the

40. Kozak 2017: 205 notes the "masterfully subtle subterfuge of [the] simile, allowing Hektor, for the first time in this long encounter, to become the predator ... while Achilles seemingly becomes the prey."

41. As with Odysseus, however, we never see Hector land and, like the other occurrences of *oimaō* and the noun *oima* in Homer, his swoop is unsuccessful. For all the gloriousness of Hector's flight, its trajectory breaks off as Achilles cuts in: ὡρμήθη δ' Ἀχιλεύς (299).

42. On Hector as a self-conscious performer, see Murnaghan 1997: 31–32: "Hector is the character who dwells most on his own future glory."

43. There is also something traditional and normative about this gesture, in the sense that it allows Odysseus to turn back into their correct positions bodily postures that have been "much turned" and twisted in the course of his journey home. Twice, for example, he has to save himself in the fantastic world of Books 9–12 by crouching upside down. On quotation and priority, see Bakker 2013: 157–69. I would argue both that Odysseus is quoting Hector here, and that Hector is quoting Odysseus. See also Pucci 1987: 131–33, for the comparison of Odysseus' leap (*thrōskō*) in *Od.* 22.303 with Achilles' in *Il.* 21.18.

circumstances that Aeneas finds himself in at the very end of Vergil's poem, at the moment when he is hesitating about whether to kill Turnus or not (*Aeneid* 12.938–52):

> stetit acer in armis
> Aeneas volvens oculos dextramque repressit;
> et iam iamque magis cunctantem flectere sermo   940
> coeperat, infelix umero cum apparuit alto
> balteus et notis fulserunt cingula bullis
> Pallantis pueri, victum quem vulnere Turnus
> straverat atque umeris inimicum insigne gerebat.
> ille, oculis postquam saevi monimenta doloris   945
> exuviasque hausit, furiis accensus et ira
> terribilis: "tune hinc spoliis indute meorum
> eripiare mihi? Pallas te hoc vulnere, Pallas
> immolat et poenam scelerato ex sanguine sumit."
> hoc dicens ferrum adverso sub pectore condit   950
> fervidus; ast illi solvuntur frigore membra
> vitaque cum gemitu fugit indignata sub umbras.

> Aeneas stood fierce in his armor,
> turning his eyes this way and that, and he checked his right hand,
> and now as he was hesitating more and more the words [of Turnus]   940
> began to bend him, when the unlucky baldric became visible
> high on his shoulder, and the belt of the boy Pallas gleamed with the
>   studs he knew,
> whom Turnus had conquered and laid low with a wound,
> and was now wearing his enemy's emblem on his shoulders.
> He, after he had drunk in with his eyes the trophies, the memorials 945
> of his savage grief, burning with fury and terrible in his anger:
> "Are you to escape me from here, you dressed in the spoils of
> my own? Pallas makes a sacrifice of you with this wound, and Pallas
> exacts compensation from criminal blood."
> So saying he plunges the sword in his enemy's chest,   950
> raging; the limbs of Turnus dissolve in cold,
> and his life, indignant, flees with a groan beneath the shades.

As many scholars have shown,[44] the end of this poem picks up in interesting ways on the end of the *Odyssey* and the killing of Hector in *Iliad* 22.[45] But

---

44. Knauer 1964; Hardie 1997: 139–62; Putnam 2011; Dekel 2012; Tarrant 2012.
45. As also on Menelaus' killing of the suppliant Adrestus at *Il.* 6.61–65.

it is also possible to see in the end of the *Aeneid* a doubling of the Achilles scene from *Iliad* 1, where Aeneas' *dextramque repressit* ("and restrained his right hand") succinctly rewrites "so speaking he checked his heavy hand on the silver hilt / and back into the scabbard he pushed the great sword" (ἐπ' ἀργυρέῃ κώπῃ σχέθε χεῖρα βαρεῖαν / ἂψ δ' ἐς κουλεὸν ὦσε μέγα ξίφος) from *Iliad* 1. Aeneas' passionate disavowal not only of the norms of Roman *pietas* but also the codes of epic is almost averted when he, like Achilles, at first obeys the directions laid down for him by the text and stays the hand that has reached for his sword.

Just as Homer did for Achilles, Vergil expands the moment of Aeneas' hesitation, capturing it in slow motion through his doubling of the word "now." The final iteration of *iam iamque* here dwells on precisely how the plot could have been different, just at that moment when Aeneas began to change his mind.[46] Caught in the same moment of uncertainty as Achilles when he turned around to face Athena, yet unable to contain his anger at the sight of the baldric, Aeneas not only imitates the Achilles of Book 22, but also, and more specifically, corrects Achilles' decision from Book 1, by pulling out his sword and killing his adversary. In this way—by first staying his hand on the hilt of his sword and then, following *Iliad* 22, refusing to grant his opponent mercy—Aeneas re-enacts both versions of Achilles at once in the space of twelve short lines (938–51). In doing so, he decisively claims the very last action of the epic before the "dissolution" of Turnus' limbs in the poem's final two lines (951–52). Somewhat paradoxically, the *Aeneid* ends by referencing not only the moment of murderous rage that killed Hector, and which was far from bringing closure to the *Iliad,* but also the moment in Book 1 when the plot was forcibly directed onto its proper course with the plunging of a sword back into a scabbard.

Odysseus' leap to nowhere at the very end of the *Odyssey* could thereby be read as a prototype of Aeneas' more serious challenge to paternal and textual authority at the very end of the *Aeneid.* For like Achilles, who pulls his sword out by degrees, and like the *iam iamque magis cunctantem* of the *Aeneid,* Odysseus' moment of curling into a crouch before the spring suggests the potentiality of

---

46. As Emily Gowers points out to me, there is a discrepancy between Aeneas' action of indecisively rolling his eyes around (*volvens*) and decisively thrusting his sword back (*repressit*). There is also a difference in the coordination of eyes and hands between Aeneas and Turnus, for the latter had previously cast his eyes down and stretched his hands out (*Aen.* 12.930–31: *ille humilis supplex. occulos dextramque precantem / pretendens,* "he, humble suppliant, stretches out his eyes and his praying right hand"), such that the two actions can be covered by the same participle, *protendens* (the syntax is difficult—see Lovatt 2013: 340 n.80). On Turnus' inability to look Aeneas in the eye (12.894, 896, 908–9, 913–18) before this moment, see Lovatt 2013: 339–40.

the present; the body's sense of reacting to the here and now and making its own choice about how to respond.[47]

Crouching turns on the line between active and passive, defensive and aggressive behavior, drawing the body into a temporary position of immobility and uncertainty. Because it is often associated with waiting (μένω) or anticipating (ποτιδέχομαι), it draws our attention—not least because the position is uncomfortable—to the duration of the present. The croucher's purpose is to pause and wait for action, to look forward to the plot's next adventure. In narratological terms, it is a strongly self-reflexive stance, inasmuch as the character, like the reader, is focused on nothing but what is coming next in the text. It has affinities with the notion of the Muybridge stop-motion picture or sports photograph insofar as it decelerates the time of action into the moment of "just before"—what I earlier referred to as "the elasticity of the almost," a still moment in narrative time that is often tied to deliberation. As with *iam iamque* we are stilled and drawn into not only the "now" of action but also the "now" of reading (or listening); pressed to ask, with the croucher himself, which way will the plot go?

For Odysseus, this sense of the plot's focus on the present moment is an especially pressing issue. For he is a character and narrator who has spent much of the *Odyssey* twice removed from his own story, via plots that he either narrates after the fact (Books 9–12), or learns of ahead of time (his conversation with Athena in Book 13).[48] By contrast, the crouch at *Odyssey* 24.538 represents a moment when Odysseus might break into the now, even into the fiction of living his story as it happens, by acting spontaneously and going off-script.[49] This kind of improvisation-at-the-end is on the one hand part of the dynamics of any move toward closure, as Tim Whitmarsh has argued for the Greek novel. The push-pull between restraint and innovation must find some way of achieving quiescence in closure, however, some way

---

47. Note Hardie on the "last recorded moment of the epic present" in his discussion of the *Aeneid* (1997: 143).

48. See Burgess 2012: 269–90 on Odysseus as a belated hero.

49. The fantasy of the time of the *histoire* (or event) and the time of the *récit* (its narration) ever coinciding was brilliantly exposed by Laurence Sterne, as Shklovsky explained, through the stooping posture of his mother left eavesdropping at a door for several pages, as Sterne catches up with another storyline taking place in the kitchen. At times Sterne will suddenly remember that he left his mother at the door: "I am a Turk if I had not as much forgot my mother," etc., but—like all characters in stories—she is left to wait there until the business of narrating has caught up with her. What Sterne does, though, is to focus on the physical discomfort of Shandy's mother—through her posture, frozen in a painful stoop, we are made aware of the passage of time. As Shklovsky writes, "Sterne, by repeatedly mentioning and reminding us of the fact that his mother has been standing in a stooped position for the whole time, forces us to notice his handling of it" (1965: 36).

of "finding the right end" and reaching a point where the "now" of the story is finally over.[50]

The crouch that occurs ten lines before the end of the *Odyssey* represents a moment of suspense, shot through with impermanence and anticipation, a posture of resistance and kinetic uncertainty that translates into a sudden disruption of how we thought the poem would end. That uncertainty can be carried over to other aspects of the ending, too, in which we see Athena acting somewhat inscrutably, perhaps also rebelliously, in relation to her father, and where the cursory "afterwards she made oaths on both sides" (ὅρκια δ' αὖ κατόπισθε μετ' ἀμφοτέροισιν ἔθηκε, 546) after Odysseus' leap leaves the poem in a politically ambiguous space.[51] As Donald Lateiner's work on proxemics has shown, in crouching you attempt to regulate or negotiate the distance between yourself and what is in front of you; it is a position that is most associated with horizontality (1992: 144–56). Odysseus' crouch at the end of the poem is thus also an attempt to negotiate the distance toward the end, whether we are to imagine Odysseus' leap passing over the *Odyssey*'s boundary or not.[52]

Reading Odysseus' ending through Hector's also reminds us that it is not only the eagle who crouches before swooping, but also the hare (πτώξ, from πτώσσω, *to crouch*), who gathers herself in so as to ward off attack. These two contradictory impulses are dramatized in the turn from tenor to vehicle in the simile describing Hector's leap (*Il.* 22.308–10):

οἴμησεν δὲ ἀλεὶς ὥς τ' αἰετὸς ὑψιπετήεις,
ὅς τ' εἶσιν πεδίονδε διὰ νεφέων ἐρεβεννῶν
ἁρπάξων ἢ ἄρν' ἀμαλὴν ἢ πτῶκα λαγωόν·

and he leapt having crouched like a high-flying eagle,
who goes along the plain and through the dark clouds
in order to snatch either a soft lamb or crouching hare.

50. Whitmarsh 2011: 177–213. On finding the right end see Brooks 1984: 140 and D. A. Miller on closure (cited in Whitmarsh 2011: 191): "the closural settlement accommodates the narratable only by changing its status, that is by putting it into a past perfect tense and declaring it 'over'" (Miller 1981: 98).

51. As Pietro Pucci points out to me, Athena's final arrival on Ithaca appears to contravene the order of Zeus to accomplish a truce (ὅρκια πιστά, 24.483) "as is fitting" (ὡς ἐπέοικεν, 481). Instead, she actively encourages the fight and initially calls on only one side (the "Ithacans," Ἰθακήσιοι, 531) to stop, claiming—after Laertes has killed Eupeithes—that they should part without blood (ἀναιμωτί, 532). Indeed, given her conversation with Zeus at *Od.* 24.472–86, why does Athena encourage Laertes to cast his spear at 24.518–19 (she behaves similarly at *Il.* 4.92–103, when encouraging Pandarus to break the truce, but there she is explicitly following Zeus' instructions)? Thanks also to Ben Radcliffe for helpful discussion on the political problems at the poem's end.

52. The assimilation of Odysseus to an eagle in the poem's final simile is also noteworthy, and recalls Odysseus as eagle looking over the dead suitors at *Od.* 22.381–89 (cf. Telò 2011: 589, who observes [591] that the eagle's actions are always repetitive—no sooner has it swooped down on its prey than it will find a high vantage point from which to spy out its next victim). The A scholia discuss the confusion between the swoop (*oimat'*) and gaze (*ommat'*) of Achilles as eagle at 21.252 (ΣA *Il.* 22.308a; Erbse vol. 5: 324).

In both cases, the crouch suggests anticipation, and both look forward to the same event. In Homer, we frequently see small animals such as hares or fawns crouching in order to hide or wait out a moment of danger, and heroes on the battlefield do the same.[53] Although the verb πτώσσω is typically used to denote the cowardice of a Homeric warrior, this kind of defensive crouching can also indicate good battle strategy, just as an opponent places himself in position and either waits for an opportune moment or anticipates an oncoming attack.[54]

In the end, of course, Odysseus' leap fades away. It is a benign gesture that results neither in his death nor anyone else's, and even though I have been calling it a rebellion it is one that few readers remember. As the final gesture of a man who spent most of the *Odyssey* crouching either to save or hide himself (on his knees on Scheria, upside down crouching beneath Polyphemus and Charybdis' fig tree, or bent over as a beggar [literally "croucher," πτωχός]) and who finally gets to stretch out his limbs with a leap back onto his own threshold at the beginning of *Odyssey* 22,[55] Odysseus' brief reperformance of his Iliadic self at the very end of his poem speaks both to the continuation of the epic tradition and to its need to adjust its movement vocabulary to new times and landscapes. For perhaps it is relevant, as Richard Martin argues (1993), that it is old Laertes rather than young Telemachus who gets to make the final kill; perhaps the kinetic possibilities of the "old epic" are beginning to recede. The acute attention paid to memory in the last two books of the *Odyssey*—particularly remembering things from long ago that are beyond Telemachus' ken—reinforces a sense of anxiety and nostalgia for the way things used to be. This is partly, I think, why it is so hard for the epic to find its own ending, and why it builds its own resistance to that ending into the various poses of Odysseus even up to and beyond the epic's closing lines.

---

53. To cower in, hide, or retreat from battle: *Il.* 4.371; 5.634; 7.129 (all terms of reproach; cf. Irwin 2005: 37–39 on the crouch in Tyrtaeus); 13.408; 16.402–3; 20.278, 427; 21.14, 26, 571; *Od.* 22.304, 362. Of beggars: *Od.* 17.227; 18.363. Of animals: *Il.* 17.676; 22.310 (hare [πτώξ]); *Il.* 5.476 (dogs); *Il.* 8.136 (horses cringing [καταπτήτην]); *Il.* 21.571 (leopard). Of Paris springing from his hiding place: *Il.* 11.379 (ἐκ λόχου ἀμπήδησε); to be in a hidden position: *Il.* 13.277, 285; to crouch in a posture of defense (ἕζομαι): *Il.* 22.275; *Od.* 14.31; of bending double in death: *Il.* 20.418, 420 (λιασθείς / λιαζόμενον ποτὶ γαίῃ).

54. *Il.* 13.404–10; 16.360, 401–4; Friedrich 1956, 2003: 138. Smart defense: Agenor *Il.* 21.571–82; Aeneas *Il.* 20.278–85; Hector *Il.* 22.93–97.

55. On which see my Chapter 5.

5

Standing

> I often return to a neutral standing position between moves. It is, for me, a
> way of measuring where I have been and where I am going.
> —Trisha Brown, *Dance and Art in Dialogue*: 1961–2001

UNLIKE FALLING OR CROUCHING, STANDING IS DIFFICULT TO TALK
about in any systematic way in the Homeric poems, in part because it is an in-
between state that every human and divine body assumes countless times. It
is a micro-gesture that prefigures falling, is rapidly passed through in walking,
and can signal both the start and the middle of several different types of action
(Telemachus "rose up" from his bed; Agamemnon "stood up" to speak, Hector
"stood waiting" on the battlefield ...). Standing on two feet is the default gesture
not only for being human,[1] but also for making oneself heard or for engaging
in battle or competition. Standing, which shares a conceptual space with lying
down and sitting, is set apart from the other gestures in this book insofar as it
is inherently motionless, thus drawing more on proxemics and deictics than it
does on movement through space or action and plot.[2]

In this chapter, I study two different and marked forms of standing. First,
Achilles' in the *Iliad*, beginning with the stance he adopts at 1.6 when he and
Agamemnon simultaneously stand apart from each other (διαστήτην), and then
moving through a sequence of standings on or near the battlefield that, through
their relational aspect, figure the loneliness of the warrior after the structure of
"standing beside" (παρίστημι) has been broken. Second, I examine Penelope's
iconic "standing beside the stathmos" in the *Odyssey*, a pose that draws the
reader into a time of contemplation, pause, and reflection of both the future and
the past, and that frames a different register of action for the poem. I argue that
when Penelope stands by the stathmos, as when Odysseus stands amongst the
dead bodies in the hall in Eurycleia's description in Book 23, we might think in
generic terms of a new kind of stance: one that resembles the staged tableau of
tragedy.

Standing occupies a complicated position in a book that is about repetition.
Since able-bodied human beings move into a standing position hundreds of

---

1. As Oedipus recognized in solving the riddle of the Sphinx. See further Buchan 2004: 21–49.
2. Related is the notion of one's stance as self. Thus Archilochus fr. 114W, Solon, fr. 5W, etc., which
draw out the Homeric notion of "standing fast" in battle (see my discussion of Ajax and Menelaus over
the body of Patroclus in *Iliad* 17 later in this chapter).

times a day, how can we talk about the act of standing in terms of repetition at all? In Homeric epic, the act seems to be *too* repetitive to count as meaningful in any systematic way.[3] To complicate matters further, there is a seemingly endless variety of ways to indicate standing in Homer, not just because *histēmi* has so many forms, but because it is also joined in compounds with several different prepositional prefixes (beginning with *dia-*, and including, but not limited to, *para-*, *amphi-*, *anti-*, and *ana-*).[4]

Finally, there is the relation between standing and movement to consider. In the *Republic,* Socrates argues that the same thing cannot stand still and move *at the same time and in the same part of itself* (ἑστάναι ... καὶ κινεῖσθαι τὸ αὐτὸ ἅμα κατὰ τὸ αὐτὸ),[5] but elsewhere in Greek thought standing and movement are sometimes interchangeable. Thus it is something of a paradox, as Nicole Loraux has argued, that the Greek word for civil war (*stasis*) comes from the verb *histēmi,* to stand still, but in meaning is often synonymous with movement (*kinēsis*).[6] Thucydides, Aristotle, and Plato all talk of *stasis* as something that is connected to movement or change (*kineō*), with such contradictory formulations as στάσιν κινοῦσιν ("they bring a *stasis* into movement").[7] The question is important not so much for how it applies to the physical act of standing in Homer, but for how it illuminates the issue of narrative progression; whereas we would expect standing to be nothing but a stilling device for a plot, it ends up moving narrative forward in sometimes surprising ways.[8]

In *Beginnings,* Edward Said writes, "Even when it is repressed, the beginning is always a first step ..." (1975: xii). Yet in the *Iliad* the simultaneous acts of stepping apart *and* standing, represented by *dia* + *histēmi* in the poem's opening lines, lead to a long period of immobility and inaction for the plot's protagonist. In the *Odyssey,* too, the plot from Penelope's perspective cycles around a curious combination of repetition and stasis, comprised of her four times standing in

3. As such, it falls at the least significant end of Bakker's "scale of interformularity" (2013: 159), as discussed also in my Introduction and Chapter 4.

4. *LfgrE,* s.v. ἵστημι. The perfect of *bainō* also denotes "taking a stand."

5. Pl., *Rep.* 436c5. Socrates says that it is possible for only *one part* of a man to be standing and *another part* of him (say his hands or head) to be moving at the same time: τὸ μέν τι αὐτοῦ ἕστηκε, τὸ δὲ κινεῖται (436d1). See, differently, the choreographer Steve Paxton on standing as a "small dance" (1986), which focuses attention on the many minor forms of vestibular or proprioceptive movement that the body continually engages in as part of its work in keeping itself upright. On stillness as action see Lepecki 2006.

6. As Hawhee notes, *stasis* can be used to indicate a bodily position, such as the stance a boxer takes (2004: 34).

7. Loraux [1997] 2002: 93–122; Thuc. 3.82.1; Pl., *Rep.* 8.545c8–d6; Ar., *Pol.* 5.4.1304a36.

8. Olsen 2017b notes that "ἵστημι in early Greek usage is persistently associated with the organization of choral performance" (8, with further references). As she shows, Homer's use of this verb to describe choral dance expresses a double signification of stillness and movement at once.

front of the suitors for brief but key periods, and then returning to a room where she lies down to weep.

There is a balance, in other words, an unexpressed correlation, between standing and moving, and a tacit understanding that a plot will not let the neutral standing (or "resting") parts go on for too long.[9] Standing's inherent dullness, its sense of being situated outside the intensity of the now, means that this chapter forms an inverse pair with the one on crouching. It would seem to make more sense to begin a narrative with a leap and end one with a standstill, but at the beginning of the *Iliad* and the end of the *Odyssey* respectively, exactly the opposite happens. At the same time, the *Iliad* opens with division: the fracturing of a unit from one to two. The dual form of *diastētēn* (1.6) calls into question how the proximal relation between one man and another will be framed in the poem; the start of a thread stitched through paired conversations and duels in the epic as a whole. The *Iliad,* for all its scenes of amassed armies and assemblies, likes to think in twos, and frequently settles on scenes that figure the relationship between a pair of individuals. One movement I trace in this chapter, therefore, runs from the *Iliad*'s initial foregrounding of the dual verb in *diastētēn* through to the final scenes between Achilles and the shade of Patroclus in Book 23, as individuals from different "sides" try fleetingly to close the gap.[10] This is one of the ways in which I suggest that standing, although difficult to pin down in terms of narrative action, nevertheless clues the reader in to how the poem works spatially and relationally, through what we might call a poetics of adjacency.[11]

What standing also reveals is that the *Odyssey* (despite the *homophrosynē* shared by husband and wife) is *not* particularly invested in thinking in twos. In this poem, the second category—the thing in relation to which one stands—is most often the house or an object within it.[12] Although loyalty between characters (as between Athena and Odysseus) is indexed by the phrase "s/he came and stood near him," using some variation of ἄγχι παραστάς, it is more typically a column (κιών), roof pillar (σταθμός), threshold (οὐδός), or door jamb (φίλτρος) that will provide the supporting role for a standing character in this poem. If the most important description of standing in the *Iliad* is ἐξ οὗ δὴ τὰ

9. We can turn here to another piece by Steve Paxton (n.5, this chapter), *State* (1968), in which forty-one performers simply stand still on stage. Banes argues, following Robert Morris, that the use of standing in this work challenges the notion of theatrical time, "reduc[ing] the incidence of action and distribut[ing] it in an uneventful, even way" (Banes 1987: 61 and n.7).

10. On Hector standing before the Scaean gates at the beginning of Book 22, see my Chapter 3, and on Achilles and Priam in Book 24, Chapter 6.

11. Cf. Manning 2009: 43–47.

12. Gil: "All gesture is, in itself, an assemblage. But in general gesture assembles the body *with* an object or with other bodies" (2006: 29, emphasis mine).

πρῶτα διαστήτην ἐρίσαντε / Ἀτρεΐδης τε ἄναξ ἀνδρῶν καὶ δῖος Ἀχιλλεύς ("from the time when they first stood apart in strife, / the son of Atreus, lord of men, and shining Achilles"), then the *Odyssey*'s counterpart is an equally well-known phrase: στῆ ῥα παρὰ σταθμὸν τέγεος πύκα ποιητοῖο ("she stood beside the pillar of the well-built roof"). The verse occurs five times in the *Odyssey*, once to describe Nausicaa and four times to describe Penelope. I explore in this chapter how the fourfold repetition of a static scene, in which Penelope descends from her room, appears, and then retreats back up to it, maps out a particularly restricted route, and set of expressions, for the human body. More so than other female characters (Andromache runs, falls, turns, walks; Nausicaa travels by cart, plays catch with a ball, and makes a crucial decision about how to hold her body when first encountering Odysseus), Penelope's physical range is limited. In general, her movement patterns reach no further than back and forth along the length of the loom and up and down the steps of her house.

Later on, I discuss the correspondence between these two iterative and seemingly endlessly reversible movement pathways. Indeed, Penelope's repetitive kinetics have become so tightly braided over time that it is hard to untie the knot that results. She is caught in (but also fights to maintain) a world where everything is the same, where she seems doomed to repeat the same sequences of appearing and disappearing next to the column of the house. The two words, στῆ ῥα, which announce her public persona emblematize standing as a form of inaction, just as her private trick at the loom once sought to undo time's progressive and teleological nature.

Homer's replaying of the scene in which Penelope "stands by the stathmos" draws us into a place where repetition happens in the same place, and to the same character, over and over again. This is not the typical kind of type scene, such as arming, which shifts between characters and locales.[13] Instead, Penelope descends and ascends the same staircase each time. What she says changes with each occurrence, but her movement, posture, and setting do not. This pattern means that we will have to confront a form of repetition that we have not yet explored. I am thinking here of a situation wherein the same character performs the same action, in the same place, on four different occasions, what we might consider as the kind of repetition in which a character is "stuck" and cannot move forward. At the same time, we will have to consider the consequences for Penelope's agency if so many of her appearances are structured by a gesture not only of standing, but also of repeating.

---

13. Arend discusses the importance of variation and fixity in the Homeric type scene ("der Wechsel von fester Form und verschiedener Ausschmückung," [1933] 1975: 27).

In my reading of first the *Iliad* and then the *Odyssey* in this chapter, I am concerned with standing as a form of stopping; but also as a small, physical readjustment that invites the reader to think, in lateral terms, about how characters align themselves in relation to other bodies and objects in the text.

ILIAD

1. διαστήτην (*Il.* 1.6)

Μῆνιν ἄειδε, θεά, Πηληϊάδεω Ἀχιλῆος
οὐλομένην, ἣ μυρί' Ἀχαιοῖς ἄλγε' ἔθηκε,
πολλὰς δ' ἰφθίμους ψυχὰς Ἄϊδι προΐαψεν
ἡρώων, αὐτοὺς δὲ ἑλώρια τεῦχε κύνεσσιν
οἰωνοῖσί τε πᾶσι, Διὸς δ' ἐτελείετο βουλή,
ἐξ οὗ δὴ τὰ πρῶτα διαστήτην ἐρίσαντε
Ἀτρεΐδης τε ἄναξ ἀνδρῶν καὶ δῖος Ἀχιλλεύς.

Sing, goddess, the anger of Peleus' son Achilles
and its devastation, which put pains thousandfold upon the Achaeans,
hurled in their multitudes to the house of Hades strong souls
of heroes, but gave their bodies to be the delicate feasting
of dogs, of all birds, and the will of Zeus was accomplished
since that time when first the two stood in division of conflict
Atreus' son the lord of men and brilliant Achilleus.

— *Iliad* 1.1–7, trans. Lattimore (adapted).

The *Iliad*'s first position, before the confusion wrought by anger's "placing" (ἔθηκε) and "hurling" (προΐαψεν) has begun, is of two men standing apart: διαστήτην.[14] Indeed, before we even know who the two are, the dual aorist form of the verb signals the key information as to how things are now: divided and at a standstill. In formal terms, the proem signals the importance of this opening gesture in three different ways. First, the fracture between the two heroes spreads phonically through the poem's opening via the diaeretic splinterings of Πηληϊάδεω, Ἄϊδι, προΐαψεν, and Ἀτρεΐδης. Second, the verb for "standing apart" sets in motion an anagrammatic shuffling through and beyond the line's end: διαστήτην ἐρίσαντε / Ἀτρεΐδης, in which every letter in each word recurs in at least one of the other words in the set, and more

---

14. διίστημι is relatively unusual in Homer, occurring seven times in the *Iliad* (1.6; 12.86; 13.29; 16.470; 17.391; 21.436; 24.718) and never in the *Odyssey*. It appears at only one other time in the third-person dual of the aorist (16.470) but with a slightly different meaning—there the two divine horses of Achilles *together* (i.e., in the dual) separate from their slain trace horse, Pedasos.

typically in both, provided we pay attention to quality of vowels, not quantity.[15] Finally, the δια- of διαστήτην is highlighted by its correspondence with Διός in the verse that precedes it; both occur in the same metrical position in successive lines and both are followed by similar sounds: DIOSDETE and DIASTETE, with the only difference being o ~ a and d ~ t.[16] Add this to the adjective δῖος in line 7, and the result is a chiastic structuring of *di-* sounds in the last three lines of the proem, with *dia-* gaining extra prominence from its position in the middle (Διὸς ... διασ- ... δῖος).[17] The sequence is especially noteworthy insofar as it resembles a more explicit pun of the same kind at the opening of Hesiod's *Works and Days,* but here the emphasis falls on separation rather than the god.[18]

All of this, combined with a preponderance of word-opening vowels, creates a rush at the poem's start, as if everything were hurtling toward διαστήτην, that thing that the proem wants to tell us happened "first."[19] Yet the epic no sooner introduces the dual form than it splits it open, driving in a wedge with δια- that forces preposition and person ending to compete within a single word.[20] The verb's lexical meaning of standing apart—the poem's initial and defiant

15. So epsilon ~ eta. The words are almost complete anagrams of each other, except that the δ in ἐρίσαντε has been effectively hidden by the σ (the verb is based on a dental stem, cf. ἔρις, ἔριδος) and the second τ of διαστήτην is replaced by a new letter, ρ, in ἐρίσαντε and Ἀτρεΐδης. See also Parry (1930: 117ff.) for the *Iliad*'s opening lines.

16. Both *d* and *t* are dental stops, and respectively voiced and unvoiced equivalents. I am grateful to Joshua Katz for helping me with this material and for pointing out to me the correspondence between Διὸς δ' ἐτελ- and διαστήτ-. As he also suggests to me, the alternate reading of 1.5, οἰωνοῖσί τε δαῖτα, would add yet another combination of delta, iota, and alpha to these lines.

17. There is a variation in the third category, insofar as the iota in δῖος is long (contrasting with the short iota of Διὸς and διαστήτην), but, as with my previous discussion of epsilon and eta, what matters here is quality, not quantity.

18. Hes., *WD* 1–4: Μοῦσαι Πιερίηθεν, ἀοιδῇσι κλείουσαι, / δεῦτε, Δί' ἐννέπετε, σφέτερον πατέρ' ὑμνείουσαι, / ὅν τε διὰ βροτοὶ ἄνδρες ὁμῶς ἄφατοί τε φατοί τε / ῥητοί τ' ἄρρητοί τε Διὸς μεγάλοιο ἕκητι. As Katz notes, "the preposition διά in verse 3 is a probable etymological play on Δί(α), in exactly the same metrical position in the previous verse" (2013b: 16). See further West 1978: 138–39; Watkins 1995: 99, with n.4 (as cited in Katz 2013b).

19. There is a large number of initial alphas (ἄειδε, Ἀχιλῆος, Ἀχαιοῖς, ἄλγε', Ἄϊδι, αὐτοὺς, Ἀτρεΐδης, ἄναξ [ignoring digamma], ἀνδρῶν, Ἀχιλλεύς), epsilons (ἔθηκε, ἑλώρια, ἐτελείετο, ἐξ, ἐρίσαντε), etas (ἥ, ἡρώων), and omicron "diphthongs" (οὐλομένην, οἰωνοῖσι, οὐ) in the proem, compared to a relatively small number of initial consonants (according to the sequence μ, π, μ, π, ψ, π, τ, κ, π, δ, β, δ, τ, π, δ, δ and dominated by patterns involving first π and then δ). On the significance of vowels at the openings of archaic song, especially with ἄειδε, see Katz 2013a, 2013b, esp. 17ff; and 2018. On the proem's rhythm, see Kahane 1997 and 1994: 40–41 and n.54, esp. for the more dynamic vv. 6–7 and the clash between meter and sense at ἄναξ ἀνδρῶν. See also Schein 2015: 301–9.

20. As Buchan has written (2012: 9), "[a] strain is placed on the use of the dual form in line 7." He goes on to show that there are not two people at issue in this scene, but three, for the Atreid pair of Menelaus and Agamemnon lurks continually in the background, disrupting the ordered pairing of Achilles and Agamemnon. Cf. his discussion at 48–49, 126, 132. Also on duals see Scodel 2002: 162–72.

pose—thereby undercuts the dual's inherent assumption that two men can act together.[21]

The events of *Iliad* 1 that lead up to *diistēmi* have been well discussed elsewhere, and are themselves initiated by a sequence of standing ups and sitting downs that characterize a regular Homeric assembly.[22] The development from *anistēmi* to *diistēmi* over the course of the argument in Book 1 can be seen first with the orderly rising (ἀνιστάμενος, ἀνέστη) to speak of Achilles, Calchas, and Agamemnon (58, 68, 101), then in Achilles' consideration of whether to break up the whole assembly (τοὺς μὲν ἀναστήσειεν, 191) by killing Agamemnon, and culminating in the irreconcilable stance of the pair at 304–5: τὼ γ᾽ ἀντιβίοισι μαχεσσαμένω ἐπέεσσιν / ἀνστήτην ("they stood against each other fighting with opposing words"). What I want to hold onto here, however, is not just the "standing" alliance between ἀνστήτην and διαστήτην, but also the poet's marked use of the dual to structure the events of Book 1. Agamemnon and Achilles find themselves frequently categorized by it, but so also does the removal of Briseis by Agamemnon's two heralds seem to showcase the grammatical form for no other reason than to drive home the point of a kind of binary poetics underlying the *Iliad*'s opening stance.[23] This formal or grammatical device, as I go on to argue, finds physical expression in the duel of Book 3, the first fight staged on the *Iliad*'s battlefield, especially insofar as the phrase "fighting with antagonistic words," ἀντιβίοισι μαχεσσαμένω ἐπέεσσιν (that described Agamemnon and Achilles at 1.304) prefigures the invitation to ἀντίβιον μαχέσασθαι, made by Paris and Hector in their separate challenges to the Achaeans for a duel in Books 3 and 7 respectively.[24]

---

21. On the importance of διαστήτην, see also Tsagalis 2012: 98, who observes that "the very use of a spatial verb ... prefigures the role of space in presenting the conflict between Agamemnon and Achilles, whose names are, almost symbolically, pushed to the two edges of the next line." As he also points out (2012: 98, n.11), the verb recurs, as διάσταν, in Stesichorus' *Iliou Persis* (fr. S88.11 [PMGF]).

22. For discussion of the argument in Book 1, see most recently Barker 2009: 40–52; Elmer 2013: 63–78, with extensive bibliography. On whether the scene in Book 1 counts as an assembly or not, see Elmer 2013: 63. On the alternate dynamics of standing and sitting in relation to the assembly, see Montiglio 2000: 46–54 and my discussion, this chapter, on *Iliad* 19. On standing up to speak in Book 1 cf. 58, 68, 101 (it is worth noting that *Il.* 1.58–59 [=19.55–56]: τοῖσι δ᾽ ἀνιστάμενος μετέφη πόδας ὠκὺς Ἀχιλλεύς / Ἀτρεΐδη is changed elsewhere in Book 19 from τοῖσι δ᾽ ἀνιστάμενος to τὸν δ᾽ ἀπομειβόμενος (145, 198)).

23. Dual forms are used at *Il.* 1.321, 322, 323, 327, 328, 331, 332, 335, 336, 338, 347 to describe Talthybios and Eurybates (Buchan 2012: 42). Later in the book, the dual recurs to underscore the relations between Agamemnon and Menelaus (375), Zeus and Thetis (531), and Zeus and Hera (574).

24. *Il.* 3.20; 7.40, 51. As does the adverb ἀντίον, used of speaking here, and fighting elsewhere in the poem. On flyting speech, which typically precedes physical fighting see Martin 1989: 65–77; Barker 2009: 49–50 and n.30.

In both cases, it is clear how much the vocabulary of the assembly in *Iliad* 1 shades into that of the battlefield in the succeeding books.[25] Despite the attention that has been paid to the role of the *individual* in the poem's opening argument, therefore, διαστήτην sets a tone for the epic that is reflected in the books that follow through pairs of men who stand either too close to each other or too far apart. The proxemics of one-on-one combat, especially, will prove instructive to the *Iliad*'s action,[26] although it is not the only pattern in the *Iliad*. In the general flow of *androktasiai* (man-killing scenes), we often see men fighting in threes, dying in twos, or spooling through the typical sequences that Fenik (1968) has identified (A kills B, C kills A ... or A kills, B, C, D, E, F, G ...). But thinking about the proximity of bodies in twos in the *Iliad* underscores the importance of the dual form in the proem's opening lines.[27]

This duality is especially true given that the first formal battlefield scene in the poem is a contest between two men, Paris and Menelaus, in a space that is carefully divided for the purpose: χῶρον μὲν πρῶτον διεμέτρεον (3.315). In this case, the standing apart of Paris and Menelaus displaces the *dia* from *diastētēn* onto the communally sanctioned space in which their disagreement can be resolved (3.344–45):

καί ῥ' ἐγγὺς <u>στήτην</u> <u>διαμετρητῷ</u> ἐνὶ χώρῳ
σείοντ' ἐγχείας ἀλλήλοισιν κοτέοντε.

They stood close in the apportioned space,
shaking their spears at each other in anger.

The scene presents a counterpart to *Il.* 1.6 insofar as what divides the men—a dispute over a woman—here brings them closer (ἐγγὺς στήτην). Their pose at this moment is a prelude to action—one of the two, Menelaus claims, will die, and thus lead to a resolution and longed-for separation (διακρινθήμεναι, 3.98, 102) between the armies. The carefully measured space of the duel suggests that the story of the war, although it has barely started, is about to reach an ending. The stance between Agamemnon and Achilles at the beginning of the poem, by contrast, indicates stalemate and division. Usually, when two men stand together-and-apart like this in the *Iliad*, the most viable option is for them to come closer together and for one of them to die, something that Achilles considers but is pulled away from by Athena, as we saw in Chapter 4.

---

25. See, in addition to works already cited, Cairns 2001: 203–19; Edwards 1980: 1–28; Nagler 1988: 81–90.

26. See, e.g., 5.568–69; 6.119–22.

27. Buchan (2012: 9): "Indeed, the repeated use of the duals in episodes where two heroes act together ... suggests that this grammatical form gestures toward a wider Iliadic fantasy of male like-mindedness and solidarity that functions as a counterpart to the *Odyssey*'s fantasy of like-mindedness between husband and wife (*Od.* 6.180–85)." See also Buchan 2012: 114–29.

If death is not an option between Agamemnon and Achilles, then what is? The immobility embedded in *diastētēn* explains the stop-start nature of the poem's first four books, whose action is choppy and erratic, with false dreams, famously untimely scenes, and premature rushes toward the end. But at the same time, as those books progress, new possibilities for *dia* emerge that start to initiate movement. At 2.785, the Achaeans march for the first time as an army, "cutting swiftly through the plain" (μάλα δ' ὦκα διέπρησσον πεδίοιο), in a phrase that is repeated at 3.14. More importantly, during the duel in which one of the two standing characters is supposed to fall, *dia* reappears in particularly marked fashion, charting the swift movement of a spear thrown by Menelaus (3.357–63):[28]

διὰ μὲν ἀσπίδος ἦλθε φαεινῆς ὄβριμον ἔγχος
καὶ διὰ θώρηκος πολυδαιδάλου ἠρήρειστο·
ἀντικρὺ δὲ παραὶ λαπάρην διάμησε χιτῶνα
ἔγχος· ὁ δ' ἐκλίνθη καὶ ἀλεύατο κῆρα μέλαιναν.
Ἀτρεΐδης δὲ ἐρυσσάμενος ξίφος ἀργυρόηλον
πλῆξεν ἀνασχόμενος κόρυθος φάλον· ἀμφὶ δ' ἄρ' αὐτῷ
τριχθά τε καὶ τετραχθὰ διατρυφὲν ἔκπεσε χειρός.

The heavy spear went <u>through</u> [Paris'] shining shield
and forced its way <u>through</u> his much-decorated breastplate.
Straightaway then the spear passed <u>through</u> his corselet next to his side,
but he leaned away and avoided black death.
Then the son of Atreus drew his silver-studded sword
and holding it high struck the crest of [Paris'] helmet, but around it
broken <u>apart</u> in three and four pieces the sword fell from his hand.

Dia creates division into discrete entities, and this differentiation is necessary for any narrative beginning: there needs to be a divergence in order for a plot to start.[29] The duel in Book 3 goes some way to reframing the problem of *diastētēn* by playing with various configurations of standing alongside, until—with the launch of the spear—the passage of the word through three lines of verse leads to an increased sense of proximity, urgency, and speed. The spear's swift flight through the layers of armor brings with it the potential to cut straight through to the death of Paris, the surest and most efficient way of ending the poem.

Dia works hard, therefore, to direct the *Iliad*'s plot in the opening books, both through its lexical connection to divergence and directionality and in terms of

---

28. Cf. *Il.* 4.135–38 for a similar use of *dia*.
29. Loraux [1997] 2002; O'Connell 2005: 90–94; *DELG ad loc.*; Said 1975; Brooks 1984.

how, in the two passages I have considered here, it stakes out the charged space between men who stand in twos. The prefixing of *dia* in these instances to a select number of verbs (ἵστημι, μετρέω, ἔρχομαι, ἐρείδω, ἀμάω, θρύπτω [*stand, measure, go, thrust, cut, break*]) brings the plot back to essentially where it started; with his sword broken (διατρυφέν), Menelaus ends Book 3 in search of a vanished opponent. In fact, of the three occasions in which *dia* occurs in a threefold progression marking the teleological drive of a weapon, none results in that weapon reaching its goal.[30] In this sense *dia* is a narrative tease; it digs in its heels and resists the pull toward proximity.

According to the reading I have suggested, Achilles and Agamemnon are positioned in a kind of inverse duel, in which *dia* pulls them apart rather than toward each other. This corresponds, perhaps, to the somewhat paradoxical relationship between *kinēsis* and *stasis* in Greek thought that I mentioned previously.[31] In Plato's *Republic*, Socrates seems to interpret Homer's διαστήτην ἐρίσαντε as a byline for *stasis* in his misquotation of *Iliad* 16.112–13 (where Homer sings "tell me, Muses, … how fire first fell on the ships of the Achaeans [ὅππως δὴ πρῶτον πῦρ ἔμπεσε νηυσὶν Ἀχαιῶν)]"), by means of a reversion to the poem's opening (Pl., *Rep.* 545d8–e1):[32]

ἦ βούλει, ὥσπερ Ὅμηρος, εὐχώμεθα ταῖς Μούσαις εἰπεῖν ἡμῖν ⟨⟨ὅπως δὴ πρῶτον στάσις ἔμπεσε⟩⟩ … ;

or do you prefer, like Homer, that we pray to the Muses to tell us "how first stasis fell upon. . ."?

Even though *stasis* (civil war) is not a Homeric word, the equivalence that Plato draws between it and *diastētēn* invites us to consider the ways in which the static nature of standing reads as an irritation or provocation. On the one hand, then, by beginning with standing Homer agitates the plot into an impetus for beginning, but on the other hand his choice removes the poem's protagonist from mobility and action for the epic's first eighteen books. As we will go on to see in the next section, this play on the idea of two men standing against each other, in a duel of words or weapons, is underscored by a more traumatic strain of standing in the poem, after Achilles resists the heroic impetus to stand beside Patroclus, his best-loved companion.

30. *Il.* 3.135–38 (the unresolved duel between Paris and Menelaus, quoted previously); 4.127–40 (Pandaros' arrow grazes Menelaus); 7.251–54 (unresolved duel between Hector and Ajax).

31. Although the paradox may be resolved somewhat by the prefixing of *dia*. See Heraclitus, fr. 125 DK: "Even the *kukeōn* drink separates (διίσταται) when it is not in motion (μὴ κινούμενος)," as discussed in Loraux 2002: 108.

32. Loraux 2002: 120. Note also Plato, *Laws*, 744d4: "*diastasis* would be a more correct term for civil war than stasis," ὃ διάστασιν ἢ στάσιν ὀρθότερον ἂν εἴη κεκλῆσθαι.

2. παρίστατο (*Il.* 16.2)

As has been noted, Achilles sits and lies around, a bystander of his own plot, for over half of the epic.[33] Only after the death of Patroclus is he compelled to rise,[34] announcing his return simply by standing alone at the ditch that separates Achaeans from Trojans, and from there shouting (18.215–17):

στῆ δ' ἐπὶ τάφρον ἰὼν ἀπὸ τείχεος, οὐδ' ἐς Ἀχαιοὺς
μίσγετο· μητρὸς γὰρ πυκινὴν ὠπίζετ' ἐφετμήν.
ἔνθα στὰς ἤϋσ', ...

He stood at the ditch, having come from the wall, nor did
he mix with the Achaeans, for he was following the strong command of
    his mother.
Standing there, he shouted, ...

Achilles' solitary stance upon re-entering the battlefield (στῆ δ' ἐπὶ τάφρον, "he stood at the ditch") poignantly recalls Patroclus' last stance in life: στῆ δὲ ταφών ("he stood stunned") after having been hit from behind by Apollo at the end of Book 16.[35] By this point in Book 18, Achilles has already lamented that he was not present to protect his friend (18.98–100). Instead, when Patroclus last stood next to him (παρίστατο, 16.2) and pleaded for help, Achilles reproached him with the simile of a girl pulling on her mother's dress and clamoring to be lifted up (16.7–11, especially 8–9):

νηπίη, ἥ θ' ἅμα μητρὶ θέουσ' ἀνελέσθαι ἀνώγει,
εἰανοῦ ἁπτομένη, καί τ' ἐσσυμένην κατερύκει

[you are like] a foolish girl, who running alongside her mother begs to
    be lifted up,
pulling on her mother's dress and slowing her down as she hurries

Only looking back from Book 18 do we fully understand the implications of this simile, since the entire length of *Iliad* 17 encompassed a slow struggle first to pull Achilles' armor from the dead Patroclus and then to lift his body from

---

33. Montiglio 2000: 46–54.

34. On Achilles' posture in Book 18, see 104, 121, and 178. In the last case, Iris instructs him with ἀλλ' ἄνα, μηδ' ἔτι κεῖσο ("Rise up! Stop lying there!"). At 9.247–48, Odysseus tried a similar injunction ἀλλ' ἄνα, εἰ μέμονάς γε καὶ ὀψέ περ υἷας Ἀχαιῶν / ... ἐρύεσθαι ("Rise up, if you were ever eager to protect the Achaeans even at the last moment!"). The imperative ἀλλ' ἄνα is also used at *Il.* 6.331 and 18.178 and *Od.* 18.13.

35. 16.806, also at the start of the line (as always with στῆ). As Mario Telò points out to me, Achilles too will be killed by Apollo. Therefore, this line not only recalls Patroclus' death but also possibly foreshadows his own (see following note).

the battlefield. Although we are led to expect that Patroclus' corpse will initially be dragged from the fray (ἕλκω, 17.126, 289, ἐρύω, 104, 230, 235, 287, 396, 419, 581, 635=713), he is in the end "lifted up" into the arms of Menelaus and Meriones (ἀείραντες, 17.718, ἀγκάζοντο, 722, αἴροντας, 724; cf. ἀναιρέω at 16.8, 10).[36] We might compare here the lifting (ἀείρας) of Sarpedon's body from the battlefield by Apollo at *Il.* 16.678, in a scene that Keith Stanley pairs with Book 16's opening simile in that both characters are represented as the children of parents who are unable to save them.[37] Finally, in two prominent similes in Book 17 when an Achaean stands over Patroclus' body and protects him, that warrior is compared to a mother animal defending her young.[38] It is all the more noteworthy, therefore, that Achilles, in the simile from Book 16, is figured as a hurrying mother who dislikes being pulled to a standstill by her child. The childish clutching of her body and clothing there prefigures the more violent grasping for Achilles' armor from the body of Patroclus at the beginning of the subsequent book.

In a very real sense, too, Patroclus—like the girl in the simile—"slows down" (κατερύκει) the *Iliad*. Scholars have commented on the laborious and drawn-out nature of Book 17, which is anchored throughout by the fight for Patroclus' body through a sequence of scenes that are both repetitive and slow paced.[39] At *Iliad* 6.518–19, in a parallel construction to Achilles' καί τ' ἐσσυμένην κατερύκει / δακρυόεσσα (16.9–10), Paris apologizes to Hector for slowing *him* down, as he catches him up on his way back to the battlefield: ἠθεῖ', ἦ μάλα δή σε καὶ ἐσσύμενον κατερύκω / δηθύνων ("Brother, I with my dallying am slowing you down as you hurry").[40] Their absence from the battlefield was not so much caused by Paris, however, as by Hector's conversation with Andromache standing before the Scaean gates.[41] In Book 17 a similar kind of standing delay is transposed

---

36. The verbs are not the same but their action in this case is. The scene of the fight around Patroclus' body compares to the lifting (ἀναιρέω) of Achilles' body from the battle after a full day of fighting, as described in *Od.* 24.37–43 and in Proclus' summary of the *Aethiopis* (*Chr.* Allen V 106.9–11: καὶ περὶ τοῦ πτώματος γενομένης ἰσχυρᾶς μάχης Αἴας ἀνελόμενος ἐπὶ τὰς ναῦς κομίζει). See further Willcock 1987: 192–93.

37. Stanley 1993: 173. On Achilles as maternal protector of Patroclus, see Gaca 2008; Warwick forthcoming 2019.

38. Menelaus compared to a cow, 17.3–8, Ajax to a lion (17.132–7). For the structural symmetry of these two scenes, see Fenik 1968: 160–61. See again Warwick (forthcoming 2019) on how these similes express Achilles' dual nature as maternal protector/neglecter, in a work that was conceived prior to my own and that has had a direct influence on my thoughts here.

39. See especially Fenik 1968: 159–89, who explains that "essentially the same thing happens four times" in Book 17, and that the fighting takes on a "simple and repetitive form" (159).

40. These are the only two occurrences of paired ἐσσύμενον/ἐσσυμένην and κατερύκω in Homer.

41. 6.399–495. Andromache "stands" before and beside Hector at 399 and 405. See also my Chapter 3 (72).

to the battlefield itself, during a day of fighting that has been ongoing since Book 11, and that for almost all of Book 17 is dominated by the immobile posture of warriors standing astride or around a corpse.[42]

In the long buildup to the death of Patroclus and the torching of the ships, Greeks and Trojans stand together to fight (ἐφέστασαν ἀλλήλοισιν, "they stood against one another," 15.703; ἀλλ' οἵ γ' ἐγγύθεν ἱστάμενοι, ἕνα θυμὸν ἔχοντες, "they stood near [to one another], all having one spirit," 15.710), with Ajax, in particular, standing continually fast in defense of the Achaeans (ἔνθ' ἄρ' ὅ γ' ἑστήκει δεδοκημένος, ἔγχεϊ δ αἰεὶ / Τρῶας ἄμυνε νεῶν, "he stood there waiting, always with his spear / warding the Trojans off from the ships," 15.730).[43] After Patroclus' death, the thematic importance of collective, protective standing is intensified in the fight over his body, which the Achaeans are repeatedly said to "stand over," predominantly with the prepositions ἀμφί and περί and the verbs ἵστημι and βαίνω. There are almost twenty instances of this usage in Book 17 alone, as, for example, at 17.132–33:[44]

Αἴας δ' ἀμφὶ Μενοιτιάδῃ σάκος εὐρὺ καλύψας
ἑστήκει ὥς τίς τε λέων περὶ οἷσι τέκεσσιν ...

Ajax covered the son of Menoitios with his broad shield
and stood over him like a lion over her cubs ...

17.510:

ἀμφ' αὐτῷ βεβάμεν καὶ ἀμύνεσθαι στίχας ἀνδρῶν

to stand over him and defend him against the ranks of men

42. For stepping over a dead body as a means of protecting it in the *Iliad,* see Fenik 1968: 160. Clay (2011: 90–95) discusses how the corpse of Patroclus occupies an immobile position in the middle (ἐν μέσῳ, 17.375) of this book's spatial organization. As she puts it, "Patroclus, like an unmoved mover, is both the cause and origin of all the activity around him. Each incident revolves, departs, and returns to that central point" (2011: 94–95). Finally, Lynn-George (1993:3) notes the prominent use of ἀμφιβέβηκας in Chryses' speech in *Iliad* 1, in his discussion of the prominence of the theme of protection in the epic's opening book.

43. At 11.571 Ajax stands (ἱστάμενος) "like a stubborn donkey," blocking the Trojans from making it on to the ships. On the repetitive nature of Ajax's standing pose in Books 15 and 16, see Purves 2015.

44. In the first example ἀμφί can be joined with both καλύψας and ἑστήκει. See also 17. 4, 6, 80, 114, 120–21 (with σπεύδω), 137, 138–39, 266–67, 345, 355, 359, 369, 510, 563–64, 574 (βῆ δ' ἐπί), and 706. At 286, the Trojans adopt the same pose (οἵ περὶ Πατρόκλῳ βέβασεν) in trying to drag him off; at 313 Ajax stands over (περιβάντα) the body of Hippothoos. At 732–33, Menelaus and Meriones stand fast against the Trojans who try to attack them as they carry off Patroclus' body (μεταστρεφθέντε κατ' αὐτοὺς / σταίησαν).

17.563–64:

τῷ κεν ἔγωγ' ἐθέλοιμι <u>παρεστάμεναι</u> καὶ ἀμύνειν
Πατρόκλῳ·

I at least would choose to stand over and defend
Patroclus.

The key to the Achaeans' success, over the long haul of Book 17, is their act of standing so close to one another as to form an impenetrable fence with their shields.[45] At a certain point in the fighting, Ajax forbids the men from moving either backward or forward; they are simply to stand still and fight at close quarters (17.354–59):

σάκεσσι γὰρ ἔρχατο πάντῃ
ἑσταότες περὶ Πατρόκλῳ, πρὸ δὲ δούρατ' ἔχοντο.
Αἴας γὰρ μάλα πάντας ἐπῴχετο πολλὰ κελεύων·
οὔτε τιν' ἐξοπίσω νεκροῦ χάζεσθαι ἀνώγει
οὔτε τινα προμάχεσθαι Ἀχαιῶν ἔξοχον ἄλλων,
ἀλλὰ μάλ' ἀμφ' αὐτῷ βεβάμεν, σχεδόθεν δὲ μάχεσθαι.

They were fenced in by shields on all sides,
standing around Patroclus, and holding their spears before them.
Ajax would go among them all issuing many orders
that no man should draw back from the corpse
nor should anyone step out from the others and fight in the foreground,
but they should stand over it, and fight at close quarters.

The strategy of *standing with* or *close*, especially when understood in contrast to the Trojans' act in Book 17 of *standing against*,[46] closes the gap that Achilles first opened when he stood apart from Agamemnon and called on Zeus to help the Trojans win (1.408–10). It takes almost all of the Achaeans (Agamemnon, because he is wounded, is notably absent) to repair it, but not without the loss of Achilles' own armor. It is no surprise, moreover, that the book ends with so many characters acting in twos (and forms of the dual), a further reparative strategy to the *diastasis* of Achilles and Agamemnon.[47]

45. See Fenik 1968: 123, 177ff. on Homeric battlefield "phalanx formation." See also 17.267–68: ἔστασαν ἀμφὶ Μενοιτιάδῃ ἕνα θυμὸν ἔχοντες, / φραχθέντες σάκεσιν ("they stood around the son of Menoitios having one spirit, / forming a barricade with their shields") and 412–13: οἱ δ' αἰεὶ περὶ νεκρὸν ἀκαχμένα δούρατ' ἔχοντες / νωλεμὲς ἐγχρίμπτοντο ("Holding continually their sharp-edged spears over the corpse, / they pressed unceasingly on").

46. ἵστημι is joined with ἄντα, ἄντιος/ν, and ἐναντίοι to denote *standing against*, and with ἐγγύς and ἄγχι (among other prepositions) for *standing with*.

47. On the division of labor into pairs in the last section of *Iliad* 17, see Willcock 1987: 192. (Menelaus and Meriones carry Patroclus away while the two Ajaxes remain to fight the Trojans off.) The two Ajaxes,

The fight over the corpse brings that part of the narrative, as I have discussed, to a prolonged standstill, an immobility that is reflected in the pose of Achilles' divine horses as they also refuse to move either forward or backward (17.432–37):

τὼ δ᾽ οὔτ᾽ ἂψ ἐπὶ νῆας ἐπὶ πλατὺν Ἑλλήσποντον
ἠθελέτην ἰέναι οὔτ᾽ ἐς πόλεμον μετ᾽ Ἀχαιούς,
ἀλλ᾽ ὥς τε στήλη μένει ἔμπεδον, ἥ τ᾽ ἐπὶ τύμβῳ
ἀνέρος ἑστήκῃ τεθνηότος ἠὲ γυναικός,
ὣς μένον ἀσφαλέως περικαλλέα δίφρον ἔχοντες,
οὔδει ἐνισκίμψαντε καρήατα·

They refused to go back to the ships on the broad Hellespont,
and refused to go into battle with the Achaeans,
but like a grave monument (*stēlē*) they remained steadfast,
one that stands on the tomb of a deceased man or woman.
So they waited, immobile, holding the beautiful chariot,
and grazing the ground with their heads.

Here, the horses-as-grave-marker substitute for the immobile poses of Menelaus and Ajax over a dead body.[48] Both kinds of standing are rooted in the immobility of death (like Patroclus' own στῆ δὲ ταφών at 16.806), arising from the premature ending of the *Iliad*'s first plot: Achilles' plan has been completed, despite the misery he will experience when he learns its outcome, and Patroclus, the surrogate for the poem's protagonist, lies dead. From Book 18 on Achilles will start again, rising up from the ground, making peace with Agamemnon, and attempting to reconcile the Achaeans.

Homer subtly displaces Agamemnon's ability to regain his posture in the final books while still allowing him to save face. Thus the leader of the Achaeans famously and problematically remains seated (19.77) when offering a formal apology to Achilles, and during the last event in the funeral games for Patroclus his act of standing up to compete (23.886–88) is annulled by Achilles'

---

in particular, who fight side by side ὡς αἰεὶ Αἴαντε μάχην ἀνέεργον ὀπίσσω / Τρώων ("so always the two Ajaxes were restraining the Trojans behind them"), are joined homophonically (αἰεὶ Αἴαντε) as well as martially, to the extent that in this verse the two become indistinguishable. Cf. 13.701–8, where they are compared in a simile to a pair of oxen pulling a plough, with only the length of the polished yoke between them. So too are Menelaus and Ajax linked by similes that emphasize their co-operation (17.742–46). On reparative strategies in literature see now Mueller (forthcoming).

48. As commentators have noted, at *Il.* 13.437–8, Alcathous is depicted at his death as a στήλην … ἀτρέμας ἑστάοτα. This is the closest parallel to the description of the horses in *Iliad* 17, an otherwise highly unusual passage (Fenik 1968: 180; Schein 2002a: 193–205). But compare also Patroclus' pose after the first death blow (*Il.* 16.806), discussed previously.

delicate refusal to let him do so.[49] Instead it is Achilles who makes a formal "stand" ten times in Book 23, as if to signal his own methodical and repetitive attempt to repair the division between himself and his community first instituted by διαστήτην.[50] Standing alone, in a formalized resolution (as has often been noted) of Book 1, Achilles selects contestants, settles disputes, awards prizes, and orders events, thus correcting both his own sitting and lying for the epic's first eighteen books and Agamemnon's decision not to stand in *Iliad* 19.[51]

While Achilles stands and speaks from "the middle" to organize the games for Patroclus, he also, by refusing to participate in the competitions, does not stand face to face with any single individual to form a dual bond. Only with Patroclus' shade at the beginning of the book does he attempt to do so. As he says to him then (23.97),

> ἀλλά μοι ἆσσον στῆθι· μίνυνθά περ ἀμφιβαλόντε
> ἀλλήλους ὀλοοῖο τεταρπώμεσθα γόοιο.

But stand closer to me! For even if only for a brief moment
by embracing each other we can satisfy our terrible mourning.

Achilles' desire, which remains unfulfilled, follows immediately on Patroclus' request that Achilles bury both sets of their bones together (84–92). Achilles' ἀμφιβαλόντε (note the dual and ἀμφί's primary meaning of "on both sides") continues Patroclus' ἀμφικαλύπτοι and ἀμφιφορεύς from those lines (84–85, 91–92):

> μὴ ἐμὰ σῶν ἀπάνευθε τιθήμεναι ὀστέ᾽, Ἀχιλλεῦ,
> ἀλλ᾽ ὁμοῦ, ὡς τράφομέν περ ἐν ὑμετέροισι δόμοισιν
> . . .
> ὣς δὲ καὶ ὀστέα νῶϊν ὁμὴ σορὸς ἀμφικαλύπτοι
> χρύσεος ἀμφιφορεύς, τόν τοι πόρε πότνια μήτηρ.

Do not place my bones apart from yours, Achilles,
but put them together, just as we were raised together in your house.
. . .

49. On Agamemnon's apparent failure to stand see Edwards 1991: ad loc.; Clay 1995: 72–75; Lateiner 1995: 97–98 and n.9; Barker 2004: 33–35. Scholars usually take this gesture as Agamemnon's final jab at Achilles, a pulling rank on Agamemnon's part, and it is hard not to agree with this interpretation. On the other hand, a certain ambiguity remains, especially in this case, in which the status value of standing versus sitting in Homeric poetics has become deliberately obfuscated. On status and elevation, see Lateiner 1995: 93–103. On Agamemnon's attempt to participate in the funeral games, see Scodel 2008: 153–57.

50. Achilles standing in *Il.* 23 after 155: στῆ δ᾽ ὀρθὸς καὶ μῦθον ἐν Ἀργείοισιν ἔειπεν (271, 657, 706, 752, 801, 830), στὰς δ᾽ ἄρ᾽ ἐν Ἀργείοις ἔπεα πτερόεντ᾽ ἀγόρευε (535), αὐτὸς ἀνίστατο (491, 734). Cf. 141, 194, 617.

51. Barker 2004: 36. In the assembly in Book 19, as Barker observes, "no two speakers respond directly to each other" (35) and Agamemnon avoids looking at Achilles directly" (34, n.98). As Clay 1995 points out, Agamemnon stands to make an offering to the gods in *Iliad* 19, following Odysseus' suggestion.

So may the same urn cover over (*amphikaluptoi*) both of our bones,
the gold jar (*amphiphoreus*), which your revered mother gave you.

Patroclus' use of the first-person dual (νῶϊ), his stressing of words for togetherness (ὁμοῦ/ὁμή), and his close juxtaposition of ἐμά and σῶν, each antithetically reinforce Achilles' statement to Hector at 22.265–66, where ἐμὲ καὶ σὲ and νῶϊ are strongly negated in response to Hector's plea for a proper burial:

> ὣς οὐκ ἔστ' ἐμὲ καὶ σὲ φιλήμεναι, οὐδέ τι νῶϊ
> ὅρκια ἔσσονται ...

> There will be no love between me and you, nor between the two of us
> will there be sworn pacts ...

The correspondence between the two passages brings to light again the lost opportunity represented by Patroclus' παρίστατο at 16.2.

That lost opportunity is refracted by the poem's own gesturing toward the intimacy of enemies who fight in pairs during the sequence that leads to the death of Hector in *Iliad* 22.[52] When Athena comes to stand beside Hector disguised as his brother Deiphobus, Homer slots her into the familial body language of battlefield compatriots by his use of the phrase ἀγχοῦ δ' ἱσταμένη (and the verse is the same as the one used to describe her standing beside Achilles, as a true ally, just a few lines earlier, 22.228=22.215):[53]

> ἀγχοῦ δ' ἱσταμένη ἔπεα πτερόεντα προσηύδα

> She stood beside him and addressed him with winged words

---

52. It is often noted that Hector considers offsetting his impending fight with Achilles by removing his armor and approaching him unarmed (γυμνόν) with the promise of returning Helen and many gifts besides, although he quickly realizes that the idea is futile (22.124–28). On the intimate relationship between adversaries on the battlefield, see Slatkin [1988] 2011; Buchan 2012: 114–29.

53. To stand beside (ἀγχοῦ, ἄγχι, ἐγγύς, παρά) can be either a hostile or supportive gesture, but it is more usually supportive, expressing the assistance of a friend, ally, family member, or god. Only the phrase στῆ δὲ μάλ' ἐγγύς ... (six times, *Iliad*) is always hostile. Twice in the *Iliad* death is said to "stand close beside" (ἄγχι παρέστηκεν) a character (16.853; 24.132). In the vast majority of other cases ἄγχι + παρίστημι (eight times, *Iliad*; nine times, *Odyssey*) presents itself as a friendly gesture (the exceptions are *Il.* 15.442; 16.114). Similarly, ἀγχοῦ + ἵστημι (nine times, *Iliad*, including the two examples of ἀγχοῦ δ' ἱσταμένη discussed previously; three times, *Odyssey*) consistently denotes a supportive stance, especially from gods to mortals. Hector rejoices at Deiphobus' arrival, saying ἀλλ' ἄγε δὴ στέωμεν καὶ ἀλεξώμεσθα μένοντες (22.231; the same phrase is shared between Odysseus and Diomedes at 11.348). Finally, note also the deliberate ambiguity of Priam's stance in relation to Achilles at 24.477–79: τοὺς δ' ἔλαθ' εἰσελθὼν Πρίαμος μέγας, ἄγχι δ' ἄρα στὰς / χερσὶν Ἀχιλλῆος λάβε γούνατα καὶ κύσε χεῖρας / δεινὰς ἀνδροφόνους, αἵ οἱ πολέας κτάνον υἷας ("great Priam, entering, escaped the notice of [the others], and standing / next to Achilles he took hold of his knees with his hands, and kissed his terrible man-killing hands, / which had killed many of his sons").

The formulaic language by which Homer expresses Athena's stance beside Hector underscores that neither in speech nor action does she betray anything of her true intentions. The expectation of familiarity and predictability that the gesture of Athena sets in play is thus all the more effective when, with her sudden disappearance, it is revealed as a trick by the unfamiliar and unformulaic line ending ὁ δ' οὔ τί οἱ ἐγγύθεν ἦεν ("he was nowhere near him," 22.294–95):[54]

Δηΐφοβον δὲ κάλει λευκάσπιδα μακρὸν ἀΰσας·
ἤτεέ μιν δόρυ μακρόν· ὁ δ' οὔ τί οἱ ἐγγύθεν ἦεν··

[Hector] summoned Deiphobus of the white shield, by shouting,
and asked him for his long spear. But he was nowhere near him.

Finally, Homer describes the treatment of Hector's body as it lies on the battlefield by using an unusual reframing of the gesture of "standing beside" (371):[55]

οὐδ' ἄρα οἵ τις ἀνουτητί γε παρέστη.

there was no one who stood beside him who did not stab him.

In both of these examples, words for "near" (ἐγγύθεν) and "beside" (παρά) are engaged in a brutal transfer of allegiances. We have already seen how a fight between two men can be compared to a tryst or murmuring between lovers and how a duel can shade into its own form of intimacy. But if standing in pairs allows us to see intimacy and enmity as two sides of the same coin, part of Homer's strategy is also to make those sides sometimes ruthlessly interchangeable.

One might compare here the stance that Athena takes behind Achilles (στῆ δ' ὄπιθεν) when she holds him by the hair and prevents him from killing Agamemnon at *Il.* 1.197, as discussed in Chapter 4:

στῆ δ' ὄπιθεν, ξανθῆς δὲ κόμης ἕλε Πηλείωνα
οἴῳ φαινομένη·

She stood behind him, and grabbed the son of Peleus by the blond hair,
visible to him alone.

---

54. The closest match to this phrase occurs in Book 17, to denote, again, Athena in disguise, this time standing next to Menelaus in order to urge him on in his protection of Patroclus' corpse (553–54): πρῶτον δ' Ἀτρέος υἱὸν ἐποτρύνουσα προσηύδα, / ἴφθιμον Μενέλαον· ὃ γάρ ῥά οἱ ἐγγύθεν ἦεν, "Urging on the son of Atreus she addressed him first, / strong Menelaus, for he was next to her."

55. See also *Il.* 22.375: ὣς ἄρα τις εἴπεσκε καὶ οὐτήσασκε παραστάς. Willcock 1970: 2 summarizes readers' general discomfort with Athena's "unsporting" behavior against Hector here.

The same phrase occurs at *Il.* 17.468 to depict warriors supporting one another in battle:

στῆ δ' ὄπιθεν δίφροιο, καὶ Αὐτομέδοντα προσηύδα·

he stood behind the chariot and addressed Automedon ...

Yet it is also the stance that Apollo adopts when killing Patroclus, a god who to this warrior is not visible at all (16.791–92):[56]

στῆ δ' ὄπιθεν, πλῆξεν δὲ μετάφρενον εὐρέε τ' ὤμω
χειρὶ καταπρηνεῖ, στρεφεδίνηθεν δέ οἱ ὄσσε.

he stood behind him, and struck him on the back and broad shoulders
with the flat of his hand, and his eyes spun.

In the instances from Books 1 and 17, στῆ δ' ὄπιθεν appears to be a supportive stance between allies. Is Apollo manipulating that stance in Book 16, then, when he kills Patroclus (in much the same way as Athena [or Homer] manipulated ἀγχοῦ δ' ἱσταμένη in Book 22)? The shape of the quotations from Books 1 and 16 is very similar, sharing the same metrical structure in the first line and ending at the B2 caesura in the second. Or is this kind of interchangeability between hostile and supportive battlefield stances in itself unremarkable, part of the expected range of contexts for such a gesture? The phrase occurs only three times in Homer, but two of the three are at charged moments in the poem.[57]

What is clear is that Patroclus offers Achilles the chance to re-engage with the Achaeans and to reforge the bonds of *philotēs* precisely through the epic gesture of "standing beside"—παρίστατο—at the beginning of Book 16.[58] Achilles' explicit rejection of that posture, by way of the simile comparing himself to a harried mother, slowly works its way to a tragic conclusion in the poem as a whole. A gestural invitation passes between Patroclus and Achilles at a key moment of possible reversal for the plot, using body language so common as to go unnoticed in the minds of both the audience and the poem's characters. At the same time, Patroclus' παρίστατο struggles to bridge that in-between space between bodies where Gregory Seigworth and Melissa Gregg locate the kinetic and paralinguistic force of affect (2010: 8–13). The empathy that Patroclus attempts to kindle in his

---

56. As noted in Pucci 1998: 72–73.

57. Cf. Bakker here on interformularity (2013: 157–69).

58. Buchan 2012: 49 on Achilles not "standing by" his companion when he was killed. On the solitary state of the Homeric hero as it is "deictically fluctuated" through the rhythm of the Homeric hexameter, see Kahane 1997.

plea to Achilles is only fully realized in retrospect, culminating in the use of παρίστημι to depict the abandonment of Hector in Book 22—in a scene that is all the more devastating because it is staged as if it were happening between brothers. The *Iliad* quietly, even mundanely, lays bare the full extent of Achilles' despair by means of this series of minor oscillations between standing together and standing apart.

3. διαστήτην/διὰ στήτην (Σ ad *Il*. 1.6)

Sometimes … instead of becoming welded together, words loosen their intimate ties. Prefixes and suffixes—especially prefixes—become unwelded: they want to think for themselves.

—Gaston Bachelard, *Poetics of Space*, p. 213

One ancient critic was unhappy enough with the *Iliad*'s initial emphasis on standing that he offered an altogether new reading of *Iliad* 1.6. He proposed severing *diastētēn* entirely and replacing it with a different kind of intimacy: the kind introduced by a woman. Upon this scholiast's rewriting, therefore, διαστήτην ἐρίσαντε became διὰ στήτην ἐρίσαντε [διὰ τὴν στήτην, διὰ τὴν γυναῖκα] ("having quarreled *because of a woman*").[59] This attempt to fix a perceived problem in the text starting with *diastētēn* draws attention to the poem's own insistence on leaving the woman out. The suggested emendation—what we might call *dia*'s final act of rebellion in the *Iliad*'s long tradition—is impossible but ingenious for its reframing of the *Iliad*'s priorities.[60] If the woman matters more than the men, then much of the tension we have identified in *dia*'s pull across the dual number is lost. By drawing attention to the poet's omission, the scholiast not only reminds us that the *Iliad* wants to work in twos; he also invites us to consider how women "stand beside," or how a woman might stand in relation to a man.

ODYSSEY

στῆ ῥα παρὰ σταθμὸν (*Od*. 1.333; 8.457; 16.415; 18.209; 21.64)

Repetition is a beloved wife of whom one never tires…

—Kierkegaard, "Repetition," (trans. Piety) p. 4.

---

59. Eust. *Il*. 21.43, Sch. DT p. 11H. Note Buchan on the dual as "a grammatical form which gestures toward a wider Iliadic fantasy of male like-mindedness and solidarity" (2012: 9).

60. The scholiast's reading, as Joshua Katz suggests to me, also points to the separability of *dia* in the Greek mindset. I thank Seth Schein for drawing the scholiast's misreading to my attention.

στῆ ῥα παρὰ σταθμὸν τέγεος πύκα ποιητοῖο,
ἄντα παρειάων σχομένη λιπαρὰ κρήδεμνα·
ἀμφίπολος δ' ἄρα οἱ κεδνὴ ἑκάτερθε παρέστη.

she stood beside the roof pillar of the well-built house
holding a gleaming veil over her cheeks,
and a trusty serving girl stood one on each side of her.
—Homer, *Odyssey* 1.333–35[=16.415–16]=18.209–11=21.64–66.

Homeric scholarship has well accounted for the repetitive motion of bodies in the *Iliad*'s battle books, as well as for repetition in language, formula, and verse structure.[61] But what about the same character repeating exactly the same (still) pose, in exactly the same place, over and over again in a single work?[62] To do so is to go beyond the kind of iteration we are used to seeing in Homeric formulas and type scenes, because that kind of repetition thrives on variation of character and context.[63] Penelope, by contrast, lends out her signature "standing by the stathmos" scene only once (to Nausicaa, and only its first verse, at 8.458), before reclaiming and repeating it another three times in the poem.[64]

In the last section of this chapter, I place Penelope's standing in oblique juxtaposition to what I have looked at so far in the *Iliad*, and consider how her repositioning of ἵστημι around the inner structure of the house changes the terms by which we can understand both narrative movement and gendered movement within the epics. As Marion Young's celebrated 1980 essay "Throwing Like a Girl" makes clear, women move their bodies differently because they have been socially and culturally trained to hold back from an early age. Her reading dovetails with Butler's articulation of a social script about subjectivity and power, wherein gender is constituted through a "stylized repetition of acts through time."[65] Such gestures will also register differently in the eye of the beholder, meaning that it is impossible for an audience not to perceive a woman standing differently from the way they would perceive a man.

61. Fenik 1968; Kahane 1994 (also discussed in my Introduction).

62. Calhoun 1933: 1.

63. As Nagy (2004: 141) puts it: "From the standpoint of oral poetics, the 'thrill' is not only in hearing a *notionally* word-for-word repetition of what has just been heard but also in apprehending the changes that are being made within this repetition. For example, there are changes that are required by the *shifting* of first/second/third persons in pronouns and verbs as the composer recomposes." It is not just the thrill that matters here, but also the development in meaning that comes through repetition.

64. The formula also appears at *Hom. Hymn Dem.* 186.

65. Young [1980] 2005: 27–45; Butler 1988: 520. See also Ahmed on gender and repetition and on how the gendered body occupies space and shapes objects (2010: 251ff.).

Figure 5.1. Trisha Brown Dance Company, "For M.G.: The Movie," 1991. *Source:* Photograph of TBDC by Mark Hanauer.

In a discussion between choreographers Yvonne Rainer and Trisha Brown about the latter's thirty-minute piece *For M.G.: The Movie* (1991, Figure. 5.1), in which one of the dancers stands upstage with his or her back to the audience for the entire performance, Brown noted the markedly different reactions elicited by the gender of the stander:[66]

> **TB:** ... I learn things after I make these [casting] choices, and I might
> add that I've tried a woman in the standing position, and when the
> man turns around to take the bow at the end of the piece, the crowd

---

66. Rainer 1993: 29. Many of Trisha Brown's early works explored the boundary between standing and movement, such as *Roof Piece* (1971), *Accumulation* (1971), and *For M.G.: The Movie* (1991). Note also Steve Paxton's "small dance," a Contact Improvisation exercise that involves standing, closing the eyes, and paying attention to the many tiny movements the body engages in to stay upright. The exercise materialized into a performance entitled *State* (1968, nn.5 and 9, this chapter). See further Banes 1987: 61. Rainer, Brown, and Paxton were founding members of the Judson Church Theater, one of whose many innovations was the sustained attention it paid to pedestrian movement (see further Banes 1987, 1993).

goes wild, and when the woman turns around there is just a little
applause.

YR: Isn't that weird? What do you make of that? For the man it's heroic,
and for the woman it's nothing.

TB: The man has more power automatically, standing there—he
obviously is doing something ...

YR: ... and if the woman does it she's perceived as doing nothing.

I do not mean to suggest that Penelope has no effect on her audience when she
stands beside the house's central roof pillar, but I do want to draw attention to
the equation *female is to nothing as male is to heroics/power/doing something* that
standing—as a quintessentially neutral pose—particularly illuminates. It gives
us one way, for example, of parsing the difference between Achilles and Penelope
as epic characters who adopt a standing position at crucial moments in their re-
spective plots, but also of differentiating between Odysseus and Penelope in the
Odyssey; for Odysseus too stands repetitively (if less formulaically) within the
Ithacan household, but on the threshold rather than by the roof pillar.[67] From
their respective positions, Odysseus stands and *acts*, while Penelope stands and
speaks, often ineffectually.

As the quotation from Kierkegaard with which I began this section suggests,
Penelope—as the proverbial long-standing wife and preserver of the home—is
also the *Odyssey*'s eternal iterator: the figure who retraces the same pathway
back and forth across her loom or up and down between her bedroom and
the great hall (*megaron*) below.[68] Her placement in the frame of the stathmos
scene signals—through its return to the same—the persistent unchangeability
of formulaic time when, as here, it is somehow left unaffected by the contingent
circumstances of each separate appearance. In what follows I consider each of
her appearances in turn, noting how they serve as interrupting poses that, al-
though static and unvaried, nevertheless focus the energies of the poem in a
stance of resistance to the ongoing status quo. By the time the *Odyssey* begins,
Penelope's attempt to go back over and over the same stretch of time by end-
lessly unpicking and reweaving her shroud has failed. Yet during the poem's first

67. In fact, he works up to a leap-into-stand (ἆλτο δ' ἐπὶ μέγαν οὐδόν, 22.2), from a crouching/
sitting position on the doorstep (he is depicted at 17.339 as sitting; see Steiner 2010: ad loc. on sitting
as indicative of Odysseus' helpless state [14.31, 18.395] and of Telemachus sitting helplessly at 1.114–18);
Odysseus appears at the threshold again at 17.413, 466; 18.110. The stand at 22.2 is thus triumphant and
teleological, and especially emphasized by Odysseus' pose, with one arm stretched back and the other
forward, a standing/straining of the whole body toward the *Odyssey*'s target.

68. Penelope's web has been a favorite figure for writers thinking about repetition. See Miller
1982: 6–8, on Walter Benjamin's "The Image of Proust" (2007: 202, discussing Penelope's work of recol-
lection and forgetting).

twenty-one books she moves through a new cycle, one in which she attempts to interrupt the suitors' rowdy ground-floor games via the precise and unvaried restaging of herself standing still beside the stathmos.[69]

Penelope's first entrance is presented as an interruption; she breaks in on Phemius' song about the homecoming of the Achaeans that Telemachus and the suitors are sitting for and listening to in silence (οἱ δὲ σιωπῇ / ἥατ᾽ ἀκούοντες· ὁ δ᾽ Ἀχαιῶν νόστον ἄειδε / λυγρόν, 1.325–27). Her appearance, which is introduced by verbs of movement (καταβήσετο, … ἀμφίπολοι δύ᾽ ἕποντο, … ἀφίκετο, "she descended, … two serving women accompanied her, … she arrived") followed by a tableau (στῆ ῥα, … σχομένη λιπαρὰ κρήδεμνα, … ἀμφίπολος δ᾽ ἄρα οἱ κεδνὴ ἑκάτερθε παρέστη, "she stood, … holding her shining veil … a revered serving woman stood on either side of her"), thus competes with Phemius' song. She intrudes with the actions of her body upon the affective power of his voice, setting a competition of sorts between the two: a visual staged scene versus an aural sung one. In fact, with her entrance Penelope insists that the song must be stopped because of its corporeal effects on *her*, on this body standing before them (*Od.* 1.340–42):

> ταύτης δ᾽ ἀποπαύε᾽ ἀοιδῆς
> λυγρῆς, ἥ τέ μοι αἰεὶ ἐνὶ στήθεσσι φίλον κῆρ
> τείρει, ἐπεί με μάλιστα καθίκετο πένθος ἄλαστον.

> Stop this baneful song,
> which always in my chest wears away my own heart,
> since unending suffering afflicts me especially.

Penelope's appearance materializes the notion of a body that matters. Already Athena had hinted as much to Telemachus about his own physicality—that he looks like Odysseus and is handsome and tall (1.207–9, 301)—but only in a vague way. Prior to Penelope's appearance, Athena's initial stance at the door of the Ithacan house had also set in motion the idea of a fully embodied, heroic arrival at the threshold (1.103–5):

> στῆ δ᾽ Ἰθάκης ἐνὶ δήμῳ ἐπὶ προθύροις Ὀδυσῆος,
> οὐδοῦ ἐπ᾽ αὐλείου· παλάμῃ δ᾽ ἔχε χάλκεον ἔγχος,
> εἰδομένη ξείνῳ, Ταφίων ἡγήτορι, Μέντῃ.

> She stood in the deme of Ithaca at the front doors of Odysseus,
> on the threshold of the courtyard. And she held in her hand a
>   bronze spear,
> likening herself to a guest friend, the leader of the Taphians, Mentes.

---

69. See further Marquardt 1985; Murnaghan 1986: 103–15, 1994: 76–96; Pedrick 1988: 85–101; Katz 1991; Wohl 1993: 19–50; Felson 1994; Clayton 2004; Mueller 2007: 337–62, 2010: 1–21.

Athena's pose prefigures her wish, 150 lines later, that Odysseus might appear in the same place at the door (1.255–59):[70]

εἰ γὰρ νῦν ἐλθὼν δόμου ἐν πρώτῃσι θύρῃσι
σταίη, ἔχων πήληκα καὶ ἀσπίδα καὶ δύο δοῦρε,
τοῖος ἐὼν οἷόν μιν ἐγὼ τὰ πρῶτ᾽ ἐνόησα
οἴκῳ ἐν ἡμετέρῳ πίνοντά τε τερπόμενόν τε,
ἐξ Ἐφύρης ἀνιόντα παρ᾽ Ἴλου Μερμερίδαο·

If only now, coming to the entrance of the house,
he might stand there, with his helmet and shield and two spears,
just as he was when I first saw him
in our house drinking and enjoying himself,
having arrived from Ephyre from Ilos son of Mermeros.

This vision of Odysseus sets up a fantasy that Athena cannot of course allow. It would be counterproductive for him to appear thus at the outer doors of the house, standing and armed, as a brilliant epiphany or tableau. But the image, coupled with Athena's own lingering in the same space, with *her* spear in hand, calls our attention always toward the door, as if we might still expect the absent body of the hero to materialize there.[71]

It is Penelope, though, who from within the house fills the space opened by the desire for Odysseus' body. Her physicality is insistent and her presence carefully and slowly described in a way no other character's has been so far (328–36):

τοῦ δ᾽ ὑπερωϊόθεν φρεσὶ σύνθετο θέσπιν ἀοιδὴν
κούρη Ἰκαρίοιο, περίφρων Πηνελόπεια·
κλίμακα δ᾽ ὑψηλὴν κατεβήσετο οἷο δόμοιο,   330
οὐκ οἴη, ἅμα τῇ γε καὶ ἀμφίπολοι δύ᾽ ἕποντο.
ἡ δ᾽ ὅτε δὴ μνηστῆρας ἀφίκετο δῖα γυναικῶν,
στῆ ῥα παρὰ σταθμὸν τέγεος πύκα ποιητοῖο,
ἄντα παρειάων σχομένη λιπαρὰ κρήδεμνα·
ἀμφίπολος δ᾽ ἄρα οἱ κεδνὴ ἑκάτερθε παρέστη.   335
δακρύσασα δ᾽ ἔπειτα προσηύδα θεῖον ἀοιδόν·

She heard [Phemius'] divine song from the upper chamber,
the daughter of Icarius, circumspect Penelope,
and descended the lofty staircase of her house,   330

---

70. Cf. Telemachus' earlier fantasy at 1.115–16, where he sits "seeing his good father in his mind's eye, if one day he would come home and create a scattering of the suitors in the halls."

71. On Odysseus as long absent (πολλὸν / δὴν ἀποιχόμενος), cf. 1.253, 281.

not alone, for two serving girls attended her.
When she arrived, shining among women, before the suitors,
she stood beside the roof pillar of the well-built house
holding a gleaming veil over her cheeks,
and a revered serving girl stood one on each side of her.   335
Weeping, she spoke then to the godlike singer.

Her appearance in some ways replays Odysseus' hypothetical one, with a few
lexical echoes from the first two lines of that passage spread out and expanded
through this one: δόμου and δόμοιο (255, 330); σταίη and στῆ ῥα (both at line
beginning, 256, 333); Odysseus wears a helmet (ἔχων πήληκα, 256), Penelope
a veil (σχομένη λιπαρὰ κρήδεμνα, 334); Odysseus appears with two spears,
Penelope with two servants (with δύ[ο] in the same metrical position, 256, 331).
But the differences are also telling. Penelope's stance explicitly announces her
arrival before the suitors (ἡ δ' ὅτε δὴ μνηστῆρας ἀφίκετο, 332), while the de-
scription of Odysseus avoids any such confrontation, instead veering into the
memory of a time when he sat in another man's house "drinking and enjoying
himself" (258).

   The νῦν ("now") of Odysseus' imagined appearance at the threshold thus
slips quickly into the past, but Penelope's body beside the stathmos, by contrast,
radiates with the sustained immediacy of her suffering in the present. Twice in
this passage the verbs for standing (στῆ, παρέστη) that frame her appearance
are coupled with the participle ἄρα, which Bakker has argued has a stilling and
illuminatory force within the hexameter, drawing our attention to the here and
now.[72] Still more insistently, she interrupts Phemius' song, which is rooted in
the past (ὁ δ' Ἀχαιῶν νόστον ἄειδε / λυγρόν, ὃν ἐκ Τροίης ἐπετείλατο Παλλὰς
Ἀθήνη, 326–27), and relocates it within the present: specifically the present as
experienced and suffered continually (αἰεί, 341) within her own dramatically
visible body.[73] Her *aiei* can be understood as a tributary of *aeide*, registering
Odysseus' absence in an internal and deeply personal sense. The baneful (*lugros*,
327, 341) song that causes pleasure in other listeners causes only pain for her,[74]
and her perception of time is different. Telemachus calls Phemius' song "most
recent," νεωτάτη (352) suggesting that for him it is appealing because fresh and
new, while for Penelope it is simply the marker of an enduring and ever-present
suffering.

---

   72. Bakker 1993: 1–29. Cf. Denniston on "the reality of a past event . . . presented as apprehended
either during its occurrence or at moment of speaking or writing," 36.
   73. Cf. Worman 2018.
   74. Pucci (1987: 195ff.) calls Penelope in this scene a "sober reader" and Telemachus an "intoxicated
one." On the effects of archaic song upon the listener, cf. Hes., *Th.* 98–103; Thalmann 1984: 134–84.

Penelope's appearance is thus a "standing still" within the text, the last in a series of tableaux that Athena subtly prepares for with her own arrival and then with her suggestive picture of Odysseus standing with his armor at the house's front doors. But it is Penelope's stance that first fully makes immediate the Odyssean body as a site caught in a state of suffering-through-the-present. Adopting a starkly different pose to those of the men sitting around her, Penelope stands out of place in her own home until she is sent back upstairs to "loom and distaff" by her son, to a room where she "wept for Odysseus, her dear husband, until Athena shed sweet sleep upon her eyelids" (1.363–64).[75] The phrase occurs four times in Homer, only for Penelope, and its recurrence (like the recurrence of the *standing by the stathmos* scene with which it is often paired) denotes the repetitive range of her actions within the poem, especially insofar as they are connected to her suffering.[76]

Learning from the examples of Athena and his mother and transferring their actions from the domestic frame to the masculine space of the agora, Telemachus prepares to make his own stand in Book 2 (10–11):

βῆ ῥ᾽ ἴμεν εἰς ἀγορήν, παλάμῃ δ᾽ ἔχε χάλκεον ἔγχος,
οὐκ οἶος, ἅμα τῷ γε δύω κύνες ἀργοὶ ἔποντο.

He went into the agora, holding a bronze spear in his hand,[77]
not alone, but two shining dogs accompanied him.

Like Penelope who traveled from her upper chambers "not alone, but two hand-maids accompanied her,"[78] he arrives in a similar fashion in order to make a public stand (στῆ δὲ μέσῃ ἀγορῇ, 37) and speech against the suitors. Each of these passages, I have suggested, traces a particular theme of arrival and imma-nence, a turning of the body toward a group in a gesture of defiance (Athena's in the doorway before the suitors in Odysseus' halls; Odysseus' in the same place in Athena's imagined depiction of his arrival; Penelope's beside the stathmos before Phemius, Telemachus, and the suitors; Telemachus' in the agora before the citizens of Ithaca), by means of the careful interlacing of a series of common

75. Wohl 1993: 19–50.

76. 1.363–64=16.450–51=19.602–3=21.356–57. Lowenstam (1993: 243) sums it up: "Penelope is restricted in her choice of actions."

77. The phrase παλάμῃ δ᾽ ἔχε χάλκεον ἔγχος occurs only twice in Homer, to describe Mentes' appearance at the doorway at *Od.* 1.104 and Telemachus' here.

78. Compare *Od.* 2.11: οὐκ οἶος, ἅμα τῷ γε δύω κύνες ἀργοὶ ἔποντο with *Od.*1.331: οὐκ οἴη, ἅμα τῇ γε καὶ ἀμφίπολοι δύ᾽ ἔποντο (=*Od* 18.207 [repeated passage]) and *Il.* 3.143 (of Helen). Some manuscripts have κύνες πόδας ἀργοί ("swift-footed," also the OCT) instead of δύω κύνες ἀργοί at *Od.* 2.11. See Heubeck et al. 1988: ad loc.

Iliadic formulas. Thus, although the phrase οὐκ οἴ[ος,] ἅμα τ[ῷ] γ[ε] ("not alone but together with") occurs ten times in Homeric epic,[79] and although some epic characters are typically accompanied by either dogs or serving women who travel in twos (δύω ... ἕποντο),[80] the cluster of images that accrue between *Odyssey* 1.103 and 2.11 depicts each of the poem's four major characters poised momentarily on the brink of changing things, and each time that pose is figured as a stand (ἵστημι).

When Nausicaa comes across Odysseus on the shore of Scheria, therefore (with not a door frame or roof pillar in sight), her stance is all the more pronounced for its variation on Penelope's from Book 1. For, instead of fleeing as her serving women do, Nausicaa alone stands her ground (6.139–41):

> <u>οἴη</u> δ' Ἀλκινόου θυγάτηρ μένε· τῇ γὰρ Ἀθήνη
> θάρσος ἐνὶ φρεσὶ θῆκε καὶ ἐκ δέος εἵλετο γυίων.
> <u>στῆ δ' ἄντα σχομένη·</u>

The daughter of Alcinous <u>alone</u> stood her ground. For Athena
set courage in her breast and took the fear from her limbs.
<u>She stood opposite, holding her ground.</u>

In doing so, Homer not only grafts the language of the battlefield onto Nausicaa's sphere of experience (witness some lines later her insertion of *amphipoloi* [serving women] into a typical Iliadic battle cry: στῆτέ μοι, ἀμφίπολοι· πόσε φεύγετε; 199), but he also combines it with Penelope's movement vocabulary inside the Ithacan house (1.331–34):

> οὐκ οἴη, ἅμα τῇ γε καὶ ἀμφίπολοι δύ' ἕποντο.
> ἡ δ' ὅτε δὴ μνηστῆρας ἀφίκετο δῖα γυναικῶν,
> στῆ ῥα παρὰ σταθμὸν τέγεος πύκα ποιητοῖο,
> ἄντα παρειάων σχομένη λιπαρὰ κρήδεμνα·

[Penelope descended] not alone, for two serving girls attended her.
When she arrived, shining among women, before the suitors,
she stood beside the roof pillar of the well-built house
holding a gleaming veil over her cheeks.

Whereas Penelope is οὐκ οἴη ("not alone"), Nausicaa is οἴη ("alone"); whereas Penelope stands beside the stathmos (στῆ ῥα παρὰ σταθμόν), holding (σχομένη)

---

79. *Il.* 2.745, 822; 3.143; 24.573; *Od.* 1.331=18.207; 2.11; 6.84; 15.100; 19.601. See Clark 1997: 223–24, 287 on οὐκ οἴη, ἅμα τῇ γε καὶ ἀμφίπολοι δύ' ἕποντο, and 18.206–7; 19.600–601.

80. Of slave girls (accompanying Helen or Penelope): *Il.* 3.143; *Od.* 1.331=18.207; of dogs (accompanying Telemachus): *Od.* 2.11; 17.62=20.145.

a veil before (ἄντα) her cheeks, Homer—compressing everything into a half-line—has Nausicaa stand and hold her ground before Odysseus (στῆ δ' ἄντα σχομένη). Nausicaa's form of self-presentation—as a potential bride, but also a potential warrior—shows through variation and repetition the choices that are no longer available to Penelope. Later, when she repeats the first line of Penelope's scene verbatim (8.458: στῆ ῥα παρὰ σταθμὸν τέγεος πύκα ποιητοῖο), she will stand by the stathmos as a farewell gesture that both mirrors the Ithacan tableau and supplements her own initial stance by the edge of the shore.[81]

Penelope's act of standing by the stathmos in *Odyssey* 1 as well as in 16, 18, and 21 holds at its core the notion of "standing as challenge" that both Nausicaa and Odysseus embody. But unlike Odysseus, who needs only to bide his time before he can leap into a standing position on the threshold with his son and allies beside him, Penelope repeats a single posture from which she can only ever turn away. The contrast between her stance and Odysseus' before the suitors is telling if we consider Odysseus' own "epiphany" at the end of Book 21 and the beginning of 22 (*Od.* 21.431–34; 22.1–4, 201–4):

Ἦ καὶ ἐπ' ὀφρύσι νεῦσεν· ὁ δ' ἀμφέθετο ξίφος ὀξὺ
Τηλέμαχος, φίλος υἱὸς Ὀδυσσῆος θείοιο,
ἀμφὶ δὲ χεῖρα φίλην βάλεν ἔγχεϊ, ἄγχι δ' ἄρ' αὐτοῦ
πὰρ θρόνον ἑστήκει κεκορυθμένος αἴθοπι χαλκῷ.   *(book end)*   21.434
Αὐτὰρ ὁ γυμνώθη ῥακέων πολύμητις Ὀδυσσεύς,   22.1
ἇλτο δ' ἐπὶ μέγαν οὐδόν, ἔχων βιὸν ἠδὲ φαρέτρην
ἰῶν ἐμπλείην, ταχέας δ' ἐκχεύατ' ὀϊστοὺς
αὐτοῦ πρόσθε ποδῶν, μετὰ δὲ μνηστῆρσιν ἔειπεν ...

So [Odysseus] spoke and signaled with his eyebrows. And the other one slung on
his sharp sword, Telemachus the son of godlike Odysseus,
and he took a spear in his hand, and near to him
beside his chair stood, helmeted in gleaming bronze.   *(book end)*   21.434
And then he having stripped off his rags, much-resourceful
Odysseus,   22.1
leaped onto the great threshold, holding his bow and quiver
full of arrows, and scattered the swift arrows
there before his feet, and he addressed the suitors ...

81. On Nausicaa as a preparatory double for Penelope, see Woodhouse 1930: 64–65; Lang 1969: 159–68; van Nortwick 1979: 269–76; Louden 1993: 5–33.

τὼ δ᾽ ἐς τεύχεα δύντε, θύρην ἐπιθέντε φαεινήν,   22.201
βήτην εἰς Ὀδυσῆα δαΐφρονα ποικιλομήτην.
ἔνθα μένος πνείοντες ἐφέστασαν, οἱ μὲν ἐπ᾽ οὐδοῦ
τέσσαρες ...

[The two herdsmen] put on their armor, having shut the
    shining door,   22.201
and they went to brilliant, many-wiled Odysseus.
There breathing valor they took their stand, all four of them
on the threshold ...

In each case the posture of·Odysseus and his men upon the threshold repre-
sents a turning point, as the poem looks toward the culmination of both the
return and the revenge plot. But on the edges of these frames, on the brink of
the *mnēstērophonia*, there is the promise of mobility. Penelope's presentation of
self, by contrast, matches more explicitly that of a photograph, for she does not
pass through the scene at the stathmos, as a character might do in a film frame;
she poses and remains there (as if forever).[82]

Later, when Eurycleia recounts the scene of slaughter in the halls to Penelope,
her description captures Odysseus in a standing posture that is evocative of a tragic
tableau (23.45–47):[83]

εὗρον ἔπειτ᾽ Ὀδυσῆα μετὰ κταμένοισι νέκυσσιν
ἑσταόθ᾽· οἱ δέ μιν ἀμφὶ κραταίπεδον οὐδας ἔχοντες
κείατ᾽ ἐπ᾽ ἀλλήλοισιν·

I found then Odysseus among the slaughtered corpses,
standing. And they all around him on the firm ground
lay on top of one another.

As if the central figure in an *ekkyklēma* tableau, Odysseus' final triumphant stand
on the threshold, with bodies piled around his feet, captures him in a lasting

---

82. Barthes [1980] 2010: 78, as quoted in Brinkema, 2014: 90: "[I]n the Photograph, something
has posed (*s'est posé*) in front of the tiny hole and has remained there forever (that is my feeling); but
in cinema, something *has passed* (*est passé*) in front of this same tiny hole: the pose is swept away and
denied by the continuous series of images." In her discussion of cinematic tableau, Brinkema argues
that photography and film offer different possibilities of motility for the figure in the scene, drawing on
Barthes' distinction between the two forms. See also Doane 2002: 10–29; Väliaho 2010.

83. The scene's resemblance to a tragedy in Eurycleia's telling is further enhanced by lines 40–41: "I
did not see, I was not told, but I heard only the groans / of the men being killed," words that liken her
experience of the "offstage" slaughter to that of a chorus or audience of a tragedy (Murnaghan 2018: 184).
I am grateful to Sheila Murnaghan for sharing with me her work on the tragic nature of this scene ahead
of publication.

moment of heroism that looks forward to what Athenian audiences will later see on the tragic stage.[84] As Clytemnestra proclaims over the corpses of Agamemnon and Cassandra, "I stand where I struck, with my work accomplished. / So I have acted ..." (ἕστηκα δ᾽ ἔνθ᾽ ἔπαισ᾽ ἐπ᾽ ἐξειργασμένοις· / οὕτω δ᾽ ἔπραξα ... , Aesch., *Ag.*, 1379–80), so too does Eurycleia use the perfect tense of ἵστημι to fix Odysseus against the background of his life-defining deed.

I have suggested how each of these forms of standing reflects differently on the notion of temporality. The scenes we have considered from the *Agamemnon* and Book 23 of the *Odyssey* suggest a tableau that is also a version of an ending: a final result that is rolled out for view, with the feet of the standing figure anchored by corpses as proof that the deed has been done. But Penelope's repeated stance of defiant orientation toward the suitors does not progress through the narrative as Odysseus' had. She repeats without variation the same movement phrase in Books 16, 18, and 21 that she had in Book 1, without ever standing, like Clytemnestra, in the perfect tense before a scene that has been completed.[85] Her stance, like the weaving and unweaving of her shroud at the stationary spot of her loom, puts her in a different position as agent in relation to her effect on the plot—always caught within its middle rather than at its beginning or end.

Instead, whenever she appears besides the stathmos, Penelope attempts to re-tune the house's story. Thus in Book 1, as we have already seen, she asks Phemius to sing a different tale. At her next appearance in Book 16, she bids Antinoos to desist from wooing her and plotting to murder her son (433: ἀλλά σε παύσασθαι κέλομαι καὶ ἀνωγέμεν ἄλλους), and in Book 18 (when she beguiles gifts from the suitors) she begins by reproaching Telemachus for his treatment of the beggar. Finally, in Book 21, during her last appearance at the stathmos and on the occasion when she brings Odysseus' bow with her, she is most explicit of all, complaining to the suitors that they have been continually (ἐμμενὲς αἰεί) wasting away her house with their eating and drinking, as if endlessly expanding the empty space of her husband's long absence (21.68–72):

κέκλυτέ μευ, μνηστῆρες ἀγήνορες, οἳ τόδε δῶμα
ἐχράετ᾽ ἐσθιέμεν καὶ πινέμεν ἐμμενὲς αἰεὶ
ἀνδρὸς ἀποιχομένοιο πολὺν χρόνον· οὐδέ τιν᾽ ἄλλην

---

84. Murnaghan 2018: esp. 184–86, and her discussion of Aeschylus' lost *Penelope*.

85. Or, to borrow from Barthes' terminology (n.82, this chapter), Penelope *has posed* while Clytemnestra and Odysseus *have acted*. See my discussion above for Telemachus, Odysseus, and Clytemnestra standing in the perfect (21.434: ἑστήκει, 23.46: ἑσταόθ᾽, *Ag.* 1379: ἔστηκα). In Book 18, Penelope succeeds in acquiring gifts from the suitors, but hardly presides over a change of scene.

μύθου ποιήσασθαι ἐπισχεσίην ἐδύνασθε,
ἀλλ᾽ ἐμὲ ἱέμενοι γῆμαι θέσθαι τε γυναῖκα.

Hear me, arrogant suitors, you who vex
this house with your eating and drinking, always continually—
the house of my husband so long absent. Nor were you able
to come up with any other outcome for this story,
beyond wanting to marry me and make me your wife.

This is Penelope's last attempt at redirecting the plot, and the instrument she brings with her (the bow), will finally work—but only after it has been taken out of her hands. As Victoria Wohl observes (1993: 42), "she tries one final time to take control of the circumstances and is met, once again, with Telemachus' by now familiar reply (21.350–53)." When she stands beside the stathmos, therefore, Penelope is the prelude, the preview, the interruption, the one who waits. But she is not, unlike her epic and tragic opposites, Odysseus and Clytemnestra, the one who completes an action of her own. Nor will she be present for the plot's reversal; after her appearance here, she will spend almost the entire remainder of the *Odyssey* within the house's private interior.[86]

Penelope, as I have said, stands at the stathmos repeatedly in Books 1 through 21 so that Odysseus can leap once onto the *oudos* in Book 22. To put it in the terms of Homeric composition, she, by repeating, enacts the principle of the formula, while he, by acting in this instance in an original way, embodies the notion of the *hapax*: the thing said (or in this case done) only once.[87] Or, to be more precise (because both characters' movements are deeply embedded in formularity), Penelope's pose expresses the formula's zero-sum threat: the paradox of self-referential repetition, or repetition without variation. The danger is that her pose will have no indexicality, and that Penelope thereby figures as more of a ghost or an echo within the linear sequence of diegetic time.

The patterns of that repetition emerge, I want to suggest, from the structure of the house; it is the strong allegiance between domesticity and repetition that grounds Penelope's unique status as eternal iterator. The space of home is felt or learned through a deeply engrained (and deeply comforting) process of repetition—the tracing of the same movement pathways through the home several times a day, year after year. The result, though, is that Penelope's signature scene becomes easily detachable within the time scheme of the poem. Because it is so securely anchored to the architecture of the house it threatens to float

---

86. *Od.* 21.350–53; 23.364–65; Wohl 1993.
87. In its full terminology, *hapax legomenon* ("thing said once"). For discussion of the concept of *hapax poioumena* ("things done once"), see my comments in Chapters 1 and 6.

free of time, engaging in a form of circularity that makes possible the suitors'
stunned reaction upon seeing her in Book 18 as if for the first time (18.209–13):

στῆ ῥα παρὰ σταθμὸν τέγεος πύκα ποιητοῖο,
ἄντα παρειάων σχομένη λιπαρὰ κρήδεμνα·
ἀμφίπολος δ᾽ ἄρα οἱ κεδνὴ ἑκάτερθε παρέστη.
τῶν δ᾽ αὐτοῦ λύτο γούνατ᾽, ἔρῳ δ᾽ ἄρα θυμὸν ἔθελχθεν,
πάντες δ᾽ ἠρήσαντο παραὶ λεχέεσσι κλιθῆναι.

she stood beside the roof pillar of the well-built house
holding a gleaming veil over her cheeks,
and a revered serving girl stood one on each side of her.
Their knees gave way on the spot, and the heart of each of them was
     bewitched with desire,
and all of them prayed to lie beside her in her bed.

The example reveals the paradoxical rush of limb-loosening originality that can
tumble from the exact and precise use of repetition. Yet, despite her considerable
presence, Penelope never breaks through into the action of the epic. Her stance,
although it stages a gesture of defiance, always instead ends in her own deflec-
tion ... away and back up the stairs, to a bed upon which she has wept so much that it
is stained (πεφυρμένη) by the accumulation of words and tears (17.101–3=19.594–96):

            But now I, going up to my room,
    will lie down in my bed, a bed wrought from my groans (στονόεσσα
        τέτυκται)
    and marred by my ceaseless weeping (αἰεὶ δάκρυσ᾽ ἐμοῖσι πεφυρμένη)

The bed, the house, and Penelope will all wait, worn and marred by the
traces of repetition, until Odysseus leaps onto the threshold at the begin-
ning of Book 22. The still, ongoing nature of her stance beside the stathmos
speaks finally, therefore, to the nature of her suffering and the problem of
its representation. Penelope's grief captures her in a nonspecific moment in
time, which is exhausting both for her and for us. The repetition of her stance
speaks to a duration that is similarly unspecified but emerges through the
multiple replayings of exactly the same scene. Perhaps it is her suffering that
distorts her representation in this way, so that it is not able to track forward in
the usual way through time. We are left, then, with a stance that is deeply orig-
inal in terms of its epic presentation (no other character utilizes standing as
Penelope does) at the same time as it is perplexingly repetitive, leading to little
apparent change in itself. But this stopping and starting, these forms of inter-
ruption, are important for the different elements of time and resistance they

Figure 5.2.   Étienne-Jules Marey, *Demeny Walking,* 1883. *Source:* Collège de France. Archives.

bring into the epic, showing how the body can gesture with powerful effect in a markedly different way to its masculine or "heroic" counterpart.

In an earlier chapter, I borrowed from Muybridge's experimentation with stop-motion photography to zero in on a single moment within the leap and crouch of the Homeric warrior. By contrast, as I discuss in my Introduction, Muybridge's contemporary Étienne-Jules Marey, who sought to capture a complete record on film of human physiological movement, chose not to break his images of loco-motion into separate frames but to blur them into one (Figure 5.2). The result is an image that multiplies movement onto a number of instantiations of the body, so that the same gestures appear to be shared and replayed across a number of different characters. Marcel Duchamp's *Nude Descending a Staircase, No. 2* (1912, Figure 5.3), which was inspired by both the chronophotographs of Marey and Muybridge and the development of the motion picture,[88] concentrated that reduplication into a sequence in which the instantiations of the body not only overlapped in a more concentrated and confusing form but also moved verti-cally, turning from top to bottom.[89] Duchamp's placement of the female figure inside the house paves the way for a form of movement that will later emerge, in Gerhard Richter's *Ema (Nude on Staircase)* (1966, Figure 5.4), as the blur of a single human figure. Richter's "Ema" is in motion, yes, but also—in a rendi-tion that is striking for its framing of a figure within the interior of the house—possessed of a curious stillness. She has a ghostly presence that suggests her reappearance in the same place over and again, and that is quite different from the earlier multiples of Marey and Muybridge that inspired it. In contrast to

88. "In 1912 … the idea of describing the movement of a nude coming downstairs while still retaining static visual means to do this, particularly interested me. The fact that I had seen chronophotographs of fen-cers in action and horse galloping (what we today call stroboscopic photography) gave me the idea for the *Nude.* It doesn't mean that I copied these photographs. The Futurists were also interested in somewhat the same idea, though I was never a Futurist. And of course the motion picture with its cinematic techniques was developing then too. The whole idea of movement, of speed, was in the air," Duchamp, quoted in Kuh 1965: 48; cf. Kern [1983] 2003: 117.

89. Cf. Muybridge, *Woman Walking Downstairs* (1887).

Figure 5.3. Marcel Duchamp, *Nude Descending a Staircase (No. 2)*, 1912. Oil on canvas, 147 × 89.2 cm. *Source:* Louise and Walter Arensberg Collection, 1950. Philadelphia, Philadelphia Museum of Art: inv. 1950-134-59 (© Association Marcel Duchamp/ADAGP, Paris/Artists Rights Society [ARS], New York 2018).

Figure 5.4. Gerhard Richter, *Ema, Akt auf einer Treppe (Ema, Nude on Staircase)*, 1960. Oil on canvas, 200 × 130 cm. *Source:* Museum Ludwig, Cologne, Germany (ML 01116, Köln).

the dark backgrounds employed in chronophotography to set apart the moving body, Richter's use of color and lighting blends the female body in motion *with* the staircase, so that the figure appears for the first time not as a blurring into and out of other bodies, but as a blurring out of and back into the interior of the house.[90]

I have argued in this book that a sharing and replaying of gestures between characters is intrinsic to the structure of Homeric epic, and that there is always a kind of fluidity in the repetition of formulaic gestures between bodies. Both Muybridge and Marey's sequences can be run together to create a moving image: the representation of a body moving through space in real time. By contrast, Penelope in the *Odyssey* emblematizes what some, in the study of early film, have called the "lost time" of the division between frames, where the stills of the moving picture reside.[91] Mary Ann Doane writes about this well in her book on cinematic time, explicating film's complicated relationship between movement and stillness. Like those lost interstitial fractions of time between the frames of a moving image, perhaps Penelope's presence by the roof pillar registers a different form of time for the poem, one that usually remains hidden beneath the reel of movement and action but that Homer here brings insistently to the surface.

90. Penelope's stance can profitably be situated between the twin poles of these ghostly descending figures, whose moving bodies bear a special relationship to domestic time, and the solid, unmoving, and heavy figures of women who have *become* columns: the Caryatids, as at the Erechtheum. My thanks to Meredith Safran for this suggestion.

91. Doane 2002: 172–205. See especially her discussion of Zeno's Paradox for film's complicated differentiation between movement and stillness.

6

Reaching

ἔτλην δ᾽ οἷ᾽ οὔ πώ τις ἐπιχθόνιος βροτὸς ἄλλος,
ἀνδρὸς παιδοφόνοιο ποτὶ στόμα χεῖρ᾽ ὀρέγεσθαι.

I who have endured such things as no other human being:
to reach the hands of a son-killing man to my mouth.
—*Iliad* 24.505–6

BEARING THE BODY

IN MY FINAL CHAPTER I WANT TO THINK ABOUT GESTURE ACCORDING to its very first definition in the OED; that is, as a "manner of carrying the body" (1.a.). Starting from this premise, I consider how our understanding of gesture changes when we think of it as a bearing through time as much as a movement through space. In the last book of the *Iliad*, we are invited to consider again the relationship between the time-burdened body and τλῆναι, the Greek word for endurance, but now not through the process of falling (Chapter 2) but simply through the practice of holding oneself up or carrying one's own body.[1] Agamben, relying on Varro, understands gesture as a means of "carrying" or "supporting," following the derivation of *gesture* from *gerere* ("a meaning transferred from those who *gerunt* 'carry' burdens, because they support them").[2] As he goes on to explain ([1992] 2000: 57),

> [w]hat characterizes gesture is that in it nothing is being produced [*facere*] or acted [*agere*], but rather something is being endured and supported [*gerere*].

This formulation is especially productive when it comes to understanding Priam and Achilles' gestures in the last book of the *Iliad*, for it helps us to read into their various postures something that language alone might not be able to articulate: the heaviness and slowness of grief, and its way of pressing the body

---

1. On endurance (τλῆναι) as "supporting," see especially Pucci 1987: 46–53, 66–74, 77–81. As he explains, the verb can mean "dare" in the active and "endure" in the passive, two definitions that the epics variegate in their depiction of Odysseus. Pucci, quoting Chantraine, writes (46), "the root *tla-*, *tlē-* means 'to take upon oneself,' whence on the one hand, 'to put up with [endure, support]' and on the other 'to take responsibility for'" (*DELG* 4:1088–90: "Prendre sur soi, d'ou d'une part 'supporter,' de l'autre prendre la responsabilité de").

2. Agamben [1992] 2000: 56–57, quoting Varro *On the Latin Language* 6.8.77. See also Agamben [1991] 1999b and [2005] 2007.

into new forms of expression.[3] It also helps us to make sense of the various ways in which the actions of the *Iliad*'s last book are framed by versions of holding (ἔχω, ἀνέχω, αἱρέω), holding on (λαμβάνω, ἅπτομαι, αἱρέω, γουνοῦμαι), holding up (τλῆναι), and holding out (ὀρέγω), which together articulate the key gestural coordinates of this chapter.[4]

Book 24 maps the difficulty of bearing one's own body onto the difficulty of bearing the body of others. Its opening quandary of what to do with Hector's corpse draws attention to its status as a body that cannot gesture in and of itself but that remains obstinately present as a burden for the others to orient themselves around as well as to "carry" and "bear." The dragging of Hector's body at the beginning of the book would thereby seem to speak to the drag of gesture itself: its slow undertow, even its clumsiness, its "moment of negativity," as one scholar has put it.[5] Achilles, at a loss for how to handle his own body in grief, tries out various postures for himself (many of them imitations of death) but none bring relief.[6] Instead, the body of Hector starts to bear the weight of Achilles' hopelessness, becoming a surrogate of sorts for the pain of gesture, the lifelong difficulty of bearing the body.

The corpse is, in one sense, wholly unnatural in its movements.[7] Its gestures are dragged and dead, pulled out of the human form by an external source. It is thus both perfectly responsive and entirely unresponsive or "dumb" (24.15–18):

> Ἕκτορα δ᾽ ἕλκεσθαι δησάσκετο δίφρου ὄπισθεν,
> τρὶς δ᾽ ἐρύσας περὶ σῆμα Μενοιτιάδαο θανόντος
> αὖτις ἐνὶ κλισίῃ παυέσκετο, τὸν δέ τ᾽ ἔασκεν
> ἐν κόνι ἐκτανύσας προπρηνέα·

> He would bind Hector to drag him behind his chariot,
> three times drawing him around the tomb of the dead Patroclus,
> and would stop again at the tent, letting him go
> when he had stretched him out face down in the dust.

---

3. On grief and the bending of form, I have found especially useful Brinkema 2014: 76–112.

4. I thank Victoria Wohl for helpful discussion on this point and many others in this chapter.

5. Noland 2008: xiii; on gesture's clumsiness, cf. Agamben [1992] 2000, as well as Väliaho on nervous gesture (2010: 25–51).

6. See my Chapter 2, n.26.

7. Or, as others would put it, entirely natural. The discussion of "naturalness" in relation to gesture has a complicated history, with some coming down on the side of gesture as inherently spontaneous and embodied (phenomenologists such as Merleau-Ponty), and others claiming that gestures are learned and culturally engrained practices (cultural theorists such as Bourdieu and Butler; see my Introduction for further discussion). For a good summary of the topic, see Noland 2008: xi–xii. Agamben [1992] 2000 believes that gesture was lost at the end of the nineteenth century and remained forever afterward an alienated form. See also Derrida 1978: 180 (quoted in n.95, this chapter) on Artaud. Kleist [1810] 2009 (discussed later) suggests that the corpse is a far more natural gesturer than the living, affected body.

We can reflect here on the posture of the Homeric corpse in death, and the ways in which Hector's body serves as an unwieldy double for Achilles.[8] For now, I want to draw attention to how the enforced activity of this scene emerges through various echoes of the corpse's name. "Hector" has long carried associations with "holding" (ἔχω),[9] but also in this instance we see it paired with "dragging" (ἕλκω), with iteration (the iterative tense marker -σκ- sometimes with τ, in δησάσκετο, παυέσκετο, ἔασκεν recalls the distinctive -κτ- sound in Ἕκτορα), and with the notion of lying "stretched out" (ἐκτανύσας). Hector's name, his identity, reforms under the strain of Achilles' grief into a series of gestures that threaten to repeat endlessly through time. Yet even under the pressure of this drag and haul, under the material force of earth and chariots and binding and dust, Hector does not lose his form. For Apollo "held off all unseemliness from his body" (πᾶσαν ἀεικείην ἄπεχε χροΐ, 24.19) by anointing it so that it could not be damaged or deteriorate.[10]

What, then, do we make of Hector's second-order gestures and their effect upon the poem? His corpse, as figured here, occupies the role of a sort of weighted marionette, which dumbly projects human gestures back upon its puppeteer in a partly prosthetic and partly organic way. Heinrich von Kleist's essay "On the Marionette Theater" argues that the gestures made by artificial limbs are free in a way that those of a living, affected body are not, since for the latter "an invisible and inconceivable pressure (like an iron net) seem[s] to capture the free flow of his gestures" ([1810] 2009: 268). So, Kleist's narrator argues, the living body, which cares, feels, and knows too much, can never dance as expressively as the marionette or the soldier who possesses an artificial limb. The marionette, however, is able to convey the "feeling" of the puppeteer through its own unrestricted movement—indeed, it *requires* that feeling in order to dance gracefully. Hector and Achilles share some of this gestural reciprocity between puppeteer and marionette, even if their bindings and forms are different. For in the movements of Hector, who does not dance below but drags behind, we can read the heavy toll of Achilles' affected self and his own gestural exhaustion in the trial of grief.

When Achilles first hears the news of Patroclus' death in Book 18, his reaction is to pour dust and ash down over his head, disfiguring his face and clothes. He then lies stretched out in the dust, dirtying and rending his hair with his hands. These self-deprecating gestures have attracted notice for their resemblance to

8. See my Chapter 2 on the gesture of falling in death and some of the ways in which the pose of the corpse on the battlefield is described.

9. The correspondence between the grieving self and the body in death is reflected not only in Achilles' various poses but also in Andromache's faint upon learning of the death of Hector (e.g., 22.448: τῆς δ᾽ ἐλελίχθη, "her limbs spun"), as discussed in Chapter 2.

10. Cf. *Il.* 23.184–91. Note also the repeated *ech-* sound in ἄπεχε χροΐ at 24.19.

his treatment of Hector's corpse in Books 22 and 24.[11] One can start with the depictions of Achilles' grieving body at *Il.* 18.23–27:

> ἀμφοτέρῃσι δὲ χερσὶν ἑλὼν κόνιν αἰθαλόεσσαν
> χεύατο κὰκ κεφαλῆς, χαρίεν δ' ᾔσχυνε πρόσωπον·
> νεκταρέῳ δὲ χιτῶνι μέλαιν' ἀμφίζανε τέφρη.
> αὐτὸς δ' ἐν κονίῃσι μέγας μεγαλωστὶ τανυσθεὶς
> κεῖτο, φίλῃσι δὲ χερσὶ κόμην ᾔσχυνε δαΐζων

> Taking the smoky dust with both hands
> he [Achilles] shed it down on his head, and defiled his lovely face;
> the black ash settled on his fragrant tunic.
> He himself lay stretched out in the dust, great in his greatness,
> and with his own hands tore and defiled his hair

and at 24.10–11:

> ἄλλοτ' ἐπὶ πλευρὰς κατακείμενος, ἄλλοτε δ' αὖτε
> ὕπτιος, ἄλλοτε δὲ πρηνής·

> Now [Achilles was] lying on his side, now again
> on his back, now again on his front

and compare this with his treatment of *Hector's* body at 22.401–4:

> τοῦ δ' ἦν ἑλκομένοιο κονίσαλος, ἀμφὶ δὲ χαῖται
> κυάνεαι πίτναντο, κάρη δ' ἅπαν ἐν κονίῃσι
> κεῖτο πάρος χαρίεν· τότε δὲ Ζεὺς δυσμενέεσσι
> δῶκεν ἀεικίσσασθαι ἑῇ ἐν πατρίδι γαίῃ.

> A cloud of dust arose over him as he was dragged, and on both sides his
> dark hair was spread out, and his whole head was lying in the dust,
> which before had been beautiful. For at that time Zeus granted
> for his body to be defiled by his enemies in his own homeland

and 24.17–18:

> τὸν δέ τ' ἔασκεν
> ἐν κόνι ἐκτανύσας προπρηνέα·

> letting him go
> when he had stretched him out face down in the dust.

11. They also associate him with other mourning characters, notably Priam, Hecuba, Andromache, and Briseis (Foley 1991: 158). μέγας μεγαλωστὶ (*Il.* 16.776=*Il.* 18.26=*Od.* 24.40) describes, in order of its appearance in the *Iliad* and *Odyssey* respectively, the death of Cebriones, the mourning of Achilles, and the death of Achilles.

Achilles' and Hector's face and hair are both repeatedly covered in dust and defiled (αἰσχύνω, 18.24, 27; ἀεικής, 22.395; ἀεικίζω, 22.404), their previous love-liness (χαρίεις, 18.24; 22.403) gone, and in both cases too they lie now again face down ([προ]πρηνής, 24.11, 18), now again stretched out ([ἐκ]τανύω 18.26; 24.18).[12] Hector's corpse can thus be said to capture the paradox of a body that is both worn down by the wear of endless gesturing and—because it remains inviolate—untouched by the gesture itself.[13]

The pose of his body as it is scraped and dragged, with hair in the dust and feet bound,[14] thereby creates an image of intense suffering that travels beyond individual bodies or single selves. Here Aby Warburg's art-historical concept of the *Pathosformel* ("pathos formula"), which reads into the form of a particular gesture the expression of extreme emotion, provides a language for talking about the intensity of suffering as it is encoded within gesture.[15] For Warburg, the "typical pathos-laden language of gestures" ("Die typische pathetische Gebärdensprache") in Classical art gives external form to the internal psychic "engrams" that he sees as constants in human experience.[16] As I discuss in the Introduction, Warburg's encyclopedic constellations of the body in motion in his unfinished *Mnemosyne Atlas* contribute to our understanding of both the recording and repetition of gesture.[17] What is apposite to the material in *Iliad* 24 is Warburg's fascination with gesture as an expression of intensity over meaning. Many of the gestures he identifies, such as the upraised arm,[18] changed their meaning over time and through the course of several different representations, but what mattered to Warburg was that the gesture itself always embodied a passionate intensity; a "formula" that emerges through the process of motion. Without drawing a correspondence between any specific gesture described in the *Iliad* and depicted in the *Atlas* (although Panel 47 intriguingly explores the various senses of "bearing"), I want to touch on the notion of the *Pathosformel*

---

12. On αἰσχύνω and the motif of "feared desecration" (cf. 24.411–23), which is put to rest in Book 24, see Foley 1991: 163–68.

13. The notion of "wearing" gesture, as if it were an item of clothing, can also be found in James [1890] 1950: 105, citing Dumont on "[the] acquired habits exhibited by dead matter."

14. The scene of the dragging is described in more detail at 22.395–404, although there the act is specifically said to bring "unseemliness" (ἀεικέα 395, 404) upon the body.

15. Warburg would say "pre-stamped" (*vorgeprägt*). See Johnson 2012: 21.

16. Johnson 2012: 62–63, quoting from Warburg's 1905 essay on Dürer's "Death of Orpheus." Warburg borrowed the term *engram* ("memory trace") from Richard Seman's account of memory. See also Gombrich 1986: 283–306; Michaud [1995] 2004; Warburg and Rampley 2009: 273–83.

17. See Väliaho 2010: 153–56; Noland 2008: ix–xxviii and 2009; Stern 2008: 185–215. For a good example of the dead gesturing under the pressure of the living, see the hand of the corpse in Rembrandt's *Anatomy Lesson of Dr. Nicolaes Tulp*, included in Plate 75 of Warburg's *Atlas*.

18. Barasch 1991: 119–27. "The movement of the raised right arm, seemingly a small motif, contains in a nutshell the great tragic tension that pervades the theme as a whole" (1991: 124).

to explore the dynamic between form and passion that Warburg believed was crystallized in these images ("the act of restitution remained positioned between *impulsive self-release* and a conscious and *controlled use of forms*, in other words, between Dionysus and Apollo ...."),[19] because it circles back to the intensity of suffering that Achilles recurrently tries to surface on the body of Hector, even as the corpse holds onto its own unchanged sense of form.

The body of Hector, therefore, comes to represent not so much *a* gesture as something inherent *to* gesture at this particular moment in the *Iliad*—its "drag," as I have suggested, its connotations with bearing or carrying, and its connection, in this case, to the intense suffering of both Hector and Achilles.[20] The latter's repeated actions in dragging Hector prove, as Apollo puts it, that he has "lost pity and possesses no shame" (ὡς Ἀχιλεὺς ἔλεον μὲν ἀπώλεσεν, οὐδέ οἱ αἰδώς, 24.44; later he will say that Achilles even "defiles the dumb earth in his madness," κωφὴν γὰρ δὴ γαῖαν ἀεικίζει μενεαίνων, 24.54). In a sense, therefore, Hector is forced to perform a "dead gesture" as Achilles attempts to pummel the body's meaning over and over again and evacuate it of feeling, even at the same time as the gesture itself expresses nothing so much as intense form *of* feeling: an excessive demonstration of grief and care.[21] Indeed, we might also say that, for all their feeling, Achilles' own gestures are similarly "dead," insofar as he invests his energy into objects (a corpse, the mute earth) from which he is unable to elicit a response.

Hector's heavy materiality in these scenes contrasts strongly with the *Iliad*'s other version of gesturing with death: Achilles' attempt to hold the shade of Patroclus (23.99–102):

Ὣς ἄρα φωνήσας ὠρέξατο χερσὶ φίλῃσιν,
οὐδ' ἔλαβε· ψυχὴ δὲ κατὰ χθονὸς ἠΰτε καπνὸς
ᾤχετο τετριγυῖα· ταφὼν δ' ἀνόρουσεν Ἀχιλλεὺς
χερσί τε συμπλατάγησεν ...

19. Warburg and Rampley 2009: 280, emphasis mine. In his preface to the translation of Warburg's "Introduction" to the *Mnemosyne Atlas*, Rampley discusses Nietzsche's influence on Warburg, but also shows that the Apollo-Dionysus opposition was reformulated to one that contrasted "the maintenance of rationalizing distance and empathetic absorption in the objects of perception" (Warburg and Rampley 2009: 274). See also Rabaté 2016: 9–10; Michaud [1999] 2004: 30; Levine 2017. On form under pressure see Wohl 2015 (a chapter from this book given as a talk at the Barnard Aesthetics conference in 2013 first inspired me to think about form as a category) and Wolfson and Brown 2006. See further Wohl 2015: 39–62, 98–104 and 2018 on the material weight of grief in Euripides, what she describes as being "weighed down by a melancholy materiality" (2015: 100).

20. Schein says of Achilles that he "is already dead ... psychologically and ethically beyond the human pale" (1984: 158).

21. Lynn-George 1996 (discussed in more detail later in the chapter).

So speaking he reached out his own hands
but did not grasp him, for his spirit went under the earth like smoke
shrieking. Stunned, Achilles rose up,
and clapped both his hands together ...

The emptiness of Achilles' gesture, beginning with a reach of the hands that fails
to connect and ending with a hollow clap, registers the impossibility of holding
or bearing his friend. In his chapter "The Gesture of Making," Vilém Flusser
understands the hands' inability to find their object as a casting of the body into
loss ([1991] 2014: 42):

It is easy to see how lost hands are in the world when they fail to find
"their" object. When hands find no object on which to impress a form,
impose a value, the world literally has no value for the hands.

Achilles' failure to grasp the spirit of Patroclus or to "impress form" upon the
body of Hector—one might even say his failure to deform its form (*a-eikizdo*),
a practice that Apollo guards against (ἀεικείην ἄπεχε χροΐ, 24.19)—leaves him
adrift in the world.[22] Through Achilles' desperate gestural relations with these
two bodies at the end of the *Iliad*, therefore, it becomes possible to locate spirit
and corpse at opposite ends of the spectrum of the body's capacity for alienated
and redundant gesture ("empty" on the one hand and "dead" on the other), par-
ticularly as it is filtered through the formal requirements of representing suf-
fering through time.

Indeed, Achilles' unresolved reach (ὠρέξατο, 23.99) finds an echo, a little later
in the poem, in a gesture that Andromache imagines for Hector. In her final
lament she regrets—as she holds her husband's head in her hands in a ritual-
ized posture of grief[23]—not having had the chance to touch him when he died,
or more specifically that "dying, you did not reach out your hands (ἐκ χεῖρας
ὄρεξας) to me from your bed" (24.743). In Andromache's lament, as in other
places in the *Iliad*, the correspondence between Ἕκτωρ and ἔχω ("to have, hold")
is stressed ("you are gone, [the city's] protector, you who / protected it, you held
safe [ἔχες] the good wives and innocent children," 729–30).[24] Even as the corpse

---

22. Freud's essay "Mourning and Melancholia" ([1917] 1971) also provides a useful way of thinking
about mourning and the "lost object," especially insofar as the dead weigh on the living and are difficult
to release.

23. *Il.* 24.724:Ἕκτορος ἀνδροφόνοιο κάρη μετὰ χερσὶν ἔχουσα ("holding the head of man-killing
Hector in her hands"). On this as a ritual, traditionally female, gesture of lament in the *Iliad*, see Kakridis
1949: 68–70 (with parallels to vase painting and Thetis at 18.71); Lateiner 1995.

24. Lynn-George 1996: 11.

rests in Andromache's hands, she projects various gestures (holding, reaching) onto it that she also enacts herself. As it was for Achilles, the corpse becomes a redundant double onto which the gestural language of grief is carried or projected.[25] And, as it was for Achilles, Andromache's own pose during her lament is a gesture of bearing, although now the body is held differently and carefully in the hands.

The verb ὀρέγω (*reach*), both as it is used here and as it appears in the passage with the shade of Patroclus (23.99), connects the impulse to reach out the arms with the attempt to bear one's own body or the bodies of others in moments of intense emotion. As I argue in the second part of this chapter, it is an expression that becomes especially crystallized at the end of the poem as Achilles and Priam struggle to cope, by means of their hands, with the problem of grief.

Reaching

Before starting on the journey to ransom the body of his son, Priam speaks of his desire to hold Hector, to support and close his body within the bend of his arms (ἀγκάς, *Il.* 24.224–27):[26]

εἰ δέ μοι αἶσα
τεθνάμεναι παρὰ νηυσὶν Ἀχαιῶν χαλκοχιτώνων,
βούλομαι· αὐτίκα γάρ με κατακτείνειεν Ἀχιλλεὺς
ἀγκὰς ἑλόντ' ἐμὸν υἱόν, ἐπὴν γόου ἐξ ἔρον εἵην.

If it is my lot
to die by the ships of the bronze-clad Achaeans,
then so I wish it. Let Achilles kill me straightaway
once I have taken my son into the fold of my arms and
released my desire for lamentation.

The gesture speaks to the significance of arms both outstretched toward others and retracted toward oneself, as it also hints at ways in which the final book

---

25. See especially Worman 2018 on Tecmessa's handling of Ajax's body, and in general for her discussion of the positions and gestures of Sophocles' onstage characters as they relate to the touching of the body in pain.

26. ἀγκάς *into, in, or with the arms* (Cunliffe 1977 s.v.): *Il.* 5.371 (of Dione embracing Aphrodite); 14.346, 353 (Zeus embracing Hera); 23.711 (wrestling); *Od.* 7.252 (Odysseus grabbing keel in shipwreck). Brügger 2009 ad loc. importantly compares this scene with Priam's words at *Il.* 22.426: ὡς ὄφελεν θανέειν ἐν χερσὶν ἐμῇσι· / τῶ κε κορεσσάμεθα κλαίοντέ τε μυρομένω τε ("if only he had died in my arms, / then we two could have sated ourselves with weeping and lamenting") and Andromache's (just discussed) at 24.743. We might finally compare here ἀγκαλίδεσσι at *Il.* 22.503, said by the scholiast (AbT) to suit the smallness of Astyanax being held in his nurse's arms (Richardson 1993: 286; Erbse vol. 5: 360).

of the poem will move toward resolution through a sequence of touching,
reaching, and grasping.

Scholars have observed that the difference between Priam's successful suppli-
cation of Achilles in Book 24 and Agamemnon's failed one in Book 9 is the phys-
ical presence of the suppliant.[27] Where Agamemnon stayed back and sent others
forward with his offer of reconciliation, Priam goes alone, and the importance
of his individual body—not only its presence, but also its phraseology—has
rightly been construed as instrumental to the scene. One of the gestures that
Priam will enact with that body, namely drawing Achilles' outstretched arms
toward his mouth to kiss, has stood out for many readers as the most memora-
ble in the *Iliad*. The verb that Priam uses to hold this complex sequence of ac-
tions together is ὀρέγομαι: *to reach*. We have twice seen ὀρέγω/ὀρέγομαι occur
in connection with lament and grief, and here no less it can be identified as a
reaching for what Priam still does not have.

As with other gestures in this book, I consider how Priam's ὀρέγομαι reads
when placed against the background of other "reachings" within the epics. But
where my other chapters place great emphasis on situating Homeric gesture
within a repetitive sequence of actions, this chapter takes as its focus a gesture
that Priam claims is entirely unique. Similarly, while I have often focused in
other chapters on movement sequences that are quotidian or pedestrian, my
reading here differs insofar as it occurs in a highly marked and memorable mo-
ment in the text. Finally, the gesture's association with repetition is again dif-
ferent insofar as it is drawn from iterative practices specific to ritual, rather than
from the broader category of the habit or training of the body.[28] Nonetheless,
part of my aim is to break down the "specialness" of this scene by structuring
my reading within the mechanics of the body.[29]

ὀρέγω/ὀρέγομαι[30] occur in archaic poetry in a number of guises, often in
connection with the hands. Thus Persephone in the *Homeric Hymn to Demeter*
stretches out both her hands to pluck the miraculous flower that emerges from
the earth (15–16: ἡ δ' ἄρα θαμβήσασ' <u>ὠρέξατο</u> χερσὶν ἅμ' ἄμφω / καλὸν ἄθυρμα
λαβεῖν ["she, in amazement, reached out with both her hands together / to grasp

---

27. Lynn-George writes of "a space left vacant by a king who in Book 9 never made this journey of
submission to the tent of Achilles" (1988: 239). Felson 2002: 35–50 sees Agamemnon as a bad father figure,
as opposed to Priam. See also Taplin 1992: 269; Lateiner 1995: 40.

28. See my discussion in the Introduction on Bourdieu's habitus and Mauss' "techniques du corps,"
as well as Bell [1992] 2009: 69–117. On the importance of ritual to Book 24, see especially Seaford
1994: 144–90; Lateiner 1995: 31–61; Gould 1973: 74–103.

29. On nonverbal communication in Book 24, see importantly Lateiner's chapter "Probe and
Survey: Nonverbal Behaviors in *Iliad* 24" (1995: 33–62). Our approaches are different but I hope
complementary.

30. Also ὀρέγνυμι, ὀριγνάομαι (*LfgrE*: *(st)recken, reichen*; *LSJ* s.v.: *reach, stretch, stretch out*).

the beautiful plaything"]) in a typical pairing of reaching and desiring,[31] while at the opening of the *Theogony* the infant Kronos sets the succession motif in motion when he "reached out from his hiding place [for his father's genitals] with his left hand, and took the monstrous sickle in his right" (178–79: ὁ δ' ἐκ λοχέοιο πάις <u>ὠρέξατο</u> χειρὶ / σκαιῇ, δεξιτερῇ δὲ πελώριον ἔλλαβεν ἅρπην). In both, the desire of a father figure (Zeus/Hades, Ouranos) stands in a misplaced or indirect relationship to the child's act of intentionality.[32]

In Homer, ὀρέγω may occur in scenes of prayer, to denote the stretching out of hands toward the gods (e.g., χεῖρας ὀρεγνύς of Achilles to Thetis at *Il.* 1.351);[33] in scenes of pleading or supplication;[34] in battle to denote the act of reaching forward with a weapon (as with Diomedes' reach for Aphrodite with his spear in Book 5);[35] or on an occasion when one might reach out to embrace a close friend or family member.[36] There are other occasions, too, when the verb occurs outside any specific type of scene,[37] as there are instances of reaching denoted

31. A connection that Aristotle later formalized in his coining of the term *orexis*. Pearson 2012; Nussbaum 1986: 273–6.

32. In the *Theogony*, Ouranos' desire extends (over Gaia) in all directions (*Th.* 177–78: ἱμείρων φιλότητος ἐπέσχετο, καί ῥ' ἐτανύσθη / πάντῃ), whereas Kronos' is oriented, sequential, and directed (χειρί / σκαιῇ, δεξιτερῇ). For another example of reaching in archaic poetry, using ἐπικέσθαι rather than ὀρέγεσθαι, see Sappho Fr. 105a; Carson 1986: 26–28; also discussed briefly in Purves 2016.

33. Also *Il.* 15.371=*Od.* 9.527: εὔχετο χεῖρ' ὀρέγων εἰς οὐρανὸν ἀστερόεντα ("he prayed reaching out both hands to the starry sky"). ἀνέχω is, however, more common, as Martin Mueller notes: "The collocation *cheir+oregō* is less common (6-4-2) than the collocation *cheir+anechō* (14–7). Both refer to stretching out one's hand in pleading or praying. In the *Iliad*, the uses of *cheir+oregō* cluster at the beginning and end of the epic, and it is tempting to see in them a more charged and context-bound version of the phrase *cheir+anechō*." *Eumaios: A Collaborative Website for Early Greek Epic*: http://panini.northwestern.edu, "Repetition Note *ad Il.* 24.506." Mueller is referring to the use of χεῖρας ὀρεγνύς at *Il.* 22.37, where Priam implores Hector from the walls (the other use of the phrase is at 1.351), as well as to 23.99 and 24.703 (all previously mentioned). For good examples of ὀρέγω denoting pleading, see *Od.* 12.257 (of Odysseus' men from the mouth of Scylla: χεῖρας ἐμοὶ ὀρέγοντας ἐν αἰνῇ δηϊοτῆτι, "stretching out their hands to me in the grim struggle"), and 17.366 (of Odysseus' stretching out his hands as a beggar: πάντοσε χεῖρ' ὀρέγων, ὥς εἰ πτωχὸς πάλαι εἴη, "stretching out his hands in all directions, as if he had been a beggar all his life"). At *Il.* 24.301, Priam says ἐσθλὸν γὰρ Διὶ χεῖρας ἀνασχέμεν, αἴ κ' ἐλεήσῃ ("it is good to stretch one's hands up to Zeus in the hope that he will show pity."). See further Pucci 2012: 427–44.

34. *Il.* 22.37 (see previous note), and the phrase that we will study in more detail within the chapter: ποτὶ στόμα χεῖρ' ὀρέγεσθαι (*Il.* 24.506).

35. *Il.* 5.335 (ἐπορέγω). Also *Il.* 4.307; 5.851; 13.190; 16.314, 322; 23.805; Richardson 1993: ad 23.805.

36. Achilles to the shade of Patroclus (quoted earlier in the chapter, *Il.* 23.99); the shade of Agamemnon to Odysseus: πιτνὰς εἰς ἐμὲ χεῖρας, ὀρέξασθαι μενεαίνων ("spreading out his hands he was striving to reach me," *Od.* 11.392); Hector to Andromache (*Il.* 24.743, quoted earlier in the chapter); Hector to Astyanax (*Il.* 6.466, quoted later in the chapter).

37. Serpents reach (ὀρωρέχατο) on Agamemnon's shield at *Il.* 11.26; Poseidon reaches with his stride (ὀρέξατο) across mountaintops at *Il.* 13.20 (cf. the reach [ὀρωρέχαται] of Achilles' horses' steps at *Il.* 16.834); Thetis reaches back (ὤρεξε) her cup, having drunk from it at *Il.* 24.102; Odysseus hopes someone will extend (ὀρέξῃ) him some food or drink as a beggar at *Od.* 15.312 (cf. 17.407); Penelope reaches (ὀρεξαμένη) to take Odysseus' bow off the peg at *Od.* 21.53. The instances of ὀρέγω that do not involve the

by different verbs that fall within the same semantic domain (ἀνέχω, ἐπέχω, τανύω, τιταίνω, ἐγγυαλίζω), as well as by verbs that indicate the end of the reach (ἐπιμαίομαι, λαμβάνω, ἅπτομαι, ἁρπάζω) and, after that, the moment of letting go (λύω).

As we saw at the start of this section, during Priam's preparations for the ransom of Hector he wishes for only one thing: to hold his child in his arms. Insofar as he envisages this moment bringing an end both to his life (αὐτίκα γάρ με κατακτείνειεν) and his grief (ἐπὴν γόου ἐξ ἔρον εἵην), he juxtaposes the expectation of extreme danger with that of extreme satisfaction. Thus for him the carrying of objects from storeroom to wagon (228–37) and the stretching of his hands (χεῖρας ἀνασχέμεν, 301) in prayer to Zeus are all perfunctory. For it is not Zeus or objects that Priam reaches for but only the body of his son; all of the rest is a rehearsal as such, a ritual carrying-in-the-hands (χεῖρας, 301, χερσίν, 303, 304) in practice for the moment when Hector is released.[38]

In the Achaean encampment, however, the terms of that carefully prepared gesture shift somewhat, for Priam never does lift the body of Hector. Achilles is afraid to let him and instead helps to bear the body himself, out of sight of the father (*Il.* 24.583, 589–90):

νόσφιν <u>ἀειράσας</u>, ὡς μὴ Πρίαμος ἴδοι υἱόν,
. . .

αὐτὸς τόν γ᾽ Ἀχιλεὺς λεχέων ἐπέθηκεν <u>ἀείρας</u>,
σὺν δ᾽ ἕταροι <u>ἤειραν</u> ἐϋξέστην ἐπ᾽ ἀπήνην.

[the slave girls] lifted him at a distance, so that Priam would not see
   his son
. . .

Achilles himself lifting him set him on the bier,
and his companions together lifted him onto the well-planed wagon.

The verb is not the same as in Priam's formulation, but the gesture is; Achilles' hands, bearing the body of Hector, approximate the role prepared for by the Trojan king. Perhaps recuperative too is the fact that Achilles, rather than binding the corpse alone to his chariot (22.398; 24.15), now works co-operatively by helping others bear it up and onto Priam's wagon.

---

hands, such as in the constructions ὀρέγω + εὖχος, κῦδος, or τάχος (*LfrgE* 763–64) are of some interest insofar as they carry the trace of an idea of the hand of a god stretching down and bestowing glory on a warrior, but I am concerned only with the explicitly gestural manifestations of the verb here.

38. Hecuba's touching is of a different kind. She fantasizes about sinking her teeth into Achilles' liver, using προσφύω (24.213; cf. the use of ἐμφύω in Thetis' supplication of Zeus at *Il.* 1.513, discussed later).

Instead of holding his son, moreover, the king adopts a different gesture with his arms, by grasping the knees of Achilles and kissing his hands. His posture is extraordinary enough to be described twice, first by the narrator when Priam enters Achilles' hut (24.477–79):[39]

τοὺς δ' ἔλαθ' εἰσελθὼν Πρίαμος μέγας, ἄγχι δ' ἄρα στὰς
χερσὶν Ἀχιλλῆος λάβε γούνατα καὶ κύσε χεῖρας
δεινὰς ἀνδροφόνους, αἵ οἱ πολέας κτάνον υἷας.

Great Priam entered unnoticed by them, and standing close by,
with his hands he grasped the knees of Achilles and kissed his hands,
terrible, man-killing hands, which had killed many of his sons.

The scene is described again by Priam in his address to Achilles (24.503–6):

αὐτόν τ' ἐλέησον,
μνησάμενος σοῦ πατρός· ἐγὼ δ' ἐλεεινότερός περ,
ἔτλην δ' οἷ' οὔ πώ τις ἐπιχθόνιος βροτὸς ἄλλος,
ἀνδρὸς παιδοφόνοιο ποτὶ στόμα χεῖρ' ὀρέγεσθαι.

Pity me,
as you remember your father. But I am more pitiable still,
I who endured such things as no other mortal on earth ever endured,
to reach the hands of a son-killing man to my mouth.

The initial gesture of stretching the hands out to Achilles' knees conforms to the standard practice of supplication.[40] But it is during the gesture's second stage, in the complicated transition between (1) Priam's hands on Achilles' knees and (2) Achilles' hands brought by Priam's hands to Priam's mouth, that the movement from one position to the next becomes hard to track. As Priam notes, this second movement, of kissing the hands that killed the son, is scarcely to be endured (τλῆναι). Yet it holds its place in the poem as something that neither Homer nor Priam will allow the reader to let go.

First, let us consider the hands that Priam kisses, famously described by Homer as "man-killing" (χεῖρας / ... ἀνδροφόνους) at 479, using an adjective that is then rearranged in Priam's phrase ἀνδρὸς παιδοφόνοιο ... χεῖρ' at 506 (to describe the hands [χεῖρε] "of a son-killing man"). The epithet *androphonos* has an interesting history in the *Iliad*, for—as others have observed—it is almost

---

39. It is also prepared for by Hermes' instructions to Priam to "go in and grasp his knees" (εἰσελθὼν λαβὲ γούνατα (24.465) and refracted in the simile describing the wonder that held Achilles and his men upon seeing him (482–83); Heiden 1998: 1–10.

40. See esp. Gould 1973.

exclusively applied to Hector (eleven times, always in the genitive to describe Hector's person: Ἕκτορος ἀνδροφόνοιο), until a temporary switch occurs between Books 18 and 24.[41] After an escalation of occurrences of Ἕκτορος ἀνδροφόνοιο in Books 16 and 17, the adjective is transferred to Achilles' hands, but now always in the accusative: χεῖρας ἀνδροφόνους (18.317; 23.18; 24.478–79). The first two instances, which describe Achilles laying his hands on the chest of Patroclus in a ritualized expression of mourning (18.316–17=23.17–18),

> τοῖσι δὲ Πηλεΐδης ἁδινοῦ ἐξῆρχε γόοιο,
> <u>χεῖρας</u> ἐπ᾽ <u>ἀνδροφόνους</u> θέμενος στήθεσσιν ἑταίρου

> The son of Peleus started up for them the deep-sounding lament,
> placing his <u>man-killing hands</u> on the chest of his companion,

contrast strikingly with the third, in which those same hands are kissed by Priam (24.478–79),

> καὶ κύσε <u>χεῖρας</u>
> δεινὰς <u>ἀνδροφόνους</u>, αἵ οἱ πολέας κτάνον υἷας.

> and kissed his hands,
> terrible man-killing hands, which had killed many of his sons.

After this scene, moreover, *androphonos* returns to Hector, with Ἕκτορος ἀνδροφόνοιο recurring at 24.509 (τὼ δὲ μνησαμένω, ὁ μὲν Ἕκτορος ἀνδροφόνοιο, "both of them were remembering, and [Priam] was remembering man-killing Hector ...") and 724 (ἦρχε γόοιο, / Ἕκτορος ἀνδροφόνοιο κάρη μετὰ χερσὶν ἔχουσα, "[Andromache] began the lament, holding the head of man-killing Hector in her hands"). This final gesture of Andromache (and the final use of *androphonos* in the poem) has picked up some of the resonances it acquired under Achilles' hands at 18.317=23.18 above, for on each of these occasions hands care for the dead, as they also accompany the line-ending phrase -ἦρχε γόοιο. So too, in the short sequence in which *androphonos* and *andros paidophonoio* interlock in Achilles' hut (478–79, [506], 509), we can see this notion of caring and remembering unexpectedly brought into play, as Priam takes his son's epithet back from the hands of Achilles, drawing along with it an associative vocabulary of mourning and handling. These are χεῖρε that not only kill but also, in the last part of the poem especially, bear suffering for the dead.

41. *Il.* 1.242 (the first mention of Hector in the poem); 6.498; 9.351; 16.77, 840; 17.428, 616, 638; 18.149; 24.509, 724. See further Whalon 1979; Sacks 1989: 152–75; Richardson 1993: ad 24.477–79; Lynn-George 1988: 239; and esp. Brillet-Dubois 2015. Felson 2002: 45–46 compares these hands with Achilles' χεῖρας ἀάπτους at *Od.* 11.502.

The cycle from the actions of "man-killing Hector" ("Εκτορος ἀνδροφόνοιο) in Books 1–18, therefore, to the man-killing hands of Achilles that killed many sons of Priam (χεῖρας / δεινὰς ἀνδροφόνους, αἵ οἱ πολέας κτάνον υἷας) at 24.479, to those same hands described as "of a son-killing man" (ἀνδρὸς παιδοφόνοιο) at 24.506, and finally back around to Priam remembering his own (man-killing) son ("Εκτορος ἀνδροφόνοιο) at 24.509, shows how, from the very start of the description of Priam's supplication, there has been a gradual migration and return within the gesture from Hector to Achilles, killer to killed, and father to son. This sequence complicates the terms of exactly whose hands Priam is kissing.[42] The hands express a kind of reversibility, therefore, between the identities of the poem's two most strongly opposed characters.

Critics have also remarked upon the tricolon crescendo in enjambment of χεῖρας [hands] / δεινὰς [terrible] ἀνδροφόνους [man-killing], αἵ οἱ πολέας κτάνον υἷας [which had killed many of his sons] at 478–79, where the three units that describe the hands build with an increasing number of syllables along the line.[43] The verse forces us to linger on the hands, registering the time that they spend on the lips as the dawning realization of the gesture's significance is spelled out slowly along the rhythm of the line. Equally gradually, Priam's mouth must register the escalating visceral importance of the hands as they are held, felt, and kissed. As Irene de Jong observes, what we have here is a moment of embedded focalization, in which "the relative clause [αἵ] forms a kind of epexegesis of the epithet ἀνδροφόνους and gives expression to what must flash through Priam's head at the moment he kisses Achilles' hands" (1987: 119–20 and n.54).

Thus the gesture, even as it holds onto the hands, braces against the dissonance and harsh paradox of what it expresses. This is not at all what Priam articulated when he spoke of holding Hector in his arms (ἀγκάς). Yet the interlocking of Priam and Achilles through hands, knees, and mouth also works to bridge

---

42. King notes that four parent-child similes (9.323–25; 16.7–10; 18.318–22; 23.222–23) "have created an enduring feeling that Achilles' loss of Patroklos is equivalent to a parent's loss of a child" (1987: 42). Cf. Crotty 1994: 97: "the elderly Priam ... tak[es] on the childlike position of the suppliant, while the young Achilles is cast in the role of the father." Platt (forthcoming) offers a detailed reading of this scene as it is represented on the first-century BCE/CE silver cups of Cheirisophos.

43. Richardson 1993: ad loc.: "The next verse spells out the awful significance of this action"; cf. Macleod 1982: ad loc.; Felson 2002: 46. Lynn-George 1988: 238ff., is especially good on the language of this passage; he observes that the pairing of αἵ and οἱ in the middle of the hexameter has a profound effect: "two words so close, in form and in the gesture itself, and yet so far apart—the confrontation of αἵ and οἱ with reference to the hands and to the father." Also, "Priam links himself to hands that preserve the associations of the already slain" (1988: 239). As he observes, the epithet points to the absence of not only Hector but also Patroclus, whose body the hands were placed on in Books 18 and 23. See also, on this adjective, Redfield: "there is a contrast between the killing power of the hands and their gentle gesture" when laid on the chest of Patroclus (1975: 215).

various physical gaps left open earlier in the poem, as Priam's reaching of his hands back toward his own mouth forges a bending at the elbow. In Book 22, Priam had stretched his hands out to Hector from the walls of Troy, but failed to reach or persuade him (22.37: τὸν δ᾽ ὁ γέρων ἐλεεινὰ προσηύδα χεῖρας ὀρεγνύς, "the old man addressed him pitifully stretching out his hands"), just as Achilles' gesture of reaching for the shade of Patroclus in Book 23 remained unfulfilled (23.99–100: ὣς ἄρα φωνήσας ὠρέξατο χερσὶ φίλῃσιν, / οὐδ᾽ ἔλαβε, "So speaking he reached out with his own hands / but he did not grasp him").

These failures to connect can be said formally to resolve themselves in the intertwining of hands at the end of the poem. For not only does the chiastic structure of χερσίν ... χεῖρας at 478 create a doubling in the verse, but there is also the overlaying of father upon father and son upon son, as Peleus doubles for Priam and the hands of Achilles are twice marked (ἀνδροφόνος, παιδοφόνος) by their relationship to Hector. As James Redfield observes, the epithet also reminds us that "the man-slaying hands slew a man-slayer, that Achilles has done nothing to Hector which Hector did not promise Patroclus" (1975: 215). This mutually reinforcing and binding image thus seems to suggest the coincidence of touch, a reaching the end of the reach, as it were, culminating in a gesture that is often described as a moment of shared humanity between the two men.[44] And, as scholars have noted, the intricate choreography of Priam and Achilles' "embrace" brings other characters into its orbit too: not just Peleus and Hector, but also Patroclus, and—if we trace the gesture's *engram* through past and future scenes of this type—Thetis and Neoptolemus.[45] As such it offers a form of temporary resolution and reconciliation, a gathering together of characters and emotions, as well as an attempt to cross the boundary between the living and the dead. The effort to cross that divide creates the unlikely pairing of father and child-killer, with each providing a physical structure for the other to help in managing grief's gestural burden.

Yet Priam's collapsing of the narrator's contact verbs λάβε (*grasped*) and κύσε (*kissed*, 478) into the enigmatic ὀρέγεσθαι at 506 creates something of a puzzle in the text, for the line is syntactically anomalous.[46] The verb, as we have seen, means to reach, but here its agency is uncertain. According to Homer's prior description of the kiss, the whole line must mean "reach the hands (χεῖρε [accusative] ὀρέγεσθαι) of a son-killing man (ἀνδρὸς παιδοφόνοιο) to my mouth (ποτὶ στόμα)." Yet the elided final letter of χεῖρ᾽, along with the middle

44. King 1987: 37–45; Crotty 1994: 4; Segal 1971a; Crotty argues that the characters in Book 24 "experience ... an enlargement of their vision and understanding of the world" (1994: 15).

45. Lynn-George 1988: 239 notes that the epithet points to the absence of not only Hector but also Patroclus, whose body the hands were placed on in books 18 and 23.

46. Brügger says of 24.506 that the verse presents itself syntactically and pragmatically as an "ebene Schwierigkeit" (2009: ad loc.).

voice of ὀρέγεσθαι, opens up the possibility of an altogether different gesture. Grammatically, it would make more sense to translate the middle form of the verb with an instrumental dative (as with Achilles' ὡρέξατο χερσί at 23.99 and every other example so far cited), therefore "to reach [for myself] *with my hand* (χειρὶ ὀρέγεσθαι, thus χείρ' ὀρέγεσθαι) to the mouth of a son-killing man."[47]

This alternative gesture fits better with scenes of supplication that begin with the grasping of knees.[48] We can compare Thetis' supplication of Zeus in Book 1, where she is said to grasp his knees with one hand and his chin with the other (1.500–501):[49]

καί ῥα πάροιθ' αὐτοῖο καθέζετο, καὶ λάβε γούνων
σκαιῇ, δεξιτερῇ δ' ἄρ' ὑπ' ἀνθερεῶνος ἑλοῦσα

And she sat down before him and grasped his knees
with her left hand, and with her right she took hold of his chin.

Priam could then just be supplicating Achilles in an entirely traditional and un-exceptional way, but we can only see the trace of this gesture beneath the outline of the other, for Homer explicitly said "kissed" at 478, and there is no instance, as Walter Pötscher notes, of a suppliant reaching for the mouth (rather than the chin) of the supplicant.[50]

47. This is the reading supported by Leaf and possibly Eustathius. Vergil also seems to support it in his description of the frieze at Carthage at *Aen.* 1.487: *tendentemque manus Priamum conspexit inermis* ("and he saw Priam stretching out his defenceless hands," as quoted by Macleod 1982: ad 24.506). See further on the problem Richardson 1993: ad loc., who notes that the version of events wherein Priam stretches his hands to Achilles' mouth affords a less complex word order. The elided iota is more un-usual in Homer but does occur—we find the iota of the instrumental dative with χείρ' elided in χείρ' ἐπιμασσάμενος at *Od.* 9.302; 19.480, quoted in n.58, this chapter. See further *GH* vol. 1, 85–86; Monro [1882] 1891: paragraphs 373, 376.3; Sider 2005: 166, n.1. Artistic evidence supports both interpretations of the line: Priam reaches his hand to Achilles' chin (*LIMC* vol. 1.1 p. 148, no. 642; Trendall and Webster 1971: 57); Priam kisses Achilles' hand (*LIMC* p. 154, no. 687; Johansen 1967: 49–51), see also Miller 1995: 449–65; Platt, forthcoming (chap. 2). For the most detailed analysis of the gesture, see Pötscher, who argues for "reached the hands of a son-killing man to my mouth to kiss" (1992). This must be the correct interpretation, but I think the line retains aspects of both readings.

48. Richardson 1993: ad 24.477–79. "Only here in Homer does a suppliant kiss the hands, a gesture which is a sign of welcome and affection at *Od.* 21.225, 22.499–500, esp. 24.398." On scenes of supplication in Greek art, particularly in reference to the supplications in *Iliad* 1 and 24, see Neumann 1965: 68–71; Platt, forthcoming.

49. Later, at *Il.* 8.371, Athena says that Thetis "kissed Zeus' knees and took hold of his chin with her hand." Richardson 1993: ad 24.477–79; Gould 1973. The changing of the terms of a gesture is not uncommon in Homer (see also the different styles of throwing Hephaestus from Olympus in *Iliad* 1 and 18, discussed in my Chapter 2), but it would be unusual for it to take place at such close quarters in the text.

50. The T Scholia suggest the variant λάβε for κύσε at 478. See further Pötscher 1992.

The examples I have provided to explicate the difficulty of *cheir' oregesthai* have been well discussed in the scholarship, but one further possibility has not. Since Priam insistently recalls Peleus to Achilles (μνησάμενος σοῦ πατρός, 504), the gesture could also resemble the posture of a father who reaches his hands toward his son's mouth when feeding him as a child.[51] In Book 9, Phoenix talks of proffering bread and wine to Achilles as the boy sat on his knees (γούνεσσι καθίσσας, 9.488); such a gesture would of course involve reaching (ἐπισχών, 489) his own hands to the boy's mouth.[52] If we can see this gesture in the background of the first one, then the relative positions of Achilles and Priam in Book 24, although clear in one sense, can also be read in the other direction, as one of nurture between a father and a son.

The bidirectionality of the gesture speaks to an ambivalent reciprocity or reversibility, as I have already suggested, between the actors as their bodies meet in touch, which is in itself a famously indeterminate and subject-displacing form of contact.[53] Merleau-Ponty has referred to the "non-coincidence" of the left hand touching the right, insofar as they cannot meet in time ("my left hand is always on the verge of touching my right hand touching the things, but I never reach coincidence …"),[54] and so here too we find that an attempt to grasp fully the touch shared by Priam and Achilles results in an endless re-circuiting; a splitting and reconnecting between dative and accusative, singular and dual, active and middle, as between λαμβάνω, κυνέω, and ὀρέγω, and hands, knees, and mouths. In cognitive processing terms, we might consider how the brain's sensorimotor capacities and mirror neurons are misfired by these tiny and temporary kinetic confusions.[55] These confusions are important, for they open up a productive space of indeterminacy for a posture that is caught in the surround of a bewildering array of emotions, including (but not limited to) grief, hostility, intimacy, abjection, alienation, wonder, and disgust.

---

51. On the reciprocal care between father and son, see Felson 2002, who does not mention this passage but points to ways in which Achilles' desire to repay (ἀποδίδωμι) care (θρέπτρα) to his father, as well as his father substitutes such as Phoenix, contribute to Achilles' sympathetic treatment of Priam in *Iliad* 24.

52. The connection with Phoenix as a third "father" in this passage is made by others. See especially Heath 2005: 144 ff. with further bibliography for the parallels between the scene in *Iliad* 24 and the one with Phoenix in *Iliad* 9.

53. See especially Stewart 1999 and 2002; Paterson 2007 and further references in Purves 2018: 1–20.

54. Merleau-Ponty [1964] 1968: 147–48. See also Stewart 1999.

55. Bolens [2008] 2012: 17, "literature … triggers the activation of unpredicted sensorimotor configurations and surprises the mind with its own imaginative and cognitive potentialities."

In commenting on Merleau-Ponty's essay on the non-coincidence of touch, Judith Butler writes (2015: 53–54),

> I am not touched as I touch, and this noncoincidence is essential to me and to touch, but what does it mean? It means that I cannot always separate the being touched from the touching, but neither can they be collapsed into one another. There is no mirror image, and no reflexivity, but a coiling and folding, suggesting that there are moments of contact, of nonconceptualizable proximity, but that this proximity is not an identity, and it knows no closure.

The resistance that Merleau-Ponty notes in his account of touch's reach toward closure allows, in Butler's words, for an incomplete merging of the toucher and the touched, in a form of blurring that captures the back and forth between the owners of the hands and mouths in the *Iliad* passage. But what is particularly important here is that Priam and Achilles fleetingly become interchangeable in the small gap opened up not so much by touching as by reaching (ὀρέγεσθαι), in the moment *before* the gesture closes in on the clasping together of father's and son-killer's hands.[56]

There seems to be a kind of slip in language that has taken place, therefore, that mirrors a sleight of hand within the gesture itself.[57] Elsewhere in epic poetry careful attention is paid to the sequencing of left hand and right. We have already commented on the deliberateness with which Hesiod depicts Kronos' act of reaching with first one hand and then the other in the *Theogony* (ὠρέξατο χειρὶ / σκαιῇ, δεξιτερῇ ... ἔλλαβεν, "he reached with his left hand and grasped with his right," 178–79), as we have also seen the line-initial pairing of σκαιῇ, δεξιτερῇ in Thetis' supplication of Zeus (λάβε γούνων / σκαιῇ, δεξιτερῇ δ' ἄρ' ὑπ' ἀνθερεῶνος ἑλοῦσα, "she took him by the knees with her left hand, having grabbed his chin from underneath with her right," *Il.* 1.501).[58] A further example comes from the scene depicting the supplication of Achilles by Lycaon on the

---

56. As Mark Buchan points out to me, the middle voice of ὀρέγομαι reflects this interchangeability of subject and object, as it also connects to the substantial body of research on the active/passive nature of Odysseus as endurer. See Pucci 1987 (n.1, this chapter) on the active and passive meanings of τλῆναι as they relate to Odysseus as both "darer" and "sufferer"; also note the dual meaning of ὀδύσσομαι. See further Peradotto 1990; Cook [1999] 2009.

57. Note also that Achilles' hands are called "untouchable" ἄαπτους at *Od.* 11.502 (as observed by Felson 2002: 45–46 in relation to their Iliadic epithet of man- or child-slaying).

58. It occurs also at *Il.* 21.490 to describe Athena disarming Artemis in battle. Finally, Odysseus, in silencing Eurycleia, is described as χείρ' ἐπιμασσάμενος φάρυγος λάβε δεξιτερῆφι, / τῇ δ' ἑτέρῃ ἕθεν ἆσσον ἐρύσσατο φώνησέν τε ("feeling he took her throat with his right hand / and with the other drew her close to him and spoke," *Od.* 19.480–81).

battlefield at *Il.* 21.64–75, where Lycaon uses one hand and then the next (τῇ ἑτέρῃ … / τῇ δ᾽ ἑτέρῃ) in a quick-thinking series of moves:[59]

Ὣς ὥρμαινε μένων· ὁ δέ οἱ σχεδὸν ἦλθε τεθηπώς,
<u>γούνων ἅψασθαι</u> μεμαώς, περὶ δ᾽ ἤθελε θυμῷ·   65
ἐκφυγέειν θάνατόν τε κακὸν καὶ κῆρα μέλαιναν.
ἤτοι ὁ μὲν δόρυ μακρὸν ἀνέσχετο δῖος Ἀχιλλεὺς
οὐτάμεναι μεμαώς, ὁ δ᾽ ὑπέδραμε καὶ <u>λάβε γούνων</u>
κύψας· ἐγχείη δ᾽ ἄρ᾽ ὑπὲρ νώτου ἐνὶ γαίῃ
ἔστη, ἱεμένη χροὸς ἄμεναι ἀνδρομέοιο.   70
αὐτὰρ ὁ <u>τῇ ἑτέρῃ μὲν ἑλὼν ἐλλίσσετο γούνων</u>,
<u>τῇ δ᾽ ἑτέρῃ</u> ἔχεν ἔγχος ἀκαχμένον οὐδὲ μεθίει·
καί μιν φωνήσας ἔπεα πτερόεντα προσηύδα·
"<u>γουνοῦμαί</u> σ᾽, Ἀχιλεῦ· σὺ δέ μ᾽ αἴδεο καί μ᾽ ἐλέησον·
ἀντί τοί εἰμ᾽ ἱκέταο, διοτρεφές, αἰδοίοιο."   75

So he considered, waiting. And [Lycaon] came close to him, stunned,
desperate to <u>grasp his knees</u>, for he desired very much in his heart   65
to flee evil death and dark destruction.
Then brilliant Achilles held up his long spear,
eager to stab him, but Lycaon ran under and <u>took his knees</u>,
bending down, and the spear went over his back and
stood in the ground, wanting to be sated with human flesh,   70
and he having <u>grasped his knees</u> <u>with one hand</u> was beseeching,
<u>and with the other</u> he held onto the sharp-pointed spear and would
    not let go.
Speaking out winged words he addressed Achilles:
"I am <u>at your knees</u>, Achilles. Respect and pity me,
godlike one, for I am here in the place of an honored suppliant."   75

The emphasis on "holding on" in the description of Lycaon's supplication is striking. Achilles' knees appear three times as the genitive object of words for grasping (ἅπτομαι, λαμβάνω, αἱρέω, as well as once in their own verbal form [γουνοῦμαι]).[60] The reach itself is unexpressed, although prepared for by the references to desire (μεμαώς twice; ἱεμένη) and by the span of the spear's flight, under which Lycaon stretches forward and around. Once knees and spear have

---

59. On Lycaon's *Doppelgestus* here, see Friedrich 1956: 100–102; Cairns 1993: 116–18; Schein 2016: 167–70. Schein notes (169) that Simone Weil "returned again and again" to translating two scenes in particular: Priam's visit to Achilles and Lycaon's supplication. On the intertextual connection between this scene and *Od.* 22.312, see Bakker 2013: 154.

60. On *gounoumai*, see Pedrick 1982: 125–40.

been grasped, moreover, there is a determined effort not to let go (οὐδὲ μεθίει). Supplication, Lycaon teaches us, is a pose in which one wants to stay as long as possible, and optimally involves a kind of grafting onto the body of another. Thus Thetis in *Iliad* 1, when receiving no response from Zeus the first time around, remains where she is and tightens her grip, so that she "grows into" Zeus (Θέτις δ' ὡς ἥψατο γούνων / ὡς ἔχετ' ἐμπεφυυῖα, "Thus Thetis clasped his knees / and held fast, grafting herself to them," 1.512–13).[61] Only then does he assent to her wish.

In Lycaon's case the stakes are much higher: to stay holding on to Achilles' knees and spear is to stay upright and alive.[62] There is a sense in both cases of holding on and enduring through time. For Lycaon, however, as with other examples of Homeric supplication for one's life,[63] the carrying out of a gesture becomes not an action but a "bearing"—a supporting of oneself in an attempt to keep the body alive.

When Lycaon lets go of Achilles' spear and knees and submits to death, therefore, this final gesture undoes all the work of supplication that had gone before (21.114–16):

Ὣς φάτο, τοῦ δ' αὐτοῦ λύτο γούνατα καὶ φίλον ἦτορ·
ἔγχος μέν ῥ' ἀφέηκεν, ὁ δ' ἕζετο χεῖρε πετάσσας
ἀμφοτέρας·

So he spoke, and on the spot his knees went slack and his own heart.
He let go of the spear, and he sat back stretching wide his arms,[64]
both of them.

The words τοῦ δ' αὐτοῦ λύτο γούνατα ("his knees went slack on the spot") refer to Lycaon's severe emotional distress (the same phrase, *mutatis mutandis*, is used of Penelope, Laertes, and the suitors when they are overwhelmed with emotion in the *Odyssey*).[65] But the loosening of Lycaon's knees, in a phrase that recalls the formulaic λῦσε δὲ γυῖα ("he unstrung his limbs," used frequently in

---

61. See further Gould: "ἔχετ' ἐμπεφυυῖα conveys something altogether stronger (than touch), a kind of graft or symbiosis" (1973: n.13).

62. Crotty: "To the extent that supplication is expressive of subjection and domination ... Thetis' use of it is ironically distanced from the underlying reality" (1994: 22).

63. See esp. Gould 1973: 80ff. On the difference between supplication in the *Iliad* and the *Odyssey*, see Pedrick 1982.

64. I thank Seth Schein for helpful discussion on the phrase χεῖρε πετάσσας (spread wide his hands), which—as he notes—occurs elsewhere in the *Iliad* but always in connection with death. In the *Odyssey*, Polyphemus employs the same gesture when petting his ram at 9.417 (Purves 2016: 74), perhaps—as Seth Schein points out to me—signaling an association with death.

65. *Od.* 4.703; 18.212; 22.68; 23.205; 24.345. See my Chapter 5 (149) on *Od.* 18.212.

the *Iliad* of death), coincides with his own releasing of Achilles' knees, along with his spear, in the very next line.[66] Thus a strange circularity and reciprocity forms between the bodies of the beseecher and the beseeched, so that their knees seem to share in a single gesture that works in three different ways. In an overlapping sequence, Lycaon's knees go slack in fear (λύτο γούνατα), Achilles' knees are released from the suppliant's grasp, and Lycaon falls with his knees unstrung in death.[67] The formulaic *luse de guia* is importantly missing from the description of Lycaon's death, but the gesture, which is inextricably connected with falling, folds back into the initial image of supplication, forcing us to understand λάβε γούνων earlier in the passage in light of the double undoing that is to come.[68]

It now becomes easier to see how the balance between holding (λαμβάνω) and releasing (λύω) frames the ending of the poem.[69] For just as Priam had earlier conflated holding his son in his arms (ἀγκὰς ἑλών) with death and a release from suffering (ἐξίημι γόου), so throughout Book 24 we can understand that his act of seeking the release (*lusis*) of Hector's corpse is tightly bound up with the notion of holding and enduring (both φέρομαι and ἀνέχω belong within this conceptual domain, as we will see later on). Priam puts himself in the position of a suppliant who bears (*gerere*) the reach, the moment of the gesture's opening, through time.[70] So differently from the swift, even contagious iterations that drive other gestures throughout the poem, Priam's grief is framed by the slow process of contemplating and enduring a single and almost unspeakable configuration of bodies. To remember again Agamben, "what characterizes gesture is that in it nothing is being produced or acted, but rather something is being

66. The phrase is used once in the *Iliad* to denote the knees collapsing in (symbolic) death, after Athena hits Artemis on the battlefield at 21.425. See my Chapter 2 for further discussion of falling on the battlefield.

67. For a similarly complex and unexpected use of *luō*, see the attack on Patroclus at *Il.* 16.804–6: λῦσε δέ οἱ θώρηκα ... / λύθεν δ' ὑπὸ φαίδιμα γυῖα, / στῆ δὲ ταφών· Here Patroclus' breastplate is loosened ... his knees go slack ... and he stands upright. This is the first of Patroclus' three death gestures. He falls properly at 822 and will finally die thirty lines later, at 855.

68. The gesture of the outstretched arms is also particularly noteworthy, and can be interpreted in various different ways (hopelessness, acceptance, etc.; cf. Schein 2016: 168). What matters to me is that the arms have let go—stretched wide; we see that they hold on to nothing and do not fold back in again to the body.

69. The thematic importance of λύω to the end of the *Iliad* has long been recognized. Note that λῦτο is the first word of Book 24 and, even though the book divisions are post-Homeric, it is strongly programmatic.

70. Benveniste 1969, vol. 2: 9–15, posits that the Latin word *rex* may be etymologically connected to ὀρέγω, a verb that he suggests does not mean simply "stretch" but rather the reaching out from oneself toward whatever is in front in a straight line: "*orégō, orégnumi* est 'étendre en ligne droite'—plus explicitement: 'à partir du point qu'on occupe, tirer vers l'avant une ligne droite'" (13).

endured or supported."[71] In this case the poem too is bearing the weight of not only Priam's supplication but also the many others that have come before it.

But in each of those previous supplications, it was the knees that were reached for, or hands that were stretched out or down. In *Iliad* 24, by contrast, Priam transforms the gesture of the reach into a unique variation (24.503–6):[72]

> αὐτόν τ' ἐλέησον,
> μνησάμενος σοῦ πατρός· ἐγὼ δ' ἐλεεινότερός περ,
> ἔτλην δ' οἷ' οὔ πώ τις ἐπιχθόνιος βροτὸς ἄλλος,
> ἀνδρὸς παιδοφόνοιο ποτὶ στόμα χεῖρ' ὀρέγεσθαι.

> Pity me,
> as you remember your father. But I am still more pitiable,
> I who endured such things as no other mortal man ever endured:
> to reach the hands of a son-killing man to my mouth.

In describing his gesture Priam separates himself from the *Iliad*'s other formulaic bodies, for, in reaching the hands of his son's killer to his mouth, he has done "such things as no other mortal man ever (πώ) has." The king stages his act as a *hapax poioumenon*—a choreographic moment of such originality that it is both intensely memorable and scarcely to be endured.[73] In this way he suggests a gesture that is not so much iterative as cumulative: one that is shaped by the emotional charge of the various ritual acts of supplication that have already taken place in the poem, from the first entreaty of Chryses to Hector's plea for burial before he dies in Book 22.[74] As Lesley Stern explains with reference to the "pathos formula," this allows us to understand the duplication and quotation of gestures differently from a model of mechanical iteration, for in Warburg's system "gestures do not mean the same thing twice, but by virtue of their intensity, they persist, triggering somatic memory and producing pathos" (2008: 202). At the same time, Priam's gesture at this moment in the poem is a *hapax* precisely because it eschews repeatability; it stands instead as a kind of

71. Agamben [1992] 2000: 57.

72. The knees can be kissed in supplication, as at *Od.* 14.279 and in Athena's recounting of Thetis' supplication of Zeus at *Il.* 8.371 (in Book 1 Thetis only grasps the knees, however).

73. The coinage is my own, modeled on the terminology of the *hapax legomenon* (a word, such as παιδοφόνος at 506, occurring only once in the Homeric corpus), see further my Chapter 5 (148). Nagler (1974: 188) has argued that χεῖρ' ὀρέγεσθαι at 24.506 "echo the same two words in the preceding stages of the consolatio series" (i.e., Θέτις δ' ὤρεξε πιοῦσα at 102 and χειρί τέ μιν κατέρεξεν at 127).

74. As has long been noted, the *Iliad* both opens and closes with an old man coming to supplicate for the release of his child. Whitman 1958: 257–60; Redfield 1975: 219; Macleod 1982; Schein 1984: 31; Minchin 1986: 15; Crotty 1994: 94–98; Seaford 1994: 70; Lateiner 1995: 32; Wilson 2002: 128. On the sequence of supplications in the *Iliad*, see Thornton 1984: 121ff. On how "supplication structures the trajectory of Akhilleus' wrath and its eventual extinction," see Lateiner 1995, esp. 36–37.

perpetual symbol of endurance, a holding pattern that reflects on the unremitting nature of τλῆναι.

Finally, it is important to note that Priam is not just gesturing himself, but impressing a gesture *on* Achilles, by making the latter's hands move in a certain way. There is thus a kind of puppetry to his actions, which echoes and corrects the futile puppetry that Achilles performed on Hector's body at the start of the book. But while Achilles' dragging of Hector leaves the Trojan's body unchanged, Priam, by contrast, effectively reanimates Achilles' hands, starting the sequence that leads to Achilles lifting Hector's body for him. He is able to impose upon the still-living if moribund body of Achilles a gesture (ὀρέγω) through which, as we have seen, Andromache and Achilles had both failed to connect with corpses of their own. The kinaesthetic disconnect Achilles expressed in continually dragging Hector, moreover, now starts to get repaired, in what Susan Foster calls "kinaesthetic empathy"—the strange capacity of movement to convey emotional experience—both in us, the poem's audience, but also through the bodily feedback between Achilles and Priam. Achilles now "feels" the gesture that he was unable to before.

I return, then, to my attempt to think of the formula as gestural as well as verbal, and to think of it here as if it were a body in motion, reforming under the pressure of the extraordinary circumstances of Priam's supplication.[75] When Achilles afterward grabs hold of the old man by the hand and shoves him away "gently" (24.508: ἁψάμενος δ' ἄρα χειρὸς ἀπῶσατο ἦκα γέροντα), we can detect a similar affective dissonance, drawn from the paradoxical pairing of "kissing" and "killing" at 506.[76] At verses 506 and 508, in other words, Homer's breaking or forcing of language into unusual juxtapositions in the line reflects on the forcing and breaking of bodies as well, as both men attempt to bear up under the strain of what they have to endure. Priam later confesses he has not eaten or slept since his son's death, but had only been rolling in the dung (24.637–41) and ever "nursing" or "brooding on" his grief (αἰεὶ στενάχω καὶ κήδεα μυρία πέσσω, 639).[77] To remain in this state is to end up immobile and truly worn down.[78]

---

75. The hexameter is thought of in terms of "limbs" (κῶλα) or colons, but I mean to refer to the bodies of the characters in the scene, not the metaphorical limbs of the verse construction.

76. Lynn-George 1988: 238, on the pairing of "kissing" and "killing." On 24.508, see also Taplin 1992: 270.

77. The verb πέσσω (*ripen, cook, bake*) is used with χόλον at 4.513=9.565 to describe Achilles "cooking" or "brooding over" his anger, or perhaps "foment[ing]" it inside him and mak[ing] it moistly swollen like ripened fruit" (Clarke 1999: 93).

78. See esp. Lynn-George 1996 on "the inhibiting power of care and grief," which can lead to paralysis and immobility. Niobe, he says, is "immobilized by care" (1996: 15).

The process is literalized by the story of the grieving Niobe, turned to stone (ἔνθα λίθος περ ἐοῦσα θεῶν ἐκ κήδεα πέσσει, "there, as a stone, she nurses her sorrows from the gods," 24.617), who puts into practice the notion that the body might become "a kind of monument, a support that archives the gesture it has performed."[79] In contrast, the open circulation of motion and emotion that the reach of Priam establishes enables both men to escape the petrification of grief. Unlike the situation with Niobe (whose people sat for nine days immobile in stone with the gods stepping in to bury her children on the tenth and who still now sits unmoving, although she has taken in food),[80] Priam and Achilles agree on a plan for setting the ritual of grief into physical motion, restarting again the articulation of limbs into the purposeful movement first set in process by Priam's crossing to the Achaean camp and breaking the cycle of dragging, whirling, rolling, and sitting.[81] Thus they agree that the Trojans will bring wood down from the hills and lament for nine days, bury the body and feast on the tenth, build a tomb on the eleventh, and return to fighting on the twelfth (662–67).

But in order to get to this stage Priam and Achilles have to negotiate a delicate balance between holding (on) and letting go. The brief but sustained passage of their intertwining sets in motion a careful choreography, mostly involving the hands, from 24.506 until 675, when Hermes appears to escort the king back to the city. Thus Achilles takes Priam twice by the hand and once by the wrist, sometimes indicating gestures of intimacy, sometimes of barely suppressed violence,[82] but in each case responding to the initial reach (χεῖρ' ὀρέγεσθαι) of the old man at 506. Here again the hand (χείρ), the genitive object of the touch in the first two cases, mingles almost imperceptibly between subject and object.

> 508: ἁψάμενος δ' ἄρα χειρὸς ἀπώσατο ἦκα γέροντα
>
> grabbing the old man by the hand he shoved him away gently
>
> 515: αὐτίκ' ἀπὸ θρόνου ὦρτο, γέροντα δὲ χειρὸς ἀνίστη
>
> quickly he rose up from his seat, and stood the old man up by the hand

---

79. Noland 2008: xiii.

80. *Il.* 24. 610–17. Achilles too confesses to Priam that he "sits" immobile in his grief (24.542). For a fuller treatment of the Niobe passage see Heath 2005: 156–67. Kakridis argues that Niobe cannot both eat and turn to stone; he thus wants *Il.* 24,614–17 to be a later interpolation (1949: 96–103).

81. As I discuss in other chapters, Achilles often expresses dissatisfaction with his own heavy "sitting" upon the earth.

82. ἀπωθέω, *to push or shove away*, is a rough word (on Simone Weil's famous mistranslation of ἦκα in this line, see Schein 2016: 167). To take a woman "by the wrist" (χεῖρ' ἐπὶ καρπῷ) is a gesture of marriage in later Greek iconography (Oakley and Sinos 1993: 32, Figs. 84, 87, 94, and 97 and nn.70–71). See Taplin: "this gentle gesture … is the last contact between the two," as it also was between Odysseus and Penelope before he left for Troy (*Od.* 18.258) (1992: 190–92). Felson: "Using his child-slaying hands, Achilles now takes the old man by the hand (24.515) [and] offers him protection from his enemies …" (2002: 49).

671–72: ὡς ἄρα φωνήσας ἐπὶ καρπῷ χεῖρα γέροντος / ἔλλαβε δεξιτερήν

so speaking he took hold of the left hand of the old man at the wrist

Throughout the rest of the scene in Achilles' hut, moreover, there is a back and forth between verbs for releasing or letting be (λύω, ἐάω, ἐξίημι, [κατα]κεῖμαι) and verbs for holding or bearing (ἀνέχω, ἔχω, τλῆναι, φέρομαι).[83] Michael Lynn-George has written of the move toward letting go at the end of the epic, arguing that in Book 24 structures of care (κήδομαι) "negotiate with the need to 'let it be'" (1996: 1–26, especially 4). He draws attention to the prevalence of ἐάω (*allow*) in this book, a verb that signals a movement toward letting go in the process of grieving. This notion is of course both practical and metaphorical: in letting go of Hector's body (*lusis*), Achilles also lets go of his anger. Similarly, the process of both Priam and Achilles coming to a form of acceptance in their suffering is intertwined with other forms of λύω that we have seen in connection with the gesture of supplication, specifically Lycaon's releasing of Achilles' knees (λύτο γούνατα) as an acceptance of his own fate. Equally, words that cluster around the conceptual domain of "carrying," including bearing, suffering, behavior, and deportment,[84] have an effect, as we have seen, on the gestural vocabulary of the *Iliad*'s final book. The notion of "bearing," in particular, can be traced through φέρω/φέρομαι (*I bear*),[85] which refers not only to the transportation home of Hector's corpse in Book 24 (581), but more generally in Homeric epic to both the enduring of sufferings and the way in which the limbs "carry" the body.[86]

We can see in the physical forms of expression shared between Priam and Achilles, therefore, how what I earlier referred to as the "drag" of gesture, the heavy experience of bearing the body through the process of grief, is affectively transposed from the dragging of Hector's corpse to its ritual cleansing and anointing, lifting, and final carrying home. In so doing, both

---

83. In Achilles' hut: λύω, *to release, ransom*: 502, 555, 561, 576, 593, 599; ἐάω, *to let be, allow*: 523, 557, 569; ἐξίημι, *to release*: 628; [-]κεῖμαι, *to lay down, let lie, be placed*: 523, 527, 554, 600, 610, [627], 676; λέγω, *to lay down*: 635, 650; ἀνέχω, *to stretch out, bear up, endure*: 518, 549; ἔχω, *to hold, hold on, endure*: 670; τλῆναι, *to endure*: 505, 519, 565; φέρω, *to carry, bear*: 502, 556, 581; ἅπτω, *to grasp*: 508, λαμβάνω, *to hold, grasp*: 465, 478, 672.

84. See further Lakoff and Johnson 1980 for the metaphorical process of transfering language within a conceptual domain.

85. See also ὀχέω, ἔχω.

86. Achilles says at *Il.* 9.411 that he bears (φερέμεν) a twofold fate. Cf. on enduring misery *Od.* 18.135 (*LfgrE* col.850). At *Il.* 22.425, Hecuba says that her piercing grief for Hector will bear her down (καταφέρω) to Hades. The feet are often said to carry (φέρω) the body in movement. Cf. *Il.* 6.514; 13.515, of the feet bearing one swiftly, or 15.405; 17.700; 18.148; *Od.* 15.555, of the feet simply bearing one in movement. See also *Il.* 6.511=15.268, of the γοῦνα of horses (*LfgrE* 1baaa). I thank Lucien van Beek for helpful discussion on this point.

characters take back some of the responsibility for bearing their own bodies through gesture. Thus ἀνέχω is twice used to index, metaphorically, the idea of holding up under grief in Achilles' speech to Priam (518, 549), in a usage that connects if only indirectly to the phrase χεῖρας ἀνασχέμεν ("reach out the hands") at 24.301.[87] Priam's original wish to hold the body of his son in his arms, therefore, translates into a gradual acceptance of how to hold himself, both in terms of the remembering and restoring of gesture and in terms of the undoing (λύω) of postures that are too painful to endure. When Priam first articulated his desire to retrieve Hector's body, he paired holding with letting go, αἱρέω with ἵημι,[88] and it is this complementary relationship that matters most to the moving forward of Achilles and Priam in grief. The remembering and righting of gesture that comes through the combination of λύω and ἀνέχω helps us to understand, in formal terms, the gesture at 24.506, where ὀρέγεσθαι had to work so hard to bridge the gap between the two.

The resistance within that pose to the actual moment of connecting the son-killer's hands with the father's mouth speaks to a misalignment of sorts, as the gesture situates itself in relation to language, formulaic action, and meaning. Agamben refers to gesture's relationship with language as a "gag" ([1992] 2000: 59, emphasis original):

> The gesture is essentially always a gesture of not being able to figure something out in language; it is always a *gag* in the proper meaning of the term, indicating first of all something that could be put in your mouth to hinder speech, as well as in the sense of the actor's improvisation meant to compensate a loss of memory or an inability to speak.

Achilles' hands do something similar to Priam's speech, forcing the words apart in his mouth and driving "son" (πάϊς), as we have seen, between ἀνδρο- and φόνος. The king's improvised gesture, his *hapax* of both body and language, would seem to gag or choke on itself as something that the body can scarcely endure. At the same time, by placing Achilles' hands on his mouth, Priam deliberately puts gesture (with all its ambiguities) in the place of words, reaching for something beyond language. The act represents, perhaps, the struggle to find a

---

87. Lynn-George 1996: 5. ἀνέχω, like ὀρέγω, is frequently paired with the hands to denote reaching in Homeric epic, and with χεῖρας the two are often interchangeable (e.g., Chryses at *Il.* 1.450: εὔχετο χεῖρας ἀνασχών), see n.33, this chapter. Cf. ἐπισχών, used to denote Phoenix reaching out wine to the infant Achilles (9.489), discussed previously. Achilles' call to Priam to "bear up" occurs when he is also pulling him to his feet (ἀνίστη, 515; Schein 1984: 159; Lynn-George 1996: 5).

88. *Il.* 24.227, as discussed previously: ἀγκὰς ἑλόντ' ἐμὸν υἱόν, ἐπὴν γόου ἐξ ἔρον εἵην (note how the rough breathings accentuate the parallel). Cf. *Il.* 24.628.

way ("the actor's improvisation") of making the body's formulas of expression not only compatible with language, but also better able than language to express this particular intensity of feeling.[89]

We have seen, too, how epic language rights itself after this scene, and we might adapt here Stephanie Jamison's concept of "poetic repair" in the *Rigveda* to the end of the *Iliad*.[90] "This is not," as she puts it, "a structuring device but a method for producing forward momentum. The poet sets a problem—lexical, syntactic, or thematic—earlier in the hymn and then 'repairs' this problem later in the hymn by substituting the expected word, syntactic construction, or thematic element for the problematic one."[91] Similarly, at the end of the *Iliad,* both the anomalous syntactic construction of *cheir' oregesthai* and the misplacement of the adjective *androphonos* in the hand-kissing scene work as a kind of problem whose anticipated solution creates momentum for the poem. We could say, then, that the reversion of *androphonos* to its rightful owner in the aftermath of this scene and in Andromache's lament (509, 724) mends the language of the epic, establishing a "poetic" or formulaic repair as well as a psychological one for the characters involved.

The reach of Priam for Achilles is framed, as I have already suggested, as a reach of fatherhood.[92] As if Achilles were his son, the old man instructs the younger one to "remember your father." Yet this act of reaching toward one's son is a troubling and unresolved gesture in the poem. We have already seen Priam stretch out his hands to Hector to no avail from the walls of Troy (χεῖρας ὀρεγνύς, 22.37), but the reach extends further down the family line, from Hector to Astyanax. In a well-known scene from the end of Book 6, Astyanax draws back from his father's outstretched arms (6.466–71):[93]

> Ὣς εἰπὼν οὗ παιδὸς <u>ὀρέξατο</u> φαίδιμος Ἕκτωρ·
> ἂψ δ' ὁ πάϊς πρὸς κόλπον ἐϋζώνοιο τιθήνης
> ἐκλίνθη ἰάχων, πατρὸς φίλου ὄψιν ἀτυχθείς,
> ταρβήσας χαλκόν τε ἰδὲ λόφον ἱππιοχαίτην,

---

89. The violence of Priam's (self-) gagging is also doubled by his trapping of Achilles' hands as Priam places them on his own lips. Thus Priam enacts a simultaneous restraining of both gesture and speech. Cf. Buchan 2012: 46 on Antilochus' restraining of Achilles' hands at *Il.* 18.33, lest he cut his own throat upon hearing the news of Patroclus' death.

90. Jamison 2006. I thank Ian Hollenbaugh for this suggestion.

91. Jamison and Brereton 2014: 67.

92. Crotty 1994 makes the intriguing point that supplication is "the ceremony of the father's absence." As he argues, "the suppliant adopts the small stature and the importunate gestures of a child, but it is just the point of supplication that the one supplicated is *not* a kindly father and that, indeed, there is no powerful and beneficent parent," (1994: 97, italics original).

93. On the significance of the gestures at the end of Book 6, see also Kozak 2017: 65–67.

δεινὸν ἀπ' ἀκροτάτης κόρυθος νεύοντα νοήσας.
ἐκ δὲ γέλασσε πατήρ τε φίλος καὶ πότνια μήτηρ·

So speaking glorious Hector reached out for his son,
but the child shrank back into the lap of the well-girdled nurse
crying out, disturbed by the sight of his own father,
and upset at seeing the bronze and the horsehair crest of his helmet,
nodding down terribly from the very top.
His dear father and lady mother laughed …

This same child, as Jonathan Burgess has pointed out, will be taken by the hand (χειρὸς ἑλών) and thrown from the walls of Troy: ἤ τις Ἀχαιῶν / ῥίψει χειρὸς ἑλὼν ἀπὸ πύργου, λυγρὸν ὄλεθρον ("or someone of the Achaeans will throw you, having taken you by the hand, from the tower to a pitiful death," *Il.* 24.734–35).[94] Here, at the very end of the poem, we find the same genitive of touching or grasping (χειρός) that we saw earlier in Achilles' relations with Priam, now working to undo the bonds of filial protection that Priam, Hector, and Peleus all labor to maintain against the odds. That both fathers reach but fail to hold their sons, moreover (sons who are both also "let go" by the hand), invites us to see holding as a brief interval between reaching and releasing, which—rather than being opposites—stand at different ends of the same gesture.

If the gesturing body is, as some have argued, alien and "other," always "not mine,"[95] then the last book of the *Iliad* moves forcefully both to support and to challenge that idea. For it is in trying to hold onto the body that Priam and Achilles both find and lose the most support for themselves. Priam's ultimate failure to hold onto (ἀγκάς ἑλών) the corpse of his son, just as Achilles can hold no more than ash and dust in his hands (χερσὶν ἑλών) upon first hearing of Patroclus' death (18.23), points to holding's role in the poem as a posture that, as Lycaon demonstrated, cannot last through time. Instead, in stretching his arms out in supplication for the body of his son, Priam reaches, and in the act of reaching grasps hold of something ambiguous and unexpected. His gesture opens the body up to new circuits of feeling, as it redirects the practice of gesturing from the dead back to the living.

94. Burgess 2010 convincingly argues for hypertextual links between these two scenes and a fragment of the *Little Iliad* describing Astyanax's death (see also Burgess 2011: 176–82). The scene in *Iliad* 6 also becomes much less innocent once paired with Andromache's regret at missing out on Hector "stretching out his hands" (χεῖρας ὄρεξας, 743) to her from his deathbed.

95. Derrida 1978: 180, discussing the Theatre of Cruelty: "Ever since I have a relation to my body, therefore, ever since my birth, I no longer am my body. Ever since I have had a body I am not this body, hence I do not possess it. This deprivation institutes and informs my relation to my life. My body has thus always been stolen from me" (see also n.7, this chapter).

7

Conclusion

THE HOMERIC BODY IS PROGRAMMED TO MOVE IN GENERICALLY determined ways; to adopt postures, poses, and movement patterns (what I have referred to as "gestures") within a formulaic system that is both lexical and physical. I have explored in this book how the repetitive, habitual movement choices of Homeric characters—when chasing an opponent, for example, or leaping in battle, or drawing a sword—function simultaneously as kinetic reflexes for the hero and aesthetic reflexes for the poet. This exploration opens up for the epics a way of reading that is cued to the kinetic; not just a way of "reading the body" but also a means of reading *through* or *within* the body, so that its inclinations and angles, the speed at which it moves or the order in which it arranges those movements, all influence the nature of the poem's composition.

Rather than understanding gesture as a social code, therefore, I see it—like the formula to which it is intricately related—as an integral part of the poetic fabric of epic. Throughout this book, I have drawn a connection between familiar epic movements—learned through repetition, reinforced by muscle memory, and culturally engrained—and the verbal formulas through which many of these movements are conveyed. This approach has allowed me the opportunity to reconsider the nature of epic repetition, especially insofar as it relates to the sequencing of action through time. Indeed, Homeric action formulas may be said to offer two "takes" on the body—one in the third-person scenario of what action theorist Michael Thompson calls "natural-historical" time, during which Homeric man leaps, falls, or runs, in a type of atemporal, formulaic existence, and another in the first-person experience of the character enacting that formula, as a specific event unfolding within the time of his or her life.[1] It is clear that, for the *Iliad* and the *Odyssey,* what the body does and suffers is a central poetic concern, but there will always be a tension in epic's formulaic structure because the actions of its characters can be at the same time both individual and generic. My book has sought to situate the actions and experiences of the individual body precisely within the larger framework of how other

---

1. I take the concept of "natural-historical" time and first- and third-person experience from Thompson (2002, 2004, 2008; cf. Keenleyside 2016: 153–57, 235–38). Thompson uses the term "natural-historical judgments" to classify an atemporal form of empirical observation, often found in field guides or nature studies (on, for example, "*the* jellyfish"), and which he terms "vital" or "anti-individualistic." My thanks to Mark Payne for alerting me to this work.

bodies share in similar sufferings and actions through the Homeric corpus, not in order to detract from the first-person experiences of its characters, but to better explain their emotional effects within the constraints and pressures of the epic world to which they belong.

In terms of organization this book has been very simple in its goals: to take a single movement pattern or gesture and perform a cross-sectional reading of it through one or both of the poems. This approach means that I do not start from questions about character or story. Instead, I have sought to identify underlying patterns within the kinetic structure of the poem, which point to a new method of reading for gestures which may be unique (Priam kissing the hands of Achilles), which may be so ubiquitous as to be easily passed over ("he fell with a thud and his armor clattered about him"), or which may fall somewhere in between (Odysseus and Hector leaping "like a high-flown eagle," Penelope four times "standing beside the stathmos"). By tracking the directions and tendencies of particular movement phrases, I have pointed out moments when the gesture diverges from its expected course or takes on some form of resistance—either to the epic status quo or to the objective of the narrative.

In each chapter, by focusing on a vividly suggestive configuration of the body, I have tried to point to the liveliness of gesture, its ability to act beyond the body, and most of all its ability to act *between* bodies. Gesture's special capacity to escape the boundaries of the individual subject, to take on a sense of autonomy or agency, speaks to a capacity for limbs to move according to their own deep-seated habits and inclinations. Nowhere is this capacity more on display than within the formulaic system of Homeric epic, especially because in Homer the body is the essential core or sum of the self.

I want to conclude this book, therefore, by highlighting what we might call gesture's quiet potential to act on its own accord and to exhibit its own forms of will or agency. When Penelope stands still, Achilles pushes his sword back into his scabbard, or Priam kisses his enemy's hands, they—like the body falling in death—all act under the pressure of external forces. Yet what is important about these gestures is their ability to introduce different forms of temporality and different ways of thinking about narrative into our understanding of literary texts. If one way of understanding epic plots, along Aristotelian lines, is as a continuous sequence of causally necessary events, then gesture can be seen to work alongside this sequence, through a different kind of somatic necessity and over discontinuous intervals. By returning to the same static pose again and again, Penelope exhibits her own peculiar agency over the structure of the *Odyssey,* which holds the poem in the right temporal register until Odysseus leaps onto the threshold at the beginning of

Book 22. Similarly, the minor discrepancies between catching up and over-taking, between how close or far apart you stand from a warrior, or between whose hands touch whom at the moment of supplication, in one sense hardly matter at all to the plot of the *Iliad*. But in another sense they do, insofar as they incline us toward an underlying poetics of form and feeling that is integral to epic's positioning of the body in space.

Bibliography

Agamben, Giorgio. (1975) 1999a. "Aby Warburg and the Nameless Science." In *Potentialities: Collected Essays in Philosophy*, trans. D. Heller-Roazen. Stanford, CA: Stanford University Press, 89–103.

———. (1991) 1999b. "Kommerell, or On Gesture." In *Potentialities: Collected Essays in Philosophy*, ed. and trans. D. Heller-Roazen. Stanford, CA: Stanford University Press, 77–85.

———. (1992) 2000. "Notes on Gesture." In *Means without End: Notes on Politics*, trans. V. Binetti and C. Casarino. Minneapolis: University of Minnesota Press, 49–60.

———. (2005) 2007. "The Author as Gesture." In *Profanations*, trans. J. Fort. New York: Zone, 61–72.

Ahl, Frederick, and Hanna M. Roisman. 1996. *The* Odyssey *Re-Formed*. Ithaca, NY: Cornell University Press.

Ahmed, Sara. 2010. "Orientations Matter." In *New Materialisms: Ontology, Agency, and Politics*, ed. D. Coole and S. Frost. Durham, NC: Duke University Press, 234–57.

Alden, Maureen Joan. 2000. *Homer Beside Himself: Para-Narratives in the* Iliad. Oxford: Oxford University Press.

Anderson, Laurie. 1982. "Walking and Falling." In *Big Science*, prod. L. Anderson and R. Baran. Warner Bros. Records, Burbank, compact disc.

Andersen, Øivind. 1981. "A Note on the 'Mortality' of Gods in Homer." *GRBS* 22.4: 323–27.

Anderson, Warren D. 1957. "Notes on the Simile in Homer and His Successors: I. Homer, Apollonius Rhodius, and Vergil." *CJ* 53.2: 81–87.

Arend, Walter. (1933) 1975. *Die typischen Scenen bei Homer*. Berlin: Weidmann.

Austin, Norman. 1975. *Archery at the Dark of the Moon: Poetic Problems in Homer's* Odyssey. Berkeley: University of California Press.

Bakker, Egbert J. 1993. "Discourse and Performance: Involvement, Visualization, and 'Presence' in Homeric Poetry." *CA* 12.1: 1–29.

———. 1999. "Pointing to the Past: Verbal Augment and Temporal Deixis in Homer." In *Euphrosyne: Studies in Ancient Epic and Its Legacy in Honor of Dimitris N. Maronitis*, ed. J. N. Kazazis and A. Rengakos. Stuttgart: Steiner, 50–65.

———. 2013. *The Meaning of Meat and the Structure of the* Odyssey. Cambridge: Cambridge University Press.

Banes, Sally. 1987. *Terpsicore in Sneakers: Post-modern Dance*. Middletown, CT: Wesleyan University Press.

———. 1993. *Democracy's Body: Judson Dance Theater, 1962–1964*. Durham, NC: Duke University Press.

Barasch, Moshe. 1991. *Imago Hominis: Studies in the Language of Art*. Vienna: IRSA.

Barker, Elton T. E. 2004. "Achilles' Last Stand: Institutionalising Dissent in Homer's *Iliad*." *PCPhS* 50: 92–120.

———. 2009. *Entering the Agon: Dissent and Authority in Homer, Historiography and Tragedy.* Oxford: Oxford University Press.

Barthes, Roland. (1980) 2010. *Camera Lucida: Reflections on Photography*, trans. R. Howard. New York: Hill & Wang.

Bassett, Samuel Eliot. 1938. *The Poetry of Homer.* Berkeley: University of California Press.

Beck, Bill. 2017. "Lost in the Middle: Story Time and Discourse Time in the *Iliad*." *Yearbook of Ancient Greek Epic* 1: 46–64.

Becker, Otfrid. 1937. *Das Bild des Weges und verwandte Vorstellungen in frühgriechischen Denken.* (Hermes, Einzelschriften 4). Berlin: Wiedmannsche Buchhandlung.

Beckwith, Miles C. 1998. "The 'Hanging of Hera' and the Meaning of Greek ἄκμων." *HSCP* 98: 91–102.

Beer, Gillian. 2007. "End of the Line." 12 January. *Guardian*.

Bell, Catherine. (1992) 2009. *Ritual Theory, Ritual Practice.* Oxford: Oxford University Press.

Benjamin, Walter. (1961) 2007. *Illuminations: Essays and Reflections*, trans. H. Zohn., ed. H. Arendt. New York: Schocken.

Benveniste, Émile, 1969. *Le vocabulaire des institutions indo-européennes.* Vol. 2, *Pouvoir, droit, religion.* Paris: Les Éditions de Minuit.

Bergren, Ann. 1980. "Helen's Web: Time and Tableau in the *Iliad*." *Helios* 7.1: 19–34.

———. 1983. "Odyssean Temporality: Many (Re)Turns." In *Approaches to Homer*, ed. C. A. Rubino and C. W. Shelmerdine. Austin: University of Texas Press, 38–73.

Bergson, Henri. (1896) 1988. *Matter and Memory*, trans. N. M. Paul and W. S. Palmer. New York: Zone.

Boegehold, Alan L. 1999. *When a Gesture Was Expected.* Princeton, NJ: Princeton University Press.

Bolens, Guillemette. (2008) 2012. *The Style of Gestures: Embodiment and Cognition in Literary Narrative.* Baltimore: Johns Hopkins University Press.

Bonifazi, Anna. 2009. "Inquiring into *Nostos* and Its Cognates." *AJP* 130.4: 481–510.

Bourdieu, Pierre. (1972) 1977. *Outline of a Theory of Practice*, trans. R. Nice. Cambridge: Cambridge University Press.

———. (1980) 1990a. *The Logic of Practice*, trans. R. Nice. Stanford, CA: Stanford University Press.

———. (1987) 1990b. *In Other Words: Essays Towards a Reflexive Sociology*, trans. M. Adamson. Stanford, CA: Stanford University Press.

Bowra, C. M. 1930. *Tradition and Design in the* Iliad. Oxford: Clarendon.

Braswell, Bruce Karl. 1971. "Mythological Innovation in the *Iliad*." *CQ* 21.1: 16–26.

———. 1982. "The Song of Ares and Aphrodite: Theme and Relevance to *Odyssey* 8." *Hermes* 110.2: 129–37.

Braun, Marta. 1992. *Picturing Time: The Work of Etienne-Jules Marey (1830–1904).* Chicago: University of Chicago Press.

Braune, Wilhelm, and Otto Fischer. (1895–1904) 1987. *The Human Gait*, trans. P. Maquet and R. Furlong. Berlin: Springer-Verlag.

Brecht, Bertolt. (1930) 1992. "On Gestic Music." In *Brecht on Theater: A Development of an Aesthetic*, trans. and ed. J. Willett. New York: Hill & Wang, 104–6.

Bremmer, Jan. 1991. "Walking, Standing, and Sitting in Greek Culture." In *A Cultural History of Gesture: From Antiquity to the Present Day*, ed. J. Bremmer and H. Roodenburg. Cambridge: Polity, 15–35.

Brillet-Dubois, Pascale. 2015. "'Hector tueur d'hommes' ou 'Hector dompteur de chevaux': L'art formulaire au service du récit d'*Iliade*." Special issue, *Gaïa: Revue interdisciplinaire sur la*

Grèce Archaïque, no. 18: Πολυφόρβῃ Γαίῃ. *Mélanges de littérature et linguistique offerts à Francoise Létoublon*. Textes réunis par F. Dell'Oro and O. Lagacherie: 261–74.

Brinkema, Eugenie. 2014. *The Forms of the Affects*. Durham, NC: Duke University Press.

Brooks, Peter. 1984. *Reading for the Plot: Design and Intention in Narrative*. New York: A. A. Knopf.

Brügger, Claude. 2009. *Homers Ilias: Gesamtkommentar. Bd. VIII, Vierundzwanzigster Gesang. Faszikel 2*. Ed. Anton Bierl and Joachim Latacz. Berlin: de Gruyter.

Buchan, Mark. 2004a. *The Limits of Heroism: Homer and the Ethics of Reading*. Ann Arbor: University of Michigan Press.

———. 2004b. "Looking to the Feet: The Riddles of the Scylla." *Helios* 31.1–2: 21–49.

———. 2012. *Perfidy and Passion: Reintroducing the Iliad*. Madison: University of Wisconsin Press.

Bundrick, Sheramy. 2015. "Recovering Rhapsodes: A New Vase by the Pantoxena Painter." *CA* 34.1: 1–31.

Burch, Noel. 1990. *Life to Those Shadows*. Berkeley: University of California Press.

Burgess, Jonathan S. 2009. *The Death and Afterlife of Achilles*. Baltimore: Johns Hopkins University Press.

———. 2010. "The Hypertext of Astyanax." *Trends in Classics* 2: 211–24.

———. 2011. "Intertextuality without Text in Early Greek Poetry." In *Relative Chronology in Early Greek Epic Poetry*, ed. O. Anderson and D T. T. Haag. Cambridge: Cambridge University Press, 168–83.

———. 2012. "Belatedness in the Travels of Odysseus." In *Homeric Contexts: Neoanalysis and the Interpretation of Oral Poetry*, ed. F. Montanari, A. Rengakos, and C. Tsagalis. Berlin and Boston: de Gruyter, 269–90.

Burkert, Walter. 1960. "Das Lied von Ares und Aphrodite." *Rheinisches Museum für Philologie* 103.2: 130–44.

Burnett, Anne Pippin. 2005. *Pindar's Songs for Young Athletes of Aigina*. Oxford and New York: Oxford University Press.

Bury, J. B. 1922. "The End of the *Odyssey*." *JHS* 42.1: 1–15.

Butler, Judith. 1988. "Performative Acts and Gender Constitution: An Essay in Phenomenology and Feminist Theory." *Theater Journal* 40.4: 519–31.

———. 1997. *The Psychic Life of Power: Theories in Subjection*. Stanford, CA: Stanford University Press.

———. 2015. *Senses of the Subject*. New York: Fordham University Press.

Cairns, Douglas L. 1993. *Aidōs: The Psychology and Ethics of Honour and Shame in Ancient Greek Literature*. Oxford: Clarendon.

———. 2001. "Affronts and Quarrels in the *Iliad*." In *Oxford Readings in Homer's Iliad*, ed. D. L. Cairns. Oxford and New York: Oxford University Press, 203–19.

Calhoun, George Miller. 1933. "Homeric Repetitions." *University of California Publications in Classical Philology* 12.1: 1–26.

Carson, Anne. 1986. *Eros the Bittersweet: An Essay*. Princeton, NJ: Princeton University Press.

Caruth, Cathy. 1995. "The Claims of Reference." In *Critical Encounters: Reference and Responsibility in Deconstructive Writing*, ed. C. Caruth and D. Esch. New Brunswick: Rutgers University Press, 92–105.

Casey, Edward. "Habitual Body and Memory in Merleau-Ponty." In *A History of Habit*, ed. T. Sparrow and A. Hutchinson. Lanham, MD: Lexington Books, 209–25.

Clark, Andy. 2013. "Whatever Next? Predictive Brains, Situated Agents, and the Future of Cognitive Science." *Behavioral and Brain Sciences* 36.3: 181–204.

Clark, Christina E., Edith Foster, and Judith P. Hallett, eds. 2015. *Kinesis: The Ancient Depiction of Gesture, Motion, and Emotion*. Ann Arbor: University of Michigan Press.

Clark, Matthew. 1997. *Out of Line: Homeric Composition beyond the Hexameter*. Lanham, MD: Rowman & Littlefield.

———. 2004. "Formulas, Metre, and Type Scenes." In *The Cambridge Companion to Homer*, ed. R. Fowler. Cambridge: Cambridge University Press, 117–38.

Clarke, Michael. 1999. *Flesh and Spirit in the Songs of Homer: A Study of Words and Myths*. Oxford: Clarendon.

Clay, Diskin. 1992. "The World of Hesiod." *Ramus* 21.2: 131–55.

Clay, Jenny Strauss. 1982. "Immortal and Ageless Forever." *CQ* 77: 112–17.

———. 1983. *The Wrath of Athena: Gods and Men in the* Odyssey. Princeton, NJ: Princeton University Press.

———. 1990. *The Politics of Olympus: Form and Meaning in the Homeric Hymns*. Princeton, NJ: Princeton University Press.

———. 1995. "Agamemnon's Stance (*Iliad* 19.51–77)." *Philologus* 139.1: 72–75.

———. 1999. "A Ram among the Sheep: Some Notes on Odysseus in the *Iliad*." In *Euphrosyne: Studies in Ancient Epic and Its Legacy in Honor of Dimitris N. Maronitis*, ed. J. N. Kazazis and A. Rengakos. Stuttgart: Steiner, 363–67.

———. 2002a. "Dying Is Hard to Do." *Colby Quarterly* 38.1: 7–16.

———. 2002b. "Odyssean Animadversions." In *Omero Tremila Anno Dopo*, ed. F. Montanari and P. Ascheri. Rome: Edizioni di Storia e Letteratura, 73–83.

———. 2011. *Homer's Trojan Theater: Space, Vision, and Memory in the* Iliad. Cambridge and New York: Cambridge University Press.

Clayton, Barbara. 2004. *A Penelopean Poetics: Reweaving the Feminine in Homer's* Odyssey. Lanham, MD: Lexington Books.

Cook, Erwin. (1999) 2009. "'Active' and 'Passive' Heroics in the *Odyssey*." In *Oxford Readings in Classical Studies: Homer's* Odyssey, ed. L. E. Doherty. Oxford and New York: Oxford University Press, 111–34.

Cooper, John M. 1997, ed. *The Complete Works of Plato*. Indianapolis, IN: Hackett.

Corbeill, Anthony. 2004. *Nature Embodied: Gesture in Ancient Rome*. Princeton, NJ: Princeton University Press.

Craighero, Laila. 2014. "The Role of the Motor System in Cognitive Functions." In *The Routledge Handbook of Embodied Cognition*, ed. L. Shapiro. New York: Routledge, 51–58.

Crossley, Nick. 2013. "Pierre Bourdieu's *Habitus*." In *A History of Habit from Aristotle to Bourdieu*, ed. T. Sparrow and A. Hutchinson. Lanham, MD: Lexington Books, 291–307.

Crotty, Kevin. 1994. *The Poetics of Supplication: Homer's* Iliad *and* Odyssey. Ithaca, NY: Cornell University Press.

Cucinella, Catherine. 2010. *Poetics of the Body: Edna St. Vincent Millay, Elizabeth Bishop, Marilyn Chin, and Marilyn Hacker*. New York: Palgrave.

Cunliffe, R. J. 1977. *A Lexicon of the Homeric Dialect*. Norman, OK: University of Oklahoma Press.

Currie, Bruno. 2016. *Homer's Allusive Art*. Oxford: Oxford University Press.

Dagognet, François. (1987) 1992. *Etienne-Jules Marey: A Passion for the Trace*, trans. R. Galeta and J. Herman. New York: Zone.

Danek, Georg. 1988. *Studien zur Dolonie*. Vienna: Österreichische Akademie der Wissenschaften.

———. 1998. *Epos und Zitat: Studien zu den Quellen der* Odyssee. Vienna: Verlag der Österreichischen Akademie der Wissenschaft.

———. 2002. "Traditional Referentiality and Homeric Intertextuality." In *Omero Tremila Anni Dopo*, ed. F. Montanari and P. Ascheri. Rome: Edizioni di Storia e Letteratura, 3–19.

Dekel, Edan. 2012. *Virgil's Homeric Lens*. New York: Routledge.

De Jong, Irene J. F. 1987. *Narrators and Focalizers: The Presentation of the Story in the* Iliad. Amsterdam: B. R. Grüner.

———. 2001. *A Narratological Commentary on the* Odyssey. Cambridge: Cambridge University Press.

———. 2012. "Double Deixis in Homeric Speech: On the Interpretation of ὅδε and οὗτος." In *Homer, gedeutet durch ein grosses Lexikon*, ed. M. Meier-Brügger. Göttingen, Germany: Vandenhoeck & Ruprecht, 63–83.

De Man, Paul. 1986. *The Resistance to Theory*. Minneapolis: University of Minnesota Press.

Detienne, Marcel, and Jean-Pierre Vernant. (1974) 1991. *Cunning Intelligence in Greek Culture and Society*, trans. J. Lloyd. Chicago: University of Chicago Press.

Derrida, Jacques. 1978. *Writing and Difference*, trans. A. Bass. Chicago: University of Chicago Press.

Dickie, Matthew W. 1984. "Phaeacian Athletes." In *Papers of the Liverpool Latin Seminar, Fourth Volume*, ed. F. Cairns. Liverpool: ARCA Classical and Medieval Texts, 237–76.

Didi-Huberman, Georges. 2002. *L'image survivante: Histoire de l'art et temps des fantômes selon Aby Warburg*. Paris: Les Éditions de Minuit.

Dietrich, B. C. 1979. "Views of Homeric Gods and Religion." *Numen* 26.2: 129–51.

———. 1983. "Divine Epiphanies in Homer." *Numen* 30.1: 53–79.

Dimock, G. E., Jr. 1956. "The Name of Odysseus." *Hudson Review* 9.1: 52–70.

Doane, Mary Ann. 2002. *The Emergence of Cinematic Time: Modernity, Contingency, the Archive*. Cambridge, MA: Harvard University Press.

Dunkle, R. 1987. "Nestor, Odysseus, and the *Mētis-Biē* Antithesis: The Funeral Games, *Iliad* 23." *CW* 81.1: 1–17.

Edwards, Anthony T. 1985. *Achilles in the* Odyssey. Königstein, Germany: Anton Hain.

Edwards, Mark W. 1980. "Convention and Individuality in *Iliad* 1." *HSCP* 84: 1–29.

———. 1987. *Homer: Poet of the* Iliad. Baltimore: Johns Hopkins University Press.

———. 1991. *The Iliad: A Commentary*. Vol. 5, bks. 17–24, ed. G. S. Kirk. Cambridge: Cambridge University Press.

———. 1997. "Homeric Style and Oral Poetics." In *A New Companion to Homer*, ed. I. Morris and B. B. Powell. Leiden: Brill, 261–83.

Eide, Tormod. 1999. "Reformulated Repetitions in Homer." *Symbolae Osloenses* 74.1: 97–139.

Elmer, David F. 2010. "Kita and Kosmos: The Poetics of Ornamentation in Bosniac and Homeric Epic." *Journal of American Folklore* 123: 276–303.

———. 2013. *The Poetics of Consent: Collective Decision Making and the* Iliad. Baltimore: Johns Hopkins University Press.

———. 2015. "The 'Narrow Road' and the Ethics of Language Use in the *Iliad* and the *Odyssey*." *Ramus* 44.1–2: 155–83.

Erbse, Hartmut. (1972) 1997. "The Ending of the *Odyssey*: Linguistic Problems." In *Homer: German Scholarship in Translation*, trans. G. M. Wright and P. V. Jones. Oxford: Clarendon, 263–320.

Faraone, Christopher A. 1992. *Talismans and Trojan Horses: Guardian Statues in Ancient Greek Myth and Ritual*. Oxford: Oxford University Press.

Farron, S. 1982. "The Abruptness of the End of the *Aeneid*." *Acta Classica* 25: 136–41.

Felson, Nancy. 1994. *Regarding Penelope: From Character to Poetics*. Princeton, NJ: Princeton University Press.

———. 1999. "Paradigms of Paternity: Fathers, Sons, and Athletic/Sexual Prowess in Homer's *Odyssey*." In *Euphrosyne: Studies in Ancient Epic and Its Legacy in Honor of Dimitris N. Maronitis*, ed. J. N. Kazazis and A. Rengakos. Stuttgart: Steiner, 89–98.

———. 2002. "*Threptra* and Invincible Hands: The Father-Son Relationship in *Iliad* 24." *Arethusa* 35.1: 35–50.

Fenik, Bernard. 1968. *Typical Battle Scenes in the Iliad: Studies in the Narrative Techniques of Homeric Battle Description*. Wiesbaden, Germany: Steiner.

Flint, Kate. 2004. "Peter Walsh's Pocket-Knife." *TLS* 5262 (6 February): 12.

Flusser, Vilém. (1991) 2014. *Gestures*, trans. N. A. Roth. Minneapolis: University of Minnesota Press.

Foley, Helene. 1978. "'Reverse Similes' and Sex Roles in the *Odyssey*." *Arethusa* 11:1–2: 7–26.

Foley, John Miles. 1991. *Immanent Art: From Structure to Meaning in Traditional Oral Epic*. Bloomington: Indiana University Press.

———. 1999. *Homer's Traditional Art*. University Park: Pennsylvania State University Press.

Ford, Andrew. 1992. *Homer: The Poetry of the Past*. Ithaca, NY: Cornell University Press.

Foster, Susan Leigh. 1992. "Dancing Bodies." In *Incorporations*, ed. J. Crary and S. Kwinter. New York: Zone, 480–96.

———. 2008. "Movement's Contagion: The Kinesthetic Impact of Performance." In *The Cambridge Companion to Performance Studies*, ed. T. C. Davis. Cambridge: Cambridge University Press, 46–59.

———. 2011. *Choreographing Empathy: Kinesthesia in Performance*. London and New York: Routledge.

Foucault, Michel. (1975) 1995. *Discipline and Punish: The Birth of the Prison*, trans. A. Sheridan. New York: Vintage.

Fowler, Don P. 1997. "Second Thoughts on Closure." In *Classical Closure: Reading the End in Greek and Latin Literature*, ed. D. H. Roberts, F. M. Dunn, and D. P. Fowler. Princeton, NJ: Princeton University Press, 3–22.

Frame, Douglas. 2009. *Hippota Nestor*. Washington, DC: Center for Hellenic Studies.

Fränkel, Hermann. 1946. "Man's 'Ephemeros' Nature According to Pindar and Others." *TAPA* 77: 131–45.

———. (1931) 1955. "Die Zeitauffassung in der frühgriechischen Literatur." In *Wege und Formen frühgriechischen Denkens: Literarische und philosophiegeschichtliche Studien*, ed. F. Tietze. Munich: Beck, 1–22.

———. (1962) 1975. *Early Greek Poetry and Philosophy: A History of Greek Epic, Lyric, and Prose to the Middle of the Fifth Century*, trans. M. Hadas and J. Willis. Oxford: Blackwell; New York: Harcourt Brace Jovanovich.

Freud, Sigmund. (1917) 1971. "Mourning and Melancholia." In *The Standard Edition of the Complete Psychological Works of Sigmund Freud*. Vol. 14, trans. J. Strachey. London: Hogarth, 243–58.

Friedrich, Wolf-Hartmut. 1956. *Verwundung und Tod in der* Ilias: *Homerische Darstellungsweisen*. Göttingen, Germany: Vandenhoeck & Ruprecht.

———. 2003. *Wounding and Death in the* Iliad: *Homeric Techniques of Description*, trans. P. Jones and G. Wright. London: Duckworth.

Gaca, Kathryn. 2008. "Reinterpreting the Homeric Simile of *Iliad* 16.7–11: The Girl and Her Mother in Ancient Greek Warfare." *AJP* 129.2: 145–71.

Gagarin, Michael. 1983. "Antilochus' Strategy: The Chariot Race in *Iliad* 23." *CP* 78.1: 35–39.

Garcia, Lorenzo F. Jr. 2007. *Homeric Temporalities: Simultaneity, Sequence, and Durability in the* Iliad. PhD diss., University of California, Los Angeles.

———. 2013. *Homeric Durability. Telling Time in the* Iliad. Washington DC: Center for Hellenic Studies.

Garland, Robert. 1981. "The Causation of Death in the *Iliad*: A Biological and Theological Investigation." *BICS* 28: 43–60.

Genette, Gérard. (1972) 1980. *Narrative Discourse: An Essay in Method*, trans. J. E. Lewin. Ithaca, NY: Cornell University Press.

Gernet, L. 1948. "Jeux et droit (remarques sur le XXIII chant de l'*Iliade*)." *Revue historique de droit français et étranger* 26: 177–88.

Gil, José. 2006. "Paradoxical Body," trans. A. Lepecki. *Drama Review* 50.4: 21–35.

Gilbert, Sandra M. 1993. "Female Female Impersonator: Millay and the Theatre of Personality." In *Critical Essays on Edna St. Vincent Millay*, ed. W. B. Thesing. New York: G. K. Hall, 293–312.

Gilpin, Heidi. 1994. "Aberrations of Gravity." In *Lightness*, ed. J. Rajchman and G. Lynn. Special issue, *ANY: Architecture New York* 5: 50–55.

Gombrich, E. H. 1986. *Aby Warburg: An Intellectual Biography*. Chicago: University of Chicago Press.

González, José M. 2013. *The Epic Rhapsode and His Craft: Homeric Performance in a Diachronic Perspective*. Washington DC: Center for Hellenic Studies.

Gordon, R. L. 1979. "The Real and the Imaginary: Production and Religion in the Graeco-Roman World." *Art History* 2.1: 5–34.

Gould, John. 1973. "*HIKETEIA*." *JHS* 93: 74–103.

Graf, Fritz. 1991. "Gestures and Conventions: The Gestures of Roman Actors and Orators." In *A Cultural History of Gesture: From Antiquity to the Present Day*, ed. J. Bremmer and H. Roodenburg. Cambridge: Polity, 36–58.

Gray, H. D. F. 1954. "Metal-Working in Homer." *JHS* 74: 1–15.

Graziosi, Barbara, and Johannes Haubold. 2005. *Homer: The Resonance of Epic*. Duckworth: London.

Greene, Thomas M. 1963. *The Descent from Heaven: A Study in Continuity*. New Haven, CT: Yale University Press.

Grethlein, Jonas, and Luuk Huitink. 2017. "Homer's Vividness: An Enactive Approach." *JHS* 137: 1–25.

Griffin, Jasper. 1977. "The Epic Cycle and the Uniqueness of Homer." *JHS* 97: 39–53.

———. 1978. "The Divine Audience and the Religion of the *Iliad*." *CQ* 28.1: 1–22.

———. 1980. *Homer on Life and Death*. Oxford: Clarendon.

———. 1986. "Heroic and Unheroic Ideas in Homer." In *Chios: A Conference at the Homereion in Chios, 1984*, ed. J. Boardman and C. E. Vaphopoulou-Richardson. Oxford: Clarendon, 3–13.

Griffith, Mark. 2006a. "Horsepower and Donkeywork: Equids and the Ancient Greek Imagination. 1." *CP* 101.3: 185–246.

———. 2006b. "Horsepower and Donkeywork: Equids and the Ancient Greek Imagination. 2." *CP* 101.4: 307–58.

Gunning, Tom. 2003a. "Never Seen This Picture Before: Muybridge in Multiplicity." In *Time Stands Still: Muybridge and the Instantaneous Photography Movement*, ed. Phillip Prodger. New York: Oxford University Press, 222–72.

———. 2003b. "Re-Newing Old Technologies: Astonishment, Second Nature, and the Uncanny in Technology from the Previous Turn-of-the-Century." In *Rethinking Media Change: The Aesthetics of Transition*, ed. David Thorburn and Henry Jenkins. Cambridge, MA: MIT Press, 39–60.

———. 2008. "What's the Point of an Index? or, Faking Photographs." In *Still Moving: Between Cinema and Photography*, ed. Karen Beckman and Jean Ma. Durham, NC: Duke University Press, 23–40.

Hainsworth, J. B. 1968. *The Flexibility of the Homeric Formula*. Oxford: Clarendon.

———. 1993. *The Iliad: A Commentary*. Vol. 3, bks. 9–12, ed. G. S. Kirk. Cambridge: Cambridge University Press.

Hardie, Philip R. 1997. "Closure in Latin Epic." In *Classical Closure: Reading the End in Greek and Latin Literature*, ed. D. H. Roberts, F. M. Dunn, and D. P. Fowler, Princeton, NJ: Princeton University Press, 139–62.

————. 1999. "Metamophosis, Metaphor, and Allegory in Latin Epic." In *Epic Traditions in the Contemporary World: The Poetics of Community*, ed. M. Beissinger, J. Tylus, and S. Wofford. Berkeley: University of California Press, 89–107.

Haubold, Johannes. 2007. "Homer after Parry: Tradition, Reception, and the Timeless Text." In *Homer in the Twentieth Century: Between World Literature and the Western Canon*, ed. B. Graziosi and E. Greenwood. Oxford and New York: Oxford University Press, 27–46.

Hawhee, Debra. 2004. *Bodily Arts: Rhetoric and Athletics in Ancient Greece*. Austin: University of Texas Press.

Heath, John. 2005. *The Talking Greeks: Speech, Animals, and the Other in Homer, Aeschylus, and Plato*. Cambridge: Cambridge University Press.

Heiden, Bruce. 1998. "The Simile of the Fugitive Homicide, *Iliad* 24.480–84: Analogy, Foiling, and Allusion." *AJP* 119.1: 1–10.

Herington. James. 1985. *Poetry into Drama: Early Tragedy and the Greek Poetic Tradition*. Berkeley: University of California Press.

Heubeck, Alfred, Stephanie West, and J. B. Hainsworth, eds. 1988. *A Commentary on Homer's Odyssey*. Vol. 1, *Introduction and Books I–VIII*. Oxford: Clarendon.

Hillman, David, and Carla Mazio, eds. 1997. *The Body in Parts: Fantasies of Coporeality in Early Modern Europe*. New York: Routledge.

Hinckley, Lois V. 1986. "Patroclus' Funeral Games and Homer's Character Portrayal." *CJ* 81.3: 209–21.

Hoekstra, A. 1965. *Homeric Modifications of Formulaic Prototypes: Studies in the Development of Greek Epic Diction*. Amsterdam: Noord-Hollandsche Uitgevers Maatschappij.

Holmes, Brooke. 2007. "The *Iliad*'s Economy of Pain." *TAPA* 137: 45–84.

————. 2010. *The Symptom and the Subject: The Emergence of the Physical Body in Ancient Greece*. Princeton. NJ: Princeton University Press.

Householder, Fred, and Gregory Nagy. 1972. *Greek: A Survey of Recent Work*. The Hague: Mouton.

Ingold, Tim. 2011. *Being Alive: Essays on Movement, Knowledge and Description*. London and New York: Routledge.

Irwin, Elizabeth. 2005. *Solon and Early Greek Poetry: The Politics of Exhortation*. Cambridge: Cambridge University Press.

James, Henry. (1903) 2004. "The Beast in the Jungle." In *The Portable Henry James*, ed. J. Auchard. New York: Penguin, 236–82.

James, William. (1890) 1950. *The Principles of Psychology*. Vol. I. New York: Dover.

Jameson, Fredric. 2003. "The End of Temporality." *CI* 29.4: 695–718.

Jamison, Stephanie W. 2006. "Poetic 'Repair' in the *Rig Veda*." In *La Langue Poétique Indoeuropéene*, ed. G.-J. Pinault and D. Petit. Leuven, Belgium, and Paris: Peeters, 133–40.

————, and Joel P. Brereton. 2014, trans. *The* Rigveda: *the Earliest Religious Poetry of India*. 3 vols. New York: Oxford University Press.

Janko, Richard. 1992. *The Iliad: A Commentary*. Vol. 4, bks. 13–16, ed. G.S. Kirk. Cambridge: Cambridge University Press.

————. 1998. "The Homeric Poems as Oral Dictated Poems." *CQ* 48.1: 1–13.

Johansen, Knud Friis. 1967. *The Iliad in Early Greek Art*. Copenhagen: Munksgaard.

Johnson, Christopher D. 2012. *Memory, Metaphor, and Aby Warburg's Atlas of Images*. Ithaca, NY: Cornell University Press and Cornell University Library.

Johnson, David M. 1999. "Hesiod's Descriptions of Tartarus (*Theogony* 721–819)." *Phoenix* 53.1–2: 8–28.

Jones, Nicholas R. 1975. "'Stand' and 'Fall' as Images of Posture in *Paradise Lost*." *Milton Studies* 8: 221–46.

Kahane, Ahuvia. 1994. *The Interpretation of Order: A Study in the Poetics of Homeric Repetition*. Oxford: Oxford University Press.

———. 1997. "Hexameter Progression and the Homeric Hero's Solitary State." In *Written Voices, Spoken Signs: Tradition, Performance, and the Epic Text*, ed. E. Bakker and A. Kahane. Cambridge, MA: Harvard University Press, 110–37.

Kakridis, Johannes T. 1949. *Homeric Researches*. Lund, Sweden: C. W. K. Gleerup.

Katz, Joshua T. 2013a. "Gods and Vowels." In *Poetic Language and Religion in Greece and Rome*, ed. J. V. G. Trabazo and A. R. Pérez. Newcastle upon Tyne, UK: Cambridge Scholars Publishing, 2–28.

———. 2013b. "The Hymnic Long Alpha: Μούσας ἀείδω and Related Incipits in Archaic Greek Poetry." In *Proceedings of the 24th Annual UCLA Indo-European Conference*, ed. S. W. Jamison, H. C. Melchert, and B. Vine. Bremen, Germany: Hempen. 87–101.

———. 2018. "Μῆνιν ἄειδε, θεά and the Form of the Homeric Word for 'Goddess.'" In *Language and Meter*, ed. D. Gunkel and O. Hackstein. Leiden: Brill, 54–76.

Katz, Marilyn A. 1991. *Penelope's Renown: Meaning and Indeterminacy in the* Odyssey. Princeton, NJ: Princeton University Press.

Kay, F. L. 1957. "Aristarchus' 'τέλος,' *Odyssey* xxiii.296." *CR* 7.2: 106.

Kearns, Emily. 2004. "The Gods in the Homeric Epics." In *The Cambridge Companion to Homer*, ed. R. Fowler. Cambridge: Cambridge University Press, 59–73.

Keenleyside, Heather. 2016. *Animals and Other People: Literary Forms and Living Beings in the Long Eighteenth Century*. Philadelphia: University of Pennsylvania Press.

Kelly, Adrian. 2007a. "How to End an Orally-Derived Poem." *TAPA* 137.2: 371–402.

———. 2007b. *A Referential Commentary and Lexicon to* Iliad VIII. Oxford: Oxford University Press.

Kendon, Adam, ed. 1981. *Nonverbal Communication, Interaction, and Gesture: Selections from Semiotica*. The Hague: Mouton.

———. 2004. *Gesture: Visible Action as Utterance*. Cambridge: Cambridge University Press.

Kern, Stephen. (1983) 2003. *The Culture of Time and Space 1880–1918*. 2nd ed. Cambridge, MA: Harvard University Press.

Kirk, G. S. 1962. *The Songs of Homer*. Cambridge: Cambridge University Press.

———. 1985. *The* Iliad: *A Commentary*. Vol. 2, bks. 5–8, ed. G. S. Kirk. Cambridge: Cambridge University Press.

King, Katherine Callen. 1987. *Achilles: Paradigms of the War Hero from Homer to the Middle Ages*. Berkeley: University of California Press.

Kitchell, Kenneth F. 1998. "'But the Mare I Will Not Give Up': The Games in *Iliad* 23." *Classical Bulletin* 74.2: 159–71.

Kittler, Friedrich. 2003. "Man as a Drunken Town-Musician." *MLN* 118.3: 637–52.

Kleist, Heinrich von. (1810) 2009. "On the Theater of Marionettes." In *Selected Prose of Heinrich von Kleist*, trans. Peter Wortsman. New York: Archipelago, 264–73.

Knauer, G. N. 1964. *Die Aeneis und Homer: Studien zur poetischen Technik Vergils mit Listen der Homerzitate in der Aeneis*. Göttingen, Germany: Vandenhoek & Ruprecht.

Knox, Peter E. 1990. "In Pursuit of Daphne." *TAPA* 120: 183–202 and 385–86.

Kozak, Lynn. 2017. *Experiencing Hektor: Character in the* Iliad. London: Bloomsbury.

Kretler, Katherine. Forthcoming 2019. *One Man Show: Poetics and Presence in the* Iliad *and* Odyssey. Washington, DC: Center for Hellenic Studies.

Kuh, Katherine. 1965. *Break-Up: The Core of Modern Art*. New York: Graphic Society.

Kukkonen, K. 2014. "Presence and Prediction: The Embodied Reader's Cascades of Cognition." In *Cognitive Literary Study: Second Generation Approaches*, ed. K. Kukkonen and M. Caracciolo. Special issue, *Style* 48.3: 367–84.

Kukkonen, K., and M. Caracciolo, eds. 2014. *Cognitive Literary Study: Second Generation Approaches*. Special issue, *Style* 48.3.

Kullman, Wolfgang. 2001. "Past and Future in the *Iliad*." In *Oxford Readings in Homer's* Iliad, ed. D. L. Cairns. Oxford and New York: Oxford University Press, 385–408.

Kyle, Donald G. 1993. *Athletics in Ancient Athens*. Leiden: Brill.

———. 2007. *Sport and Spectacle in the Ancient World*. Malden, MA, and Oxford: Blackwell.

Lakoff, George, and Mark Johnson. 1980. *Metaphors We Live By*. Chicago: University of Chicago Press.

Lang, Mabel L. 1969. "Homer and Oral Techniques." *Hesperia* 38.2: 159–68.

———. 1983. "Reverberation and Mythology in the *Iliad*." In *Approaches to Homer*, ed. C. A. Rubino and C. W. Shelmerdine. Austin: University of Texas Press, 140–64.

Lateiner, Donald. 1992. "Heroic Proxemics: Social Space and Distance in the *Odyssey*." *TAPA* 122: 133–63.

———. 1995. *Sardonic Smile: Nonverbal Behavior in Homeric Epic*. Ann Arbor: University of Michigan Press.

———. 2002. "Pouring Bloody Drops (*Iliad* 16.459): The Grief of Zeus." *Colby Quarterly* 38.1: 42–61.

Lattimore, Richmond. 1951. *The* Iliad *of Homer*. Chicago: University of Chicago Press.

———.1953. "The Eumenides." In *Aeschylus I*, ed. D. Grene and R. Lattimore. Chicago: University of Chicago Press, 133–71.

———. 1965. *The* Odyssey *of Homer*. New York: Harper & Row.

Lefebvre, Henri. (1992) 2004. *Rhythmanalysis: Space, Time and Everyday Life*, trans. S. Elden and G. Moore. London and New York: Continuum.

Lepecki, André. 2006. *Exhausting Dance: Performance and the Politics of Movement*. New York and London: Routledge.

Lesky, Albin. 1961. *Göttliche und menschliche Motivation im homerischen Epos*. Heidelberg: Winter Verlag.

Létoublon, Françoise. 1985. *Il allait, pareil à la nuit: Les verbes de mouvement en Grec; Suppletisme et aspect verbal*. Paris: Klincksieck.

Levine, Caroline. 2017. *Forms: Whole, Rhythm, Hierarchy, Network*. Princeton, NJ: Princeton University Press.

Levy, Harry L. 1979. "Homer's Gods: A Comment on their Immortality." *GRBS* 20.3: 215–18.

Lloyd, G. E. R. (1966) 1987. *Polarity and Analogy: Two Types of Argumentation in Early Greek Thought*. Reprint. Indianapolis, IN: Hackett.

Lohmann, Dieter. 1970. *Die Komposition der Reden in der* Ilias. Berlin: de Gruyter.

Loraux, Nicole. 1986. "Le corps vulnérable d'Arès." In *Corps des Dieux*, ed. C. Malamoud and J.-P. Vernant. *Le temps de la réflexion* 7, 335–54.

———. (1997) 2002. *The Divided City: On Memory and Forgetting in Ancient Athens*, trans. C. Pache with J. Fort. New York: Zone.

Lord, Albert B. (1960) 2000. *The Singer of Tales*. 2nd ed. Cambridge, MA: Harvard University Press.

Louden, Bruce. 1993. "An Extended Narrative Pattern in the *Odyssey*." *GRBS* 34.1: 5–33.

Lovatt, Helen. 2005. *Status and Epic Games: Sport, Politics, and Poetics in the* Thebaid. Cambridge: Cambridge University Press.

———. 2013. *The Epic Gaze: Vision, Gender, and Narrative in Ancient Epic.* Cambridge: Cambridge University Press.

Lowenstam, Steven. 1981. *The Death of Patroklos: A Study in Typology.* Königstein, Germany: Anton Hain.

———. 1993. *The Scepter and the Spear: Studies on Forms of Repetitions in the Homeric Poems.* Lanham, MD: Rowman & Littlefield.

Lynn-George, Michael. 1982. "Homer on Life and Death." *JHS* 102: 239–45.

———. 1988. *Epos: Word, Narrative, and the* Iliad. Atlantic Highlands, NJ: Humanities Press International.

———. 1993. "Aspects of the Epic Vocabulary of Vulnerability." *Colby Quarterly* 29: 197–221.

———. 1996. "Structures of Care in the *Iliad.*" *CQ* 46.1: 1–26.

Macleod, Colin. 1982. *Homer:* Iliad; *Book XXIV.* Cambridge: Cambridge University Press.

Manning, Erin. 2009. *Relationscapes: Movement, Art, Philosophy.* Cambridge, MA: MIT Press.

Marey, Etienne-Jules. (1873) 1893. *Animal Mechanism: A Treatise on Terrestrial and Aerial Locomotion.* New York: D. Appleton.

———. (1894) 1972. *Movement,* trans. Eric Pritchard. London: William Heinemann.

Marquardt, Patricia. 1985. "Penelope 'ΠΟΛΥΤΡΟΠΟΣ.'" *AJP* 106.1: 32–48.

Martin, Richard P. 1984. "Hesiod, Odysseus, and the Instruction of Princes." *TAPA* 114: 29–48.

———. 1989. *The Language of Heroes: Speech and Performance in the* Iliad. Ithaca, NY: Cornell University Press.

———.1993. "Telemachus and the Last Hero Song." *Colby Quarterly* 29: 222–40.

Mauss, Marcel. (1935) 1992. "Techniques of the Body." In *Incorporations,* ed. J. Crary and S. Kwinter. New York: Zone, 455–77.

Merleau-Ponty, Maurice. (1945) 1962. *Phenomenology of Perception,* trans. C. Smith. New York: Humanities Press.

———. (1964) 1968. *The Visible and the Invisible,* trans. A. Lingis, ed. C. Lefort. Evanston, IL: Northwestern University Press.

Michaud, Philippe-Alain. (1998) 2004. *Aby Warburg and the Image in Motion,* trans. S. Hawkes. New York: Zone.

Millay, Edna St. Vincent. 1956. *Collected Poems.* New York: Harper & Row.

Miller, D. A. 1981. *Narrative and its Discontents: Problems of Closure in the Traditional Novel.* Princeton, NJ: Princeton University Press.

Miller, J. Hillis. 1982. *Fiction and Repetition: Seven English Novels.* Cambridge, MA: Harvard University Press.

Miller, Margaret C. 1995. "Priam, King of Troy." In *The Ages of Homer: A Tribute to Emily Townsend Vermeule,* ed. J. B. Carter and S. P. Morris. Austin: University of Texas Press, 449–65.

Minchin, Elizabeth. 1986. "The Interpretation of a Theme in Oral Epic: *Iliad* 24.559–70." *G&R* 33.1: 11–19.

———. 2001. *Homer and the Resources of Memory: Some Applications of Cognitive Theory to the* Iliad *and* Odyssey. Oxford: Oxford University Press.

Monro, D. B. (1882) 1891. *A Grammar of the Homeric Dialect.* Oxford: Clarendon.

Montiglio, Silvia. 2000. *Silence in the Land of Logos.* Princeton, NJ: Princeton University Press.

Morrison, James V. 1999. "Homeric Darkness: Patterns and Manipulations of Death Scenes in the *Iliad.*" *Hermes* 127.2: 129–44.

Mouratidis, John. 2012. *On the Jump of the Ancient Pentathlon.* Hildesheim, Germany: Weidmann.

Mueller, Melissa. 2007. "Penelope and the Poetics of Remembering." *Arethusa* 40.3: 337–62.

———. 2010. "Helen's Hands: Weaving for *Kleos* in the *Odyssey.*" *Helios* 37.1: 1–21.

———. Forthcoming. *Sappho and Homer: A Reparative Reading*. Cambridge: Cambridge University Press.

Murnaghan, Sheila H. 1986. "Penelope's ἄγνοια: Knowledge, Power, and Gender in the *Odyssey*." *Helios* 13.2: 103–15.

———. 1992. "Maternity and Mortality in Homeric Poetry." *CA* 11.2: 242–64.

———. 1994. "Reading Penelope." In *Epic and Epoch: Essays on the Interpretation and History of a Genre*, ed. S. M. Oberhelm, V. Kelly, and R. J. Golsan. Lubbock: Texas Tech University Press, 76–96.

———. 1997. "Equal Honor and Future Glory: The Plan of Zeus in the *Iliad*." In *Classical Closure: Reading the End in Greek and Latin Literature*, ed. D. H. Roberts, F. M. Dunn, and D. P. Fowler. Princeton, NJ: Princeton University Press, 23–42.

———. 1999. "The Poetics of Loss in Greek Epic." In *Epic Traditions in the Contemporary World: The Poetics of Community*, ed. M. H. Beissinger, J. Tylus, and S. L. Wofford. Berkeley: University of California Press, 203–22.

———. 2018. "Penelope as a Tragic Heroine: Choral Dynamics in Homeric Epic," *Yearbook of Ancient Greek Epic* 2.1: 165–89.

Murray, Penelope. 1996. *Plato on Poetry*. Cambridge: Cambridge University Press.

Muybridge, Eadweard. (1887) 1979. *Muybridge's Complete Human and Animal Locomotion: All 781 Plates from the 1887 Animal Locomotion by Eadweard Muybridge*. 3 vols. New York: Dover.

Nagler, Michael N. 1974. *Spontaneity and Tradition: A Study in the Oral Art of Homer*. Berkeley: University of California Press.

Nagy, Gregory. 1988. "Toward a Semantics of Ancient Conflict." *CW* 82: 81–90.

———. 1990a. *Greek Mythology and Poetics*. Ithaca, NY: Cornell University Press.

———. 1990b. *Pindar's Homer: The Lyric Possession of an Epic Past*. Baltimore: Johns Hopkins University Press.

———. 1996a. *Poetry as Performance: Homer and Beyond*. Cambridge: Cambridge University Press.

———. 1996b. *Homeric Questions*. Austin: University of Texas Press.

———. (1979) 1999. *The Best of the Achaeans: Concepts of the Hero in Archaic Greek Poetry*. Rev. ed. Baltimore: Johns Hopkins University Press.

———. 2004. "Poetics of Repetition in Homer." In *Greek Ritual Poetics*, ed. D. Yatromanolakis and P. Roilos. Washington DC: Center for Hellenic Studies, 139–48.

Nagy, Joseph F. 2009. "Hurtling Búan and the Heroic Trajectory." In *Ulidia 2: Proceedings of the Second International Conference on the Ulster Cycle of Tales*, ed. R. Ó Huiginn and B. O Catháin, Maynooth: An Sagart, 1–17.

Nakassis, Dimitri. 2004. "Gemination at the Horizons: East and West in the Mythical Geography of Archaic Greek Epic." *TAPA* 134.2: 213–33.

Neumann, Gerhard. 1965. *Gesten und Gebärden in der griechischen Kunst*. Berlin: de Gruyter.

Newton, Rick M. 1987. "Odysseus and Hephaestus in the *Odyssey*." *CJ* 83.1: 12–20.

Nightingale, Andrea. 2011. *Once out of Nature: Augustine on Time and the Body*. Chicago: University of Chicago Press.

Noland, Carrie. 2008. "Introduction." In *Migrations of Gesture*, ed. C. Noland and S. A. Ness. Minneapolis: University of Minnesota Press, ix–xxviii.

———. 2009. *Agency and Embodiment: Performing Gestures/Producing Culture*. Cambridge, MA: Harvard University Press.

Nussbaum, Martha. 1986. *The Fragility of Goodness: Luck and Ethics in Greek Tragedy and Philosophy*. Cambridge: Cambridge University Press.

O'Connell, Erin. 2005. *Heraclitus and Derrida: Presocratic Deconstruction*. New York: Peter Lang.

O'Connell, Peter A. 2017. *The Rhetoric of Seeing in Attic Forensic Oratory*. Austin: University of Texas Press.

Oakley, John H., and Rebecca H. Sinos. 1993. *The Wedding in Ancient Athens*. Madison: University of Wisconsin Press.

Olsen, S. 2016. "Beyond Choreia: Dance in Ancient Greek Literature and Culture." PhD diss., University of California, Berkeley.

———. 2017a. "The Fantastic Phaeacians: Dance and Disruption in the *Odyssey*." *CA* 36.1: 1–32.

———. 2017b. "Kinesthetic *Choreia*: Empathy, Memory, and Dance in Ancient Greece." *CP* 112: 1–22.

———. Forthcoming. *Dance, Literature, and Culture in Ancient Greece: Representing the Unruly Body*.

Olson, S. Douglas. 1989. "*Odyssey* 8: Guile, Force and the Subversive Poetics of Desire." *Arethusa* 22.2: 135–45.

Onians, R. B. 1951. *The Origins of European Thought: About the Body, the Mind, the Soul, the World, Time and Fate*. Cambridge: Cambridge University Press.

Ormand, Kirk. 2014a. "Uncertain Geographies of Desire in the *Catalogue of Women*: Atalanta." In *Geography, Topography, Landscape: Configurations of Space in Greek and Roman Epic*, ed. M. Skempis and I. Ziogas. Berlin and Boston: de Gruyter, 137–60.

———. 2014b. *The Hesiodic Catalogue of Women and Archaic Greece*. New York: Cambridge University Press.

Osborne, Robin. 2011. *The History Written on the Classical Greek Body*. Cambridge and New York: Cambridge University Press.

Oswald, Alice. 2011. *Memorial: An Excavation of the* Iliad. London: Faber and Faber (first American edition published as *Memorial: A Version of Homer's* Iliad, New York: W. W. Norton, 2012).

Page, D. L. 1955. *The Homeric* Odyssey. Oxford: Clarendon.

———. 1959. *History and the Homeric* Iliad. Berkeley: University of California Press.

Pagès, Sylviane. 2012. "Tomber." In *Histoires de gestes*, ed. M. Glon and I. Launay. Arles, France: Actes Sud, 39–51.

Paterson, Mark. 2007. *The Senses of Touch: Haptics, Affects, and Technologies*. Oxford and New York: Berg.

Pavlovskis, Zoja. 1976. "*Aeneid* V: The Old and the Young." *CJ* 71.3: 193–205.

Paxton, Steve. 1986. "The Small Dance, the Stand." *Contact Quarterly* 11.1: 48–50.

Pearson, Giles. 2012. *Aristotle on Desire*. Cambridge and New York: Cambridge University Press.

Pedrick, Victoria. 1982. "Supplication in the *Iliad* and the *Odyssey*." *TAPA* 112: 125–40.

———. 1988. "The Hospitality of Noble Women in the *Odyssey*." *Helios* 15: 85–101.

Parry, Milman. (1928) 1971a. "The Traditional Epithet in Homer." In *The Making of Homeric Verse: The Collected Papers of Milman Parry*, ed. A. Parry. Oxford: Clarendon, 1–190.

———. (1930) 1971b. "Studies in the Epic Technique of Oral Verse-Making I: Homer and Homeric Style." In *The Making of Homeric Verse: The Collected Papers of Milman Parry*, ed. A. Parry. Oxford: Clarendon, 266–324.

Pelliccia, Hayden N. 1995. *Mind, Body, and Speech in Homer and Pindar*. Göttingen, Germany: Vandenhoek & Ruprecht.

Peradotto, John. 1990. *Man in the Middle Voice: Name and Narration in the* Odyssey. Princeton, NJ: Princeton University Press.

Platt, V. 2011. *Facing the Gods: Epiphany and Representation in Graeco-Roman Art, Literature and Religion.* Cambridge: Cambridge University Press.

——. Forthcoming. *Beyond Ekphrasis: Making Objects Matter in Classical Antiquity.*

Porter, James I. 2005. "Foucault's Ascetic Ancients." *Phoenix* 59: 121–32.

——. 2015. "Homer and the Sublime." *Ramus* 44.1–2: 184–99.

——, and M. Buchan. 2004. "Introduction." In *Before Subjectivity? Lacan and the Classics,* ed. J. I. Porter and M. Buchan. Special issue, *Helios* 31:1–19.

Pötscher, Walter. 1992. "Die Hikesie des letzten Ilias-Gesanges: (Hom. *Il.* 24,477ff.)." *Würzburger Jahrbücher für die Altertumswissenschaft* 18: 5–16.

Pucci, Pietro. 1982. "The Proem of the *Odyssey.*" *Arethusa* 15: 39–62.

——. 1987. *Odysseus Polutropos: Intertextual Readings in the* Odyssey *and the* Iliad. Ithaca, NY: Cornell University Press.

——. 1996. "Between Narrative and Catalogue: Life and Death of the Poem." *Mètis. anthropologie des mondes grecs anciens* 11: 5–24.

——. 1998. *The Song of the Sirens: Essays on Homer.* Lanham, MD: Rowman & Littlefield.

——. 2000. "Le cadre temporel de la volonté divine chez Homère." In *Constructions du temps dans le monde grec ancien,* ed. C. Darbo-Peschanski. Paris: CNRS Éditions, 33–48.

——. 2012. "Iterative and Syntactical Units: A Religious Gesture in the *Iliad.*" In *Homeric Contexts: Neoanalysis and the Interpretation of Oral Poetry,* ed. F. Montanari, A. Rengakos, and C. Tsagalis. Berlin and Boston: de Gruyter, 427–43.

Purves, Alex. 2004. "Topographies of Time in Hesiod." In *Time and Temporality in the Ancient World,* ed. R. M. Rosen. Philadelphia: University of Pennsylvania Museum of Archaeology and Anthropology, 147–68.

——. 2006. "Falling into Time in Homer's *Iliad.*" *CA* 25.1: 179–209.

——. 2010. *Space and Time in Ancient Greek Narrative.* New York: Cambridge University Press.

——. 2011. "Homer and the Art of Overtaking." *AJP* 132.4: 523–51.

——. 2015. "Ajax and Other Objects: Homer's Vibrant Materialism." *Ramus* 44.1–2: 75–94.

——. 2016. "Feeling on the Surface: Touch and Emotion in Fuseli and Homer." In *Deep Classics: Rethinking Classical Reception,* ed. S. Butler. London: Bloomsbury Academic, 67–86.

——, ed. 2018. *Touch and the Ancient Senses.* London and New York: Routledge.

Putnam, Michael C. J. 2011. *The Humanness of Heroes: Studies in the Conclusion of the* Aeneid. Amsterdam: Amsterdam University Press.

Quint, David. 2004. "Fear of Falling: Icarus, Phaethon and Lucretius in *Paradise Lost.*" *Renaissance Quarterly* 57.3: 847–81.

Rabaté, Jean-Michel. 2016. *The Pathos of Distance: Affects of the Moderns.* New York and London: Bloomsbury Academic.

Rainer, Yvonne. 1993. "Trisha Brown." *BOMB* 45: 28–33.

Ravaisson, Félix. (1838) 2008. *Of Habit,* trans. C. Carlisle and M. Sinclair. New York: Continuum.

Ready, Jonathan L. and Christos C. Tsagalis, eds. 2018. *Homer in Performance: Rhapsodes, Narrators, and Characters.* Austin: University of Texas Press.

Redfield, James M. 1975. *Nature and Culture in the* Iliad: *The Tragedy of Hector.* Chicago: University of Chicago Press. 2nd ed. 1994.

Richardson, Nicholas. 1993. *The Iliad: A Commentary.* Vol. 6, bks 21–24, ed. G. S. Kirk. Cambridge: Cambridge University Press.

Rijksbaron, Albert, ed. and trans. 2007. *Plato,* Ion or: On the Iliad. With Introduction and Commentary. Leiden: Brill.

Rizolatti, Giacomo, and Corrado Sinigaglia. 2008. *Mirrors in the Brain: How Our Minds Share Actions and Emotions,* trans. F. Anderson. Oxford: Oxford University Press.

Roberts, Deborah. 1997. "Afterword: Ending and Aftermath, Ancient and Modern." In *Classical Closure: Reading the End in Greek and Latin Literature*, ed. D. H. Roberts, F. M. Dunn and D. Fowler. Princeton, NJ: Princeton University Press, 251–73.

Roisman, Hanna M. 1988. "Nestor's Advice and Antilochus' Tactics." *Phoenix* 42.2: 114–20.

Rosen, Ralph M. 1990. "Hipponax and the Homeric Odysseus." *Eikasmos* 1: 11–25.

Rossi, L. E. 1968. "La fine alessandrina dell'*Odissea* e lo ζῆλος Ὁμηρικός di Apollonio Rodio." *RFIC* 96: 151–63.

Russo, Joseph. 1997. "The Formula." In *A New Companion to Homer*, ed. I. Morris and B. B. Powell. Leiden: Brill, 238–60.

Sacks, Richard. 1989. *The Traditional Phrase in Homer: Two Studies in Meaning, Form and Interpretation*. Leiden: Brill.

Said, Edward. (1975) 1985. *Beginnings: Intention and Method*. New York: Columbia University Press.

Schein, Seth. 1970. "Odysseus and Polyphemus in the *Odyssey*." *GRBS* 11: 73–83.

———. 1984. *The Mortal Hero: An Introduction to Homer's* Iliad. Berkeley: University of California Press.

———. 2002a. "The Horses of Achilles in Book 17 of the *Iliad*." In *EPEA PTEROENTA: Beiträge zur Homerforschung. Festschrift für Wolfgang Kullmann zum 75. Geburtstag*, ed. M. Reichel and A. Rengakos. Stuttgart: Steiner, 193–205.

———. 2002b. "Mythological Allusion in the *Odyssey*." In *Omero Tremila anni dopo*, ed. F. Montanari and P. Ascheri. Rome: Edizioni di Storia e Letteratura, 185–201.

———. 2015. "The Interpretation of *Iliad* 1.1–2: Language, Meter, Style, and Myth." Special Issue, *Gaïa* 18: Πολυφόρβη Γαίη. *Mélanges de littérature et linguistique offerts à Francoise Létoublon*. Textes réunis par F. Dell'Oro and O. Lagacherie, 301–9.

———. 2016a. *Homeric Epic and Its Reception: Interpretive Essays*. Oxford: Oxford University Press.

———. (1999) 2016b. "Homeric Intertextuality: Two Examples." In *Homeric Epic and Its Reception: Interpretive Essays*, by Seth Schein. Oxford: Oxford University Press, 81–91.

Schmitt, Jean-Claude. 1990. *La raison des gestes dans l'Occident medieval*. Paris: Gallimard.

Scodel, Ruth. 1982. "The Achaean Wall and the Myth of Destruction." *HSCP* 86: 33–50.

———. 2002. *Listening to Homer: Tradition, Narrative, and Audience*. Ann Arbor: University of Michigan Press.

———. 2008. *Epic Facework. Self-Presentation and Social Interaction in Homer*. Swansea, UK: Classical Press of Wales; Oxford: Oxbow.

Scott, William C. 1974. *The Oral Nature of the Homeric Simile*. Leiden: Brill.

———. 1997. "The Etiquette of Games in *Iliad* 23." *GRBS* 38.3: 213–27.

Seaford, Richard. 1994. *Reciprocity and Ritual: Homer and Tragedy in the Developing City-State*. Oxford: Oxford University Press.

Segal, Charles. 1971a. *The Theme of the Mutilation of the Corpse in the* Iliad. *Mnemosyne* Supplementum 17. Leiden: Brill.

———. 1971b. "Andromache's *Anagnorisis*: Formulaic Artistry in *Iliad* 22.437–76." *HSCP* 75: 33–57.

Seigworth, Gregory J., and Melissa Gregg. 2010. "An Inventory of Shimmers." In *The Affect Theory Reader*, ed. M. Gregg and G. J. Seigworth. Durham, NC: Duke University Press, 1–27.

Shapiro, H. Alan. 1993. "Hipparchos and the Rhapsodes." In *Cultural Poetics in Archaic Greece*, ed. C. Dougherty and L. Kurke. Cambridge: Cambridge University Press, 92–107.

Shapiro, Lawrence. 2011. *Embodied Cognition*. New York: Routledge.

Sheets-Johnstone, Maxine. 1999. *The Primacy of Movement*. Amsterdam and Philadelphia: John Benjamins.

Shklovsky, Victor. 1965. "Sterne's *Tristram Shandy*: Stylistic Commentary." In *Russian Formalist Criticism, Four Essays*, ed. L. T. Lemon and M. J. Reis. Lincoln: University of Nebraska Press, 25–57.

Sider, David. 2005. "Posidippus on Weather Signs and the Tradition of Didactic Poetry." In *The New Posidippus: A Hellenistic Poetry Book*, ed. K. J. Gutzwiller. Oxford: Oxford University Press, 164–82.

Sissa, Giulia, and Marcel Detienne. 2000. *The Daily Life of the Greek Gods*, trans. J. Lloyd. Stanford, CA: Stanford University Press.

Slatkin, Laura M. 1991. *The Power of Thetis: Allusion and Interpretation in the* Iliad. Berkeley: University of California Press.

———. (1988) 2011. "Les amis mortels." In *the Power of Thetis and Selected Essays*. Hellenic Studies 16. Washington DC: Center for Hellenic Studies, 120–38. Originally published in 1988 as "Les amis mortals: À propos des insultes dans les combats de *L'Iliade*." In *L'écrit du temps* 19: 119–32.

Sloterdijk, Peter. (2009). 2013. *You Must Change Your Life*. Cambridge and Malden, MA: Polity.

Snell, Bruno. 1953. *The Discovery of the Mind: The Greek Origins of European Thought*. Cambridge, MA: Harvard University Press.

Solnit, Rebecca. 2000. *Wanderlust: A History of Walking*. New York: Viking.

Sparrow, Tom, and Adam Hutchinson. 2013. "Introduction: Reflections on the Unreflected." In *A History of Habit from Aristotle to Bourdieu*, ed. T. Sparrow and A. Hutchinson. Lanham, MD: Lexington Books, 1–16.

Stanford, William B. (1948) 1998. *The* Odyssey *of Homer*. Vol. 2, bks 13–24. London: Bristol Classical Press (reprint of the 1965 edition, with alterations and additions).

Stanley, Keith. 1993. *The Shield of Homer: Narrative Structure in the* Iliad. Princeton, NJ: Princeton University Press.

Steiner, Deborah, ed. 2010. *Homer: Odyssey; Books XVII–XVIII*. Cambridge: Cambridge University Press.

Stern, Lesley. 2008. "Ghosting: The Performance and Migration of Cinematic Gesture, Focusing on Hou Hsiao-Hsien's *Good Men, Good Women*." In *Migrations of Gesture*, ed. C. Noland and S. A. Ness. Minneapolis: University of Minnesota Press, 185–215.

Stewart, Susan. 1999. "Prologue: From the Museum of Touch." In *Material Memories*, ed. M. Kwint, C. Breward, and J. Aynsley. Oxford: Berg, 17–36.

———. 2002. *Poetry and the Fate of the Senses*. Chicago: University of Chicago Press.

Stocking, Charles. 2010. "Language about Achilles: Linguistic Frame Theory and the Formula in Homeric Poetics." In *A Californian Hymn to Homer*, ed. T. Pepper. Washington DC: Center for Hellenic Studies, 131–68.

———. 2016. "The Use and Abuse of Training 'Science' in Philostratus' *Gymnasticus*." *CA* 35.1: 86–125.

Taplin, Oliver. 1992. *Homeric Soundings: The Shaping of the* Iliad. Oxford: Oxford University Press.

Tarrant, Richard J., ed. 2012. *Virgil: Aeneid Book XII*. Cambridge: Cambridge University Press.

Telò, Mario. 2011. "The Eagle's Gaze in the Opening of Heliodorus' *Aethiopica*." *AJP* 132.4: 581–613.

Thalmann, William G. 1984. *Conventions of Form and Thought in Early Greek Epic Poetry*. Baltimore: Johns Hopkins University Press.

———. 1988. "Thersites: Comedy, Scapegoats, and Heroic Ideology in the *Iliad*." *TAPA* 118: 1–28.

———. 1998. *The Swineherd and the Bow: Representations of Class in the* Odyssey. Ithaca, NY: Cornell University Press.

Thomas, Keith. 1991. "Introduction." In *A Cultural History of Gesture: From Antiquity to the Present Day*, ed. J. Bremmer and H. Roodenburg. Cambridge: Polity, 1–14.

Thompson, Michael. 2002. "The Representation of Life." In *Virtues and Reasons: Philippa Foot and Moral Theory*, ed. Rosalind Hursthouse, Gavin Lawrence, and Warren Quinn. Oxford: Oxford University Press, 247–96.

———. 2004. "Apprehending Human Form." In *Modern Moral Philosophy*, ed. Anthony O'Hear. Cambridge: Cambridge University Press, 47–74.

———. 2008. *Life and Action: Elementary Structures of Practice and Practical Thought*. Cambridge, MA: Harvard University Press.

Thornton, Agathe. 1984. *Homer's* Iliad: *Its Composition and the Motif of Supplication*. Göttingen, Germany: Vandenhoeck & Ruprecht.

Trendall, A. D., and T. B. L. Webster. 1971. *Illustrations of Greek Drama*. London: Phaidon.

Troscianko, Emily 2013. *Kafka's Cognitive Realism*. London: Routledge.

Tsagalis, Christos. 2008. *The Oral Palimpsest: Exploring Intertextuality in the Homeric Epics*. Washington DC: Center for Hellenic Studies.

———. 2012. *From Listeners to Viewers: Space in the* Iliad. Washington DC: Center for Hellenic Studies.

Väliaho, Pasi. 2010. *Mapping the Moving Image: Gesture, Thought and Cinema circa 1900*. Amsterdam: Amsterdam University Press.

Van Nortwick, Thomas. 1979. "Penelope and Nausicaa." *TAPA* 109: 269–76.

Van Wees, Hans. 1988. "Kings in Combat: Battles and Heroes in the *Iliad*." *CQ* 38.1: 1–24.

———. 1994. "The Homeric Way of War: The *Iliad* and the Hoplite Phalanx (I)." *Greece & Rome* 41.1: 1–18.

Vermeule, Emily. 1979. *Aspects of Death in Early Greek Art and Poetry*. Berkeley: University of California Press.

Vernant, Jean-Pierre. (1974) 1990. *Myth and Society in Ancient Greece*, trans. J. Lloyd. New York: Zone.

———. (1982) 1991. "A 'Beautiful Death' and the Disfigured Corpse in Homeric Epic." In *Mortals and Immortals: Collected Essays*, ed. F. I. Zeitlin. Princeton, NJ: Princeton University Press, 50–74.

———. (1986) 1991. "Mortals and Immortals: the Body of the Divine." In *Mortals and Immortals: Collected Essays*, ed. F. I. Zeitlin. Princeton, NJ: Princeton University Press, 27–49.

Vidal-Naquet, Pierre. (1981) 1986. *The Black Hunter: Forms of Thought and Forms of Society in the Greek World*, trans. A. Szegedy-Maszak. Baltimore: Johns Hopkins University Press.

Virilio, Paul. 1994. "Gravitational Space." In *Traces of Dance: Drawings and Notations of Choreographers*, ed. L. Louppe, trans. B. Holmes and P. Carrier. Paris: Dis Voir, 35–60.

Vivante, Paolo. 1982. *The Epithets in Homer: A Study in Poetic Values*. New Haven, CT: Yale University Press.

Warburg, Aby, and Matthew Rampley. 2009. "The Absorption of the Expressive Values of the Past," trans. Matthew Rampley. *Art in Translation* 1.2: 273–83.

Warwick, Celsiana. Forthcoming 2019. "The Maternal Warrior: Gender and *Kleos* in the *Iliad*." *AJP* 140.1.

Watkins, Calvert. 1995. *How to Kill a Dragon: Aspects of Indo-European Poetics*. New York: Oxford University Press.

Weber, Wilhelm, and Eduard Weber. (1836) 1992. *Mechanics of the Human Walking Apparatus*. Berlin and New York: Springer-Verlag.

Wender, Dorothea. 1978. *The Last Scenes of the* Odyssey. Leiden: Brill.

West, M. L., ed. 1966. *Hesiod: Theogony*. Oxford: Clarendon.

———. 1978. *Hesiod: Works and Days*. Oxford: Clarendon.

Whalon, William. 1979. "Is Hector *Androphonos?*" In *Arktouros: Hellenic Studies Presented to Bernard Knox*, ed. G. W. Bowersock, W. Burket, and M. J. Putnam. Berlin: de Gruyter, 19–24.

Whitman, Cedric Hubbell. 1958. *Homer and the Heroic Tradition*. Cambridge, MA: Harvard University Press.

——— and Ruth Scodel. 1981. "Sequence and Simultaneity in *Iliad* N, Ξ, and O." *HSCP* 85: 1–15.

Whitmarsh, Tim. 2011. *Narrative and Identity in the Ancient Greek Novel: Returning Romance*. Cambridge: Cambridge University Press.

Williams, Bernard. (1993) 2008. *Shame and Necessity*. Berkeley: University of California Press.

Willcock, M. M. 1964. "Mythological Paradeigma in the *Iliad*." *CQ* 14.2: 141–54.

———. 1970. "Some Aspects of the Gods in the *Iliad*." *BICS* 17.1: 1–10.

———. 1973. "The Funeral Games of Patroclus." *BICS* 20.1: 1–11.

———. 1977. "Ad Hoc Invention in the *Iliad*." *HSCP* 81: 41–53.

———. 1987. "The Final Scenes of *Iliad* XVII." In *Homer beyond Oral Poetry: Recent Trends in Homeric Interpretation*, ed. J. M. Bremmer, I. J. F. de Jong, and J. Kalff. Amsterdam: B. R. Gruner, 185–94.

Wills, Jeffrey. 1996. *Repetition in Latin Poetry: Figures of Allusion*. Oxford: Clarendon.

Wilson, Donna F. 2002. *Ransom, Revenge, and Heroic Identity in the* Iliad. Cambridge: Cambridge University Press.

Wohl, Victoria. 1993. "Standing by the Stathmos: The Creation of Sexual Ideology in the *Odyssey*." *Arethusa* 26.1: 19–50.

———. 2015. *Euripides and the Politics of Form*. Princeton, NJ: Princeton University Press.

———. 2018. "Stone into Smoke: Mortality and Materiality in Euripides' *Troades*." In *Objects and Affect: the Materialities of Greek Tragedy*, ed. M. Telò and M. Mueller. London: Bloomsbury, 17–34.

Wolfson, Susan J., and Marshall Brown, eds. 2006. *Reading for Form*. Seattle: University of Washington Press.

Woodhouse, W. J. 1930. *The Composition of Homer's* Odyssey. Oxford: Clarendon.

Worman, Nancy. 2002. *The Cast of Character: Style in Greek Literature*. Austin: University of Texas Press.

———. 2015. *Landscape and the Spaces of Metaphor in Ancient Literary Theory and Criticism*. Cambridge: Cambridge University Press.

———. 2018. "Touching, Proximity, and the Aesthetics of Pain in Sophocles." In *Touch and the Ancient Senses*, ed. A. C. Purves. London and New York: Routledge, 34–49.

Young, Iris Marion. (1980) 2005. "Throwing like a Girl: A Phenomenology of Feminine Body Comportment, Motility, and Spatiality." In *On Female Body Experience: "Throwing like a Girl" and Other Essays*, ed. I. M. Young. Oxford: Oxford University Press, 27–45.

Zeitlin, Froma I. 1996. *Playing the Other: Gender and Society in Classical Greek Literature*. Chicago: University of Chicago Press.

Zielinski, Thaddaeus. 1899–901. "Die Behandlung gleichzeitiger Ereignisse im antiken Epos." *Philologus Suppl.* VIII, no. 3: 407–49.

Ziogas, Ioannis V. 2011. "Ovid as a Hesiodic Poet: Atalanta in the *Catalogue of Women* (fr. 72–6 M–W) and the *Metamorphoses* (10.560–707)." *Mnemosyne* 64.2: 249–70.

Žižek, Slavoj. 1991. *Looking Awry: An Introduction to Jacques Lacan through Popular Culture*. Cambridge, MA: MIT Press.

Index Locorum

General Index

Achilles, 27–28, 30, 42, 49–50, 52, 67,
69–71, 75–83, 88–90, 100n15, 112–14,
115n52, 133, 154, 169. *See also under*
Agamemnon; Athena; leaping;
Priam; standing; Thetis
absence from battle of, 50,
51n44, 75, 126–27
aristeia of, 41, 51
arms of, 40n10, 45–47, 88, 127n35, 130
(*see also* drawing [sword]; Shield of
Achilles)
death of, 40, 43, 44n26, 74, 127n35,
128n36, 156n11
grief of, 44n26, 153–60, 165–67, 169,
179n89, 180
and Hector, 28, 30, 44n26, 69–71, 74–77,
83n44, 89n65, 110–11, 113, 133, 153–58
(*see also under* corpse; dragging)
and Lycaon, 170–73, 180
and Odysseus, 79–83, 88
and Patroclus, 40n10, 44n26, 78n32, 119,
126–29, 132–33, 135–36, 158–60, 167
plan of, 59n69, 131
wrath of, 174n34, 175n77, 177
actor (*hupokritēs* or on stage), 29, 31n99,
178–79
Aeneas, 42n18, 70n7, 112–13, 116n54
affect, 17, 23, 28–29, 135, 140, 155, 175,
177–78
Agamben, Giorgio, 153–54, 173–74, 178
Agamemnon, 27, 48, 117, 147
and Achilles, quarrel with, 79–80, 90,
103–5, 108, 120, 123–26, 134

and Achilles, reconciliation with, 130–32, 161
and Menelaus, 122n20, 123n23
agency, autonomy (of Homeric characters),
10–11, 28, 32, 120, 167, 182–83
aging, 26, 39, 45n29, 46, 49, 53n51, 54–55.
See also old age
Ajax (Oilean), 44n26, 78–79, 84, 89,
130n37, 160n25
Ajax (Telamonian), 48n31, 88, 117n2, 126n30,
128n38, 129–31
androktasiai, 101, 124
Andromache, 41, 70n6, 156n11, 162n36
falling, 120, 155n9
lament of, 159–60, 165, 175, 179,
180n94
meeting with Hector, 71–73, 128
animal locomotion, 99–100
in Homer, 50n39, 69n5, 73–74, 93–96,
100, 110–11
in photography, 3, 17n68, 18n71, 20,
23n79, 99, 150n88
anthropomorphism, 38–39
Antilochus, 31, 77–82, 90n67, 179n89
Antinoos, 101n19, 147
anvil, 56, 63–64
Aphrodite, 37, 39n7, 60, 62, 160n26, 162
and Ares, 80, 82, 85, 90
Apollo, 23n84, 45, 47, 49, 51, 70–71, 76n22,
89–90, 127–28, 135, 155, 158–59
Arend, Walter, 12, 105n26, 120n13
Ares, 26, 37, 39, 40n10, 47, 57–58, 60–62, 64,
69n5. *See also under* Aphrodite
Astyanax, 160n26, 162n36, 179–80